Christina Stead and the Matter of America

SYDNEY STUDIES IN AUSTRALIAN LITERATURE

Robert Dixon, Series Editor

The **Sydney Studies** in **Australian Literature** series publishes original, peer-reviewed research in the field of Australian literary studies. It offers engagingly written evaluations of the nature and importance of Australian literature, and aims to reinvigorate its study both locally and internationally. It will be of interest to those researching, studying and teaching in the diverse fields of Australian literary studies.

Alex Miller: The Ruin of Time
Robert Dixon

Australian Books and Authors in the American Marketplace 1840s–1940s
David Carter and Roger Osborne

Christina Stead and the Matter of America
Fiona Morrison

Colonial Australian Fiction: Character Types, Social Formations and the Colonial Economy
Ken Gelder and Rachael Weaver

Contemporary Australian Literature: A World Not Yet Dead
Nicholas Birns

Elizabeth Harrower: Critical Essays
Ed. Elizabeth McMahon and Brigitta Olubas

The Fiction of Tim Winton: Earthed and Sacred
Lyn McCredden

Richard Flanagan: Critical Essays
Ed. Robert Dixon

Shirley Hazzard: New Critical Essays
Ed. Brigitta Olubas

Christina Stead and the Matter of America

Fiona Morrison

SYDNEY UNIVERSITY PRESS

First published by Sydney University Press

© Fiona Morrison 2019
© Sydney University Press 2019

Reproduction and communication for other purposes

Except as permitted under the Act, no part of this edition may be reproduced, stored in a retrieval system, or communicated in any form or by any means without prior written permission. All requests for reproduction or communication should be made to Sydney University Press at the address below:

Sydney University Press
Fisher Library F03
University of Sydney NSW 2006
AUSTRALIA
sup.info@sydney.edu.au
sydney.edu.au/sup

 A catalogue record for this book is available from the National Library of Australia.

ISBN 9781743324493 paperback
ISBN 9781743324509 epub

Cover image: Christina Stead ca. 1938, C.S. Daley Photograph Collection, National Library of Australia, Pic/12605/2, nla.obj-144459442.
Cover design by Miguel Yamin.

For Michael, Julia and Elena

Contents

Acknowledgements ix

Introduction 1

1 Christina Stead's "Westward Expansion": Totality, Avant-Garde Realism and the American Folk 21

2 Fascist Miscellanies and the Allegory of the Domestic Front in *The Man Who Loved Children* 47

3 Debt, Domestic Enclosure and Daughterly Revolution in *The Man Who Loved Children* 63

4 The New York Love Market and the Picara Fortunata in *Letty Fox: Her Luck* 85

5 Men, Mobility and Capital Relations in *A Little Tea, A Little Chat* and *The People with the Dogs* 103

6 Gargantuan Contradictions and the Supercession of Limits in *I'm Dying Laughing: The Humourist* 129

Conclusion 151

Works Cited 157

Index 183

Acknowledgements

This book was written with the support of an Australian Research Council Discovery Grant "Christina Stead in America" (DP120103310). Two University of New South Wales School of Arts and Media SRG grants funded work on this project, including the symposium on Christina Stead and Elizabeth Harrower in December 2015 that emerged from this research.

I would like to acknowledge the influence of my colleagues at UNSW Australia who are working in such inspiring ways on Australian literature and Australian literary cultures.

The work of my colleagues in Stead studies has been tremendously important for this project. I would like to salute the wonderful work in the field, as well as give particular thanks to Gail Jones, Brigid Rooney, and Sue Sheridan for many memorable conversations and the energising provocations of their work. I also owe a debt of gratitude to Nicholas Birns and Margaret Harris as important Stead colleagues over many years.

At Sydney University Press, I would like to acknowledge Professor Robert Dixon for the support he has given this work and the focus and wisdom of his feedback. Thank you to the SUP team, Susan Murray, Agata Mrva-Montoya and Denise O'Dea, especially in the context of such a burgeoning time for the Press.

This project is indebted to the work undertaken by Jacqueline Bell in the great Stead transcription challenge of 2016. I would also like to acknowledge the editorial assistance of Madeleine Wilson. I owe a particular debt of gratitude to the librarians at the Tainment Library and the Robert F. Wagner Labor Archives at New York University and the People's History Museum in Manchester. Closer to home, I would like to thank two people for their willingness to walk with me in the slightly heated environment of a project close to submission: to Gavin Morrison and Larissa Edwards, a big thank you.

To my wonderful daughters, Julia and Elena, who were so patient with my almost mystically extensive project, please accept my greatest love, pride and gratitude for who you have become during the "Christina Stead in America" years.

This book carries the mark of my mother, Jan, and I hope it is one way that I may show her to you.

My final thanks go to Michael Parker, who has been the steadfast companion of this work. For his patience, his belief in the material and the time he spent on that particular New Zealand holiday, I give my gratitude and love.

Introduction

> What you feel throughout is that Miss Stead is much bigger than her novel, that she will need a stream of novels to shelter her fully, for no one novel can hold her at this point.[1]

In 1987, Hortense Calisher, New York writer and newly appointed president of the American Academy of Arts and Sciences, wrote an essay for the *Yale Review* that recalled two meetings with Christina Stead. The first meeting occurred in London in September 1956 at a time of Cold War neglect and the second at a triumphalist party held by Philip Van Doren Stern in Manhattan in early 1966, to celebrate the successful Holt, Rinehart and Winston re-issue of *The Man Who Loved Children* the year before. Calisher's essay, which followed the posthumous publication of Stead's novel about American radicals in the McCarthy years, *I'm Dying Laughing* (1986), whimsically but also tellingly imagines the benevolent Stead of the 1960s as she might have been in her Manhattan years of the 1930s and 1940s: "gawky with talent, their red-cheeked colonial".[2] At the London meeting in the mid 1950s, Calisher found the woman who Robert Lowell, Elizabeth Hardwick and Randall Jarrell so admired (Calisher had read *The Man Who Loved Children* on their advice, before 1952) to be possessed of an "intimate majesty", and while both "open and silent", she did want to know if Calisher was "political". Calisher rather coyly reports that she deduced that Stead was a fellow traveller, though she concludes from their meeting that Stead was, in her capacity as a great writer, "an observer, still". Her impression of Bill Blake, Stead's American partner, was that he was a little different, rather more "European or boulevardier" in style,[3] and that:

1　Alfred Kazin, "Overture to the Mad, Hysterical Thirties: An Ironic, Powerful Novel of a Continent Drunk with Money", Review of *House of All Nations*, *New York Herald Tribune*, 12 June 1938, 1.
2　Hortense Calisher, "Stead", *Yale Review* 76 (1987), 173.
3　Calisher, "Stead", 171–177.

The United States had quite apparently been important to them both, on terms I could only surmise. For him, possibly, a country to reject. For her, as a great colonial world to engage in with all her talents, describe compellingly, and leave.[4]

Christina Stead and the Matter of America takes up this very contention – that the United States was, for Stead, "the great colonial world to engage in with all her talents." Calisher's vision of the Australian "red-cheeked colonial" who engaged the "great colonial world" of America with European experience and preferences at hand, offers a sketch of the formative configuration of Australia, Europe and the United States that grounds Stead's American novels. Stead's anatomy of America, elaborated in her five great mid-career novels, displays one colonial provincial's substantial critical interest in another large colonial province, though one soon to emerge from the semi-periphery onto the world stage as a neo-imperial power. This is surely one of the most original and extended examples of the strange, asymmetrical and generative relationship of Australia to America in the mid twentieth-century. It was certainly an epic artistic engagement, marked by originality, ambition and complex political vision.

In notes taken during an interview with Stead in Sydney in December 1982, Tom Krause captured some of the complexities of the national and transnational negotiations evident in Stead's American sojourn and the novels that emerged from this time. When asked about the criticism that *The Man Who Loved Children* failed to quite capture America and Americans, Stead responded: "I'm glad to say … the citation from the Academy the other day said that [I was] one of the best 'American' writers of the century. 'American' – they put it in quotes … so never mind what they say. I didn't put any kangaroos in it, of course".[5] The quotation marks frame the ambiguity of her election as a foreign honorary member, as well as the challenging status of the intimacy and command of her expatriate visions of mid-century America. The election of Stead as an Honorary member of the prestigious American Academy of Arts and Sciences was a deeply significant recognition of her work and career, a recognition generated through peer review and testimonial, and represents yet another moment in her career when Americans gave generous and consequential acknowledgement of her writing.

What difference did America, "the land of boundless importunity", make to Stead's fiction?[6] What did she read, imagine and contest in her time in America

---

4   Calisher, "Stead", 175.
5   Christina Stead, interviewed by Tom Krause, December 1982, 11. Unpublished interview. Heather Stewart papers in the author's possession.
6   Christina Stead, "It Is All a Scramble for Boodle: Christina Stead Sums Up America", *Australian Book Review* 141, no. 6 (1992), 22. The phrase "boundless importunity" might derive from a number of places, but one possibility is a letter from Benjamin Franklin who thanks a military officer, James Lovell (7 October 1777), for communicating about a form of cipher, and then complains about the number of French soldiers insisting in rather

from 1935 to late 1946, and how can we account for the nature of this engagement? It was as an Australian, a political internationalist and the author of three experimental and intensely modern works that Stead came to America in July 1935. Her initial expatriation was as a colonial woman writer in a literary world system whose centres were keyed to modernism. Her aesthetic experiments and her political experiences up to and during 1935 meant that the writer who arrived in America was a committed realist with a richly textured literary background arising from her Antipodean origins and her avant-garde engagements in Paris from 1929 to 1934. Stead's artistic vision and ambition were then focused on the "matter of America" from the early years of the Popular Front, through the war years and into the early McCarthy period. America became the expansive platform upon which Stead staged her signature interests in hypocrisy, egotism, women's experience of modernity and politics in their forms of everyday alienation and oppression – often viewed through the context and environment of several striking characters. America also altered and contoured these areas of interest and aesthetic approach in turn: Stead's virtuosic literary work with vernacular speech and comic vitalism immediately come to mind. Her American novels display an evolving and restlessly experimental realism, grounded in specific genres and critically shaped by the provocations of national scale as well as key literary and political genealogies of America itself. As a result, Stead created new ways of perceiving and representing mid-century America that we are only now in a position to address properly. It is time to look at the novels of this period as a distinct group and in some detail, with the clear categorisation of Stead as a writer whose most significant genesis was in and through the aesthetic and political debates of the turbulent 1930s.

Stead's sojourn in America produced five novels that are the subject of this book: *The Man Who Loved Children* (1940), *Letty Fox: Her Luck* (1946), *A Little Tea, A Little Chat* (1948), *The People with the Dogs* (1952) and *I'm Dying Laughing* (1986). Echoing David Malouf (1982) and Margaret Harris (1992), I will suggest that these might be regarded productively as a specific set of novels that engage American political, economic and social life. Stead's anatomy of America, though modally satirical overall, works with a number of master genres inspired by the aesthetic debates on the Left with which she was increasingly familiar before she arrived in America, including domestic fiction, the picaresque and the chronicle. These are key genres because of the way in which they choreograph the focus on gendered experience and political economy throughout the American sequence. Her Australian origins contour this realism in fundamental ways, too, most

---

annoying ways that they be allowed to go to America. Stead's wry humour can also be seen in the statement that she and Blake sailed for the "land of boundless importunity" after an "extensive night-course on American society under C.B. De Mille and Sam Goldwyn" before disembarking in Boston. This is disingenuous, to say the least, since Blake was born and raised in America, and they had both read a good deal of American literature and had had mainly American friends in Paris. The continental disdain for American mass culture is making itself felt here.

significantly in her determination to integrate holistic and vitally material visions of the American social panorama as a totality, which was linked to her realist desire to draw the hidden life into view. Her American novels, folding into themselves both Antipodean and European politics and aesthetics, therefore showcase an avant-garde realist working on a world scale.

In 1965, just before Calisher's Manhattan party, Holt, Rinehart and Winston's re-issue of *The Man Who Loved Children* appeared with an introductory essay titled "An Unread Book" by the poet and literary critic Randall Jarrell.[7] In this long and impassioned essay, Jarrell set about recuperating Stead's first American novel as a neglected masterpiece that deserved to be recognised as comparable, in some sense, to the works of world literature by Dostoyevsky and Tolstoy. This was an argument that placed Stead in the category of "world writer". In pursuit of the universal attributes that would secure her world literary value, Jarrell was vague about gender, evasive about politics and noncommittal about national identity. It worked. Stead was "rediscovered" with gusto, but a number of aspects of her fiction and the shape of her writing life have meant that this categorisation as a potential great of world literature has never worked for very long.[8] Drawing Stead's American novels into view through the lens of the "transnational turn" responds to a persistent critical "blind spot" about her work, and this possibility extends the logic of Simon During's claims about Stead in *Exit Capitalism* (2009). Contemporary work in transnational and world literatures (though by no means unproblematic categories for literary analysis) reveals aspects of Stead's work in America that national paradigms have obscured.[9] Despite, or perhaps because of, the fundamental challenges to literary and national category delivered by a modern woman writer who wrote a series of critical books about a country that was not

---

7   Randall Jarrell, "An Unread Book", Introduction to *The Man Who Loved Children* by Christina Stead (1940; Harmondsworth: Penguin, 1970), 37.

8   The issue with literary category and value persisted into Stead's late career and after her death. Simon During has shrewdly argued that this is connected to her unrenounced Stalinism. Simon During, "World Literature, Stalinism and the Nation: Christina Stead as Lost Object", *Exit Capitalism: Literary Culture, Theory and Post-Secular Modernity* (London: Routledge, 2009), 57–94.

9   The key monographs on Stead account for the works set outside Australia by noting the internal signatures of theme, form or gender rather than the category of nation. If her substantial international movement is noted, it is under the sign of "nomadic" or "cosmopolitan". I am tremendously indebted to these works for their pioneering accounts of the American novels: Diana Brydon, *Christina Stead* (London: Macmillan, 1987); Jennifer Gribble, *Christina Stead* (Melbourne: Oxford University Press, 1994); Joan Lidoff, *Christina Stead* (New York: Frederick Ungar, 1982); Judith Kegan Gardiner, *Rhys, Stead, Lessing and the Politics of Empathy* (Bloomington: Indiana University Press, 1989); Susan Sheridan, *Christina Stead* (London: Harvester Wheatsheaf, 1988) and Ron Geering, *Christina Stead* (New York: Twayne Publishers, 1969). I must also acknowledge a debt to Hazel Rowley's biography of Christina Stead, which, in its scope and thoroughness, has been an invaluable resource: *Christina Stead: A Biography* (Port Melbourne: Minerva, 1994).

her own (with little acknowledgement or even apology about her position as an outsider), we can claim that Stead's American novels reveal the work of the greatest political woman writer of the mid twentieth-century. Stead's anatomy of America demonstrates a political writer in the full flower of her original and critical realism, who produced an account of American ideology and national identity that seems extraordinarily prescient, even today.

The timeliness of this reading of Stead's American novels is connected to current interest in literary transnationalism that has inspired such rich conceptual work on representations of crossing, travelling and permeabilities of all kinds, and has recast the possible shape of aesthetics and politics inside and outside the category of the nation.[10] Fifty years on from the 1965 re-issue of *The Man Who Loved Children*, the field of world literature has produced many (and more flexible) accounts of the dialectical and scalar interplay of particular and universal, national and transnational. I am following here Françoise Lionnet and Shu-mei Shih's understanding of "transnational", which they define as "a space of exchange and participation", and this definition promotes an understanding of the national as always already "inflected by a transnationality".[11] In addition, "the transnational turn has appropriately encouraged feminist scholars to consider new sites of articulation of the national and of the economic, political, and social possibilities".[12]

---

10 Robert Dixon, "Australian Literature, Scale, and the Problem of the World", *Text, Translation, Transnationalism: World Literature in 21st Century Australia*, ed. Peter Morgan (Melbourne: Australian Scholarly Publishing, 2016), 173–95. Robert Dixon, "National Literatures, Scale and the Problem of the World," *JASAL: Journal of the Association for the Study of Australian Literature* 15, no. 3 (2015): 1–10; Paul Giles, *Antipodean America: Australasia and the Constitution of U.S. Literature* (Oxford: Oxford University Press, 2013); Robert Dixon and Nicholas Birns, *Reading Across the Pacific: Australia-United States Intellectual Histories* (Sydney: Sydney University Press, 2010); Jessica Berman, *Modernist Commitments: Ethics, Politics, and Transnational Modernism* (New York: Columbia University Press, 2011); Stephen Clingman, *The Grammar of Identity: Transnational Fiction and the Nature of the Boundary* (Oxford: Oxford University Press, 2009); Matthew Hart, *Nations of Nothing but Poetry: Modernism, Transnationalism, and Synthetic Vernacular Writing* (New York: Oxford University Press, 2010); Françoise Lionnet and Shu-mei Shih, *Minor Transnationalism* (Durham, NC: Duke University Press, 2005).

11 Lionnet and Shih, *Minor Transnationalism*, 5–6. The noticeable increase in publications on world literature began in 1994 with *Reading World Literature*, edited by Sarah Lawall. Damrosch later published his article "So Much to Read, So Little Time: But Isn't That the Point?"(1999) This was shortly followed by his next article "World Literature Today: From the Old World to the Whole World" (2000). In the same year Franco Moretti published "Conjectures on World Literature"(2000) in the *New Left Review*, which instigated a dialogue that directly involved key scholars Christopher Prendergast, Jonathan Arac, and Emily Apter, among others, locating the discussion on world literature within American comparative literature departments. In 2001, Wai Chee Dimock published her article "Literature for the Planet," a precursor to her book *Through Other Continents*. In 2004 Pascale Casanova's influential work *The World Republic of Letters* added fuel to the debate and is germane for any discussion of realism and provinciality.

12 Rose Brister, "Placing Women's Bodies in Eran Riklis's *The Syrian Bride*," *Signs* 39, no. 4 (2014): 927–48. The extension of feminist work on Stead and gender into the sphere of the

Transnational literary research that has informed my work on Stead's American novels includes a wide range of work on gendered mobility, including the mobility of the colonial woman writer.[13] In addition, work on women writers such as Jean Rhysthat has been conducted under the sign of global modernisms has been particularly provocative. Yet, while the archives of work on colonial and modernist expatriate woman writers are of essential interest, Stead stands in excess of them. Her movement into and through transnational space is productively aligned with colonial and modernist examples, but exceeds and complicates them. Most importantly, Stead's mobility became "grounded", as it were, in the ideological hospitality of the fellow-travelling habitus of the Left 1930s. This introduces to transnational accounts of mobile women writers of this period the material and ideological coordinates of a writer committed to notions of international solidarity uninflected by a generalised cosmopolitanism or colonial expatriation and powered, instead, by a larger sense of informed political purpose. Stead must be seen as a writer with a pressing and layered sense of the international rather than a writer with a generalised nomadic commitment to the world, and this sense comes from a politics centred on a world-wide vision of organised revolution powered by the working class, and thus a politics grounded in the work of Marx and the writings of Lenin.

It is interesting to note, therefore, that as the flexibility and adaptability of new modernist studies has grown over the last decade, Stead, like Patrick White, has been referred to, somewhat tentatively, as a modernist. As we have seen with the expansion of exciting and detailed work on Jean Rhys, modernist is a term that can organise and regulate various literary marginalities and mobilities in the period in which Stead was first published. Modernist might well describe (and I think intends to describe) something general about Stead's experimental style, the period in which she composed her early work and the specifics of her focus on women's experience, though most applications of the term seem to run into trouble sooner rather than later. Most of all, modernist is a term intended to secure literary authority and prestige and contest her persistent neglect; a neglect related directly to gender, style and transnational ambiguities of place and kind. I will argue in this book that Stead turned away from formative early interactions with modernist writing in Sydney and Paris (seen in *Seven Poor Men of Sydney*, *The Salzburg*

---

transnational is founded on a crucial set of pioneering feminist works in the field of Stead studies by Susan Sheridan, Judith Kegan Gardiner, Joan Lidoff and Diana Brydon, all of whom considered a variety of aspects of feminine subjectivity in Stead's novels. This is important to note, since the transnational has been a category of literary study that has been infamously gender blind, but key work in this area includes work by Debra Castillo, Marian Arkin, Barbara Shollar and Margaret Higonnet. A more general but helpful work has been Laura Doyle and Laura A. Winkiel, *Geomodernisms: Race, Modernism, Modernity* (Bloomington: Indiana University Press, 2005).

13 Anna Snaith, *Modernist Voyages: Colonial Women Writers in London, 1890–1945* (Cambridge: Cambridge University Press, 2014).

Tales and *The Beauties and the Furies*) at the commencement of the Popular Front years. Stead's American novels indicate, rather, the exciting and difficult style of what we might call, following Robert Philip Shulman's argument in *The Power of Political Art: The 1930s Literary Left Reconsidered*, Left avant-garde realism.[14] Building on associated work by key American literary critics and historians, I want to reframe Stead's unconventional realism in the American sequence by attending to this growing sense that the experimental realist work on the Left, which was papered over in the 1950s by a catchall sense of the propagandist, the middlebrow and boringly tendentious, was then sealed into a clichéd opposition to modernism and lost to sight.[15] Fredric Jameson's account of the antinomy between modernism and realism[16] is writ large in the stubborn persistence of right-wing Cold War views about realism, which has meant that (since "colonial woman writer" did not really apply either) Stead has been moved quite gingerly to the category "modernist writer" in order to be made visible and legible. The exciting hub of new work in the area of peripheral realism in general, and 1930s Left realism in particular, signals that it is time to look anew at this badging in the context of her American sequence. I will contend that Stead's American sequence troubles any straightforward antinomy between modernism and realism in very substantial ways.

Although Stead's political coordinates were broadly socialist (Stead and Blake sometimes referred to themselves as "old Bolsheviks", which is both very telling and also the best overall formulation of their political position), she was careful throughout her life to avoid too close a vocal commitment to political orthodoxy, valuing the necessary autonomy and individual vision of the artist. Michael Ackland's work on Stead's socialism[17] has provided a useful corrective to the notion that Stead was not a political thinker in her own right, which was a key contention

---

14 The key interlocutors here are Michael Szalay, *New Deal Modernism: American Literature and the Invention of the Welfare State* (Durham, NC: Duke University Press, 2000); Robert Philip Shulman, *The Power of Political Art: The 1930s Literary Left Reconsidered* (Chapel Hill: University of North Carolina Press, 2000); Chris Vials, *Realism for the Masses: Aesthetics, Popular Front Pluralism and U.S. Culture, 1935–1947* (Jackson: University of Mississippi Press, 2009).

15 Michael Denning, *Culture in the Age of Three Worlds* (London: Verso, 2004) and *The Cultural Front: The Laboring of American Culture in the Twentieth Century* (London: Verso, 1998); Barbara Foley, *Radical Representations: Politics and Form in US Proletarian Fiction, 1929–1941* (Durham, NC: Duke University Press, 1993); Paula Rabinowitz, *American Pulp: How Paperbacks Brought Modernism to Main Street* (Princeton, NJ: Princeton University Press, 2014), and *Labor and Desire: Women's Revolutionary Fiction in Depression America* (Chapel Hill: University of North Carolina Press, 1991); Alan M. Wald, *American Night: The Literary Left in the Era of the Cold War* (Chapel Hill: University of North Carolina Press, 2012), *Exiles from the Future Time: The Forging of the Mid-Twentieth Century Literary Left* (Chapel Hill: University of North Carolina Press, 2002), *The New York Intellectuals: The Rise and Decline of the Anti-Stalinist Left from the 1930s to the 1980s* (Chapel Hill: University of North Carolina Press, 1987), and *Trinity of Passion: The Literary Left and the Antifascist Crusade* (Chapel Hill: University of North Carolina Press, 2007).

16 Fredric Jameson, *The Antinomies of Realism* (London: Verso, 2013).

of Hazel Rowley's 1994 biography. I would suggest that a carefully negotiated artistic autonomy, evident in Stead's letters and rehearsed in her fiction, interacted with a sharp and sometimes iconoclastic political commitment as well as a keen knowledge of politics and economics. For Stead, artistic motive forces of imagination and desire were always in some kind of productive struggle with the more systematic demands of the physical and human sciences. Stead positioned desire, imagination and art as central to political subjectivity, rather than antithetical to it. Therefore, even though Stead's wandering life produced certain kinds of resistance to a static national identity that might allow us to "place" her with greater ease, what really confounds our sense of being able to "see" Stead's work is not *only* mobility, but the seriousness, ambition and plasticity of her political critique. A lifelong artistic engagement with power, ideology and political economy operated under a broad umbrella of the resistance to oppression, declared at the time of the publication of her first novel, *Seven Poor Men of Sydney* (1934). This girded Stead's commitment to realism, as the next chapter will demonstrate.

So, Stead's writing life was inextricably bound up in a specific identity that references mobility but really declares politics – that of the "fellow traveller." Fellow traveller was a transnational identity that afforded Stead powerful stability and literary energy until at least the late 1940s. It is from this mobile yet stable location as a fellow traveller in Manhattan that Stead wrote her great works about America. Though Stead had a socialist interest in the workings of capital everywhere, America's identity as fundamentally homologous with free market forces, and the Depression-era possibilities for revolution that unstable capital had at least introduced to America, made it an irresistible subject.

The Matter of America

In a piece commemorating Stead's eightieth birthday in 1982, David Malouf announced that America was the great subject of Stead's career. Although he anticipated by a couple of months Stead's election to the American Academy of Arts and Sciences, the short article reads almost as a citation supporting this honour:

> The four books at the centre of her achievement deal with the "matter of America". They are passionate critiques of failed idealisms (*The People with the Dogs*) and of the various forms of cannibalism (*A Little Tea, A Little Chat*) of its capitalist mode. The streets of New York, the Washington area of *The Man Who Loved Children,* the Catskills, Virginia in full summer, all these are created with same identity and precise feeling for place and creature … She writes about where she is.[18]

---

17 Michael Ackland, *Christina Stead and the Socialist Heritage* (New York: Cambria Press, 2016).

Valuing Stead's American novels as "the centre of her achievement" was a move out of sync with the cultural nationalist and emerging feminist studies of Stead in the early 1980s in Australia. Malouf foregrounds politics, ideology and setting as well as noting her virtuosic flexibility in responding to her different international situations: "she writes about where she is". I want to deploy and extend Malouf's phrase – the "matter of America" – to describe Stead's American project. Malouf's phrase makes, I think, an unironic reference to America as a well-understood area of worldly concern that needs to be tested and prosecuted. The question of matter also allows for a double sense of the serious subject of nation-building that imputes political scope and gravity, as well as the importance of materiality. Stead's American novels foreground the material conditions of economic and political life in the register of the everyday and here "materiality is always something more than 'mere matter'". From her earliest work, we see in Stead's prose a vital materiality that reads as "an excess, force, vitality, relationality, or difference that renders matter active, self-creative, productive, unpredictable".[19] This is most apparent in her work with direct speech, but it is also evident in her meditations on matter as embodiment, landscape and architecture. This book will ponder the materiality of Stead's American texts under the sign of literary form and genre, the role of allegory, the centrality of gigantic figures and the nature and meaning of Stead's virtuosic commitment to direct speech.

Margaret Harris's 1992 essay "Christina Stead's Human Comedy: The American Sequence" argues that Stead's American novels form a Balzacian "sequence" and in so doing she takes up Malouf's contention in 1982 that Honoré de Balzac was the most powerful comparison for Stead's novelistic project. Harris examines Stead's American sequence of novels in light of the structure of the anatomy that organises Balzac's *La Comédie Humaine*. She makes the point that "Stead thought out sequences or thematically interacting and reinforcing groups of novels – episodes in her Human Comedy – and I will indicate ways in which the American sequence constitutes such an episode".[20] This is an invaluable essay for its measured and suggestive reading of Balzac and his typologies and this book will take up the premise of the Balzacian anatomy as the starting point for longer-form argument about genre, gender and geography. Anatomy is here understood as both a structure of connected works and a form that concentrates on a critical exposure of the state of society. Northrop Frye's use of the word in the title of his great work of typological literary criticism, *Anatomy of Literary Criticism* (1957), connotes a linked or total structure of knowledge unconfined by linearity. He also deployed

---

18 David Malouf, "Stead Is Best at Egotistical Monsters", *Sydney Morning Herald,* 17 July 1982, 32.
19 Diana H. Coole and Samantha Frost, eds, *New Materialisms: Ontology, Agency, and Politics* (Durham, NC: Duke University Press, 2010), 9.
20 Margaret Harris, "Christina Stead's Human Comedy: The American Sequence," *World Literature Written in English* 32, no. 1 (1992), 45.

it with a subversive connotation in mind; "anatomy" was also a synonym for Menippean satire, "a creative treatment of exhaustive erudition" and "a vision of the world in terms of single intellectual pattern", which has the comic implication that the encyclopaedic vision is vexed, if not outright foolish.[21] Stead's consciousness of her own use of the form of the anatomy is evident in a letter to Stanley Burnshaw, thanking him for his review of *The Beauties and the Furies* in August 1936: "many, many thanks for sending the copy of your review, in all your trouble. I find it the most satisfactory of all because it has the best view of the anatomy".[22] As early as 1936, therefore, Stead had a clear sense that her work participated in a literary tradition that sought to capture and critique the social world, and that this was a work of significant dimension and ambition.

The generally accepted view of Stead's American novels has been that they are satires, a trend that began with Joan Lidoff's ground-breaking monograph on Stead, published in 1982. The nature of Stead's satire has been further investigated by Susan Sheridan since the publication of her Stead monograph in 1988, and Anne Pender's 2002 monograph on Stead offered a book-length meditation on satire as the key genre for Stead's work more broadly.[23] However, it might be that the increased importance of criticism or critique in Stead's American novels has meant that we have confused mode for genre. Satire is modally prevalent in all the American novels as a complex amalgam of comedy and critique, but these works are formally coordinated by genres such as the domestic novel, the picaresque and the chronicle. This distinction between mode, which Alistair Fowler saw as "extensions of certain genres beyond specific and time-bound formal structures" (and as essentially generalised remnants of genre), and the more structured lineaments of genre and form is important because the more specific genres tell us something essential about Stead's critical and ideological engagement with the matter of America.[24] As Vilashini Cooppan argues: "as the sites where poetics and history, form and ideology meet, genres afford a vantage point from which to learn something about the individual societies that codify and popularize certain genres as the formal mirrors of conceptual belief."[25] There is a specificity and materiality

---

21 Northrop Frye, *Anatomy of Criticism: Four Essays* (1957; Princeton, NJ: Princeton University Press, 2000), 310–11.
22 Christina Stead to Stanley Burnshaw, 2 October 1936. In *A Web of Friendship: Selected Letters 1928–1973*, edited by R. G. Geering (Sydney: Angus & Robertson, 1992), 65.
23 Anne Pender, *Christina Stead: Satirist* (Altona, Vic.: Common Ground Publishing, 2002). Sue Sheridan has also worked with this term, particularly in her analysis of *A Little Tea, A Little Chat*, where her assessment of satire and masculinity is central: "The Woman Who Loved Men: Christina Stead as Satirist in *A Little Tea, A Little Chat* and *The People with the Dogs*", *World Literature Written in English* 32, no. 1 (1992), 2–12. Elizabeth Perkins produces an interesting take on satire in "Learning to Recognize Wicked People: Christina Stead's *A Little Tea, A Little Chat*", *World Literature Written in English* 32, no. 1 (1992), 13–25.
24 Alistair Fowler, *Kinds of Literature: An Introduction to the Theory of Genre and Modes* (Cambridge, MA: Harvard University Press, 1982), 106–7.

to Stead's choice of key genres such as the domestic novel, the picaresque and the chronicle that is lost in a wider identification of the mechanisms of satire. Though significant for reasons of political work and literary tradition, any key critical position awarded to satire also diffuses our sense of the dimensions and importance of the form of the realist novel in Stead's American project. Stead was fascinated with genus and kind from her childhood tutelage in the natural sciences. We can see some of this in the multifarious Stead archive, most often in the form of encyclopaedic framing and re-framing of her work as large interlocking typologies. This was not just the elaboration of typologies of individual characters recommended by Lukács as a hallmark of engaged realism, though there are certainly quite extensive examples of this. From these notes about character type and textual kind, we can see a prose writer with an extraordinarily restless and responsive sense of form and genre. Stead's engagement with the matter of America was sourced in her experimental work with particular genres that reflected, in a deeply responsive way, an intersection between life and art sourced in the contradictory social and cultural present of her writing.[26] As Robbie Duschinsky and Emma Wilson suggest, in the context of their work on Lauren Berlant's account of contemporary American everyday life:

> Genres … organise conventions about what might be hoped for, explicitly or secretly, and the bargains that can be made with life. Genres serve as moorings, or placeholders, for intensities within streaming experience … the concept of genre has the advantage of highlighting the dialectic of fictional and lived forms in which each animates and transduces the expectations and energy of the other.[27]

This response to Berlant's dialectical vision of contemporary American life and form takes us again to Lukács, specifically *The Theory of the Novel* (1916), where his account of literary form, and particularly the realist novel, is as something profoundly active (form is always acting, mirroring, doing) in the struggle to shape experience as a whole.

For Stead's larger project of catalogue and critique, domestic fiction in *The Man Who Loved Children*, the picaresque and its variants in the New York trilogy (*Letty Fox: Her Luck*, *A Little Tea, A Little Chat* and *The People with the Dogs*), and the strange beast that is the tragi-comic chronicle in *I'm Dying Laughing* were all genre

---

25 Vilashini Cooppan, *Worlds Within: National Narratives and Global Connections in Postcolonial Writing* (Stanford: Stanford University Press, 2009), 185.
26 Stead quoted in Susan Lever, "Christina Stead's Workshop in the Novel: How to Write a 'Novel of Strife'", *JASAL: Journal of the Association for the Study of Australian Literature* 2 (2003), 87.
27 Robbie Duschinsky and Emma Wilson, "Flat Affect, Joyful Politics and Enthralled Attachments: Engaging with the Work of Lauren Berlant", *International Journal of Politics, Culture and Society* 28, no. 3 (2015), 180.

choices intended to frame gigantic or gargantuan central characters. In this double imperative of character and genre we can also discern Stead's desire to represent the panorama of America grounded in the specifics of people she knew well from life. This desire to capture the specifics of real life reveals a profound commitment to realism. In her anatomist's work with the material of life, Stead was always negotiating what Lukács, in his other great work, *History and Class Consciousness* (1923), called "an aspiration to totality":

> The relation to totality does not need to become explicit, the plenitude of the totality does not need to be consciously integrated into the motives and objects of action. What is crucial is that there should be an aspiration towards totality.[28]

Since, for Lukács, the deep totalities of Greek epic were a distant memory of the classical world, modern representation could *only* aspire to a suitable wholeness and profound intimacy of relations between subject and world. The scale of Stead's ambition, so influenced by the great provincial writer and anatomist, Balzac, can be understood in the context of her incessant drive toward totality, despite the inevitable shortcomings of the modern novel as any kind of response to fallen modernity. We will return to notions of totality in subsequent investigations of Stead's American realism.

In addition to aspects of form, genre and the realist's aspiration to totality, what makes the claim for Stead as a great and ambitious political writer so pressing is the foundational but obscured question of gender. All three formal genres identified above engage the question of gender and the lives of women, and in so doing create new kinds of texts and new kinds of knowledge about gendered experience and gendered representation. The American sequence showcases Stead's deeply original vision of gender and American identity, and there is a thread in Stead's work we might identity as a keen and iconoclastic interest in the American girl. No matter what Stead would claim about her rejection of a specific liberation movement for women in light of larger Left struggles for equality, there can be no mistaking the fact that women's experience in modernity was a deliberate and emphatic interest, and it was tied to questions of real life and worked on with ferocious particularity. In the following comment, Stead suggests a characteristic relationship with her own aesthetics – that she simply "wrote what she saw" – and, even further, that she was interested in bringing that which had been obscured to light. Sight and social truth are often collocated in her own account of writing, and her focus on women is yoked here to her "natural sciences" account of realism familiar in her late interviews, which was meant to neutralise and naturalise the specificity of her interest in gender:

---

28 Georg Lukács, *History and Class Consciousness: Studies in Marxist Dialectics*, trans. R. Livingstone (1923; London: Merlin, 1971), 198.

Introduction

> No doubt because I was brought up by a naturalist, I have always felt an irresistible urge to *paint a true picture of society as I have seen it*. I often felt that quite well-known writings lacked truth, and this was particularly so of the pictures of women, I felt, not only because women took their complete part in society but were not represented as doing so, but because the long literary tradition, thousands of years old, had enabled men completely to express themselves, while women feared to do so. However, my object was by no means to write for women, or to discuss feminine problems, but to depict society as it was ... I wished to understand men and women equally.[29]

Stead's artistic purpose is focused on the matter and texture of women's lives as part of her creation of a truthful portrait of society. Stead's "irresistible urge to paint a true picture of society as I have seen it" is the hallmark of a committed realist, intent on verisimilitude and a vision of the whole. Stead was authorised in this work by her upbringing in the household of a father-scientist. She often repeated this formulation of aesthetic purpose as part of a scientific focus from a young age. Yet, as her novels and short stories indicate, a simplistic reflection or even slightly transparent description of society was not the work she actually produced. Despite an almost ethnographic focus on recording speech, and a willingness to reproduce stories and letters from real life, Stead's realism is a formidably complex literary hub that extends out from mere empiricism. Her early passion for fairy tales and a general taste for the Gothic attest to a passionate commitment to the imagination, and this, combined with later interests in avant-garde art, had a key part to play in her experimental realism. It is interesting that her focus on gender was explained as a desire to merely record true pictures of society as she saw it. This seemingly neutral intention reveals, rather, a profoundly important element of Christina Stead's realism: it was grounded in her rather revolutionary desire to tell the truth of gendered experience. Yet again, gender must be seen as the elided but nevertheless central aspect of both transnational women's writing and Stead's experimental realist aesthetics throughout her career. The American girl and the American woman and the theatre of gender relations in which they operated were specifically important in Stead's American novels. Her focus on gender was explained as a desire to merely record true pictures of society, but it was actually a powerful engine of Stead's artistic originality and political vision.

---

29 Stead quoted in Ron Geering, "Afterword", in *Ocean of Story: Uncollected Stories of Christina Stead* by Christina Stead, ed. R.G. Geering (New York: Viking, 1986), 547. My emphasis.

Stead, the American 1930s and Realism

One of the most persuasive assessments of Stead's realism was produced by Terry Sturm in his 1974 essay "Christina Stead's New Realism." In light of current discussions of peripheral realism in world literary studies, Sturm's essay seems more strikingly prescient than ever. He explores the way in which Stead can achieve such particularity of character, including the specific contours of psychology, whilst remaining interested in ideology. There is no mention of Lukács in this essay, but Sturm describes something similar to the critical realism that Lukács so praised in Thomas Mann. Critical realism seems at first glance to be a compelling term for Stead's work too, indicating as it does the realist work of a pro-democratic political writer who takes as his or her critical subject the middle-class of certain nations (German for Mann, British for Dickens, French for Balzac and American for Stead). Lukács application of it to Thomas Mann in his essay "In Search of Bourgeois Man" reads as uncannily apposite when applied to Stead:

> Thomas Mann is a realist whose respect, indeed reverence, for reality is of rare distinction. His detail, still more his plots, his intellectual designs may not stay on the surface of everyday life; his form is quite unnaturalistic. Yet the content of his work never finally leaves the real world.[30]

Nevertheless, Lukács had to ignore extraordinary innovation and flexibility in Mann's work in order to enshrine him as a critical realist in the style of the great nineteenth-century realists, and the same challenge definitively arises in any assessment of Stead's fiction.

In the early 1940s Stead claimed that "the essence of style in literature, for me, is experiment, invention, 'creative error' … and change: and of its content, the presentation of 'man alive'".[31] This sense of the vital and the unmediated for which Stead strove so restlessly involves elements of aesthetic experience that we associate with theatre. As the most unmediated form of mimesis, theatre can be intense, particular, kinetic and devoted to the rhythms and patterns of speech and other kinds of movement. The rhetorical quality of *enargia*, a collective name for a group of figures which strive for vivid, lively description, draws from theatrical experience and describes the almost immersive capacity of representation to make visible, palpable or manifest. This is a key element in Stead's avant-garde realism – her "man alive" aesthetics. Though Derrida's assessment of the metaphysical priority

---

30 Georg Lukács, "In Search of Bourgeois Man", in *Essays on Thomas Mann*, trans. S. Mitchell (1964; London: Merlin, 1979), 12.
31 Cited in Susan Lever and Anne Pender, "*The Man Who Loved Children* by Christina Stead". *The Encyclopedia of the Novel* (Volume 2), ed. Paul Schellinger. (London: Routledge, 1998). These are Stead's statements as first recorded in Stanley J. Kunitz and Howard Haycraft (eds.), *Twentieth Century Authors*, (New York: HW Wilson, 1961), 1330. Stead is quoting from Ralph Fox's *The Novel and the People* (1937).

for speech is significant here, it is Lukács' early work in *Soul and Form* (1908), *The History of Modern Drama* (1909)³² and *Theory of the Novel* (1916) to which Stead's aesthetics respond. Lukács' early works engage the central conundrum of the necessary relationship between form and life, such that both elements are rendered meaningful and somehow "true". The idea of form, the notion of life and the significance of tapping into a broad social totality as a commitment of aesthetic work is crucial in early Lukács:

> Lukács thus argues that modern art is caught up in the dilemma of having to achieve a harmony of life and form, either at the expense of life's intensity and potentiality, or at a purely symbolic and imaginary level – by effectively withdrawing from life (an idea he discusses in reference to *Novalis* in 1908).³³

Lukács' account of the dynamic negotiation of the porous relationship between meaningful form (the realist novel) and vital life (but without endless empirical description) in modernity describes the process of Stead's realism in general and her American novels in particular. Stead responded to the matter of America through the prism of the realist novel. A characteristic complexity at the level of structure and decorum marks all these works (in addition to virtuosic renditions of speech), as Stead works to represent her sense of genuine life, as well as expose critically the hidden contradictions of mid-century America.

Stead's first recorded assessment of America is a short essay that displays something of her experimental realist preoccupations in her American sequence. "It Is All a Scramble for Boodle" was a piece composed in 1935, presumably for promotional reasons after meeting publishers in New York, but published posthumously in *Australian Book Review* in 1992. Stead says of America that "this country is a skyrocket waiting to be let off, or Vesuvius with just a little steam coming out of the top waiting for an eruption."³⁴ "Vesuvius" and "the Mississippi" were the two figures Stead used to convey American energy, scale and material wealth. Vesuvius was a certainly a term she used more than once to describe her loquacious and learned American partner, Bill Blake, whose vitality and encyclopaedic knowledge she so valued. As a way of further establishing her positive credentials as a commentator, Stead performs another provincial orientation of Australia to America:

---

32 Georg Lukács' dissertation, *The History of Modern Drama*, (1909) was never complely translated into English. One chapter was published as *The Sociology of Modern Drama* (Oshkosh, WI: Green Mountain, 1965).
33 "Georg [György] Lukács", *Stanford Encyclopaedia of Philosophy*, first published 4 November 2013; substantive revision 18 January 2018, https://plato.stanford.edu/entries/lukacs/
34 Stead, "It Is All a Scramble for Boodle", 22.

> I come from a commonwealth which loves America, regards it as the rising English-speaking nation, which imitates its fads, whistles its way down every crotchet of tinpan alley and whose constitution is founded on your own, whose labour movement is as strong, whose love of liberty still lingers as fresh …[35]

The affectionate and deliberate use of American slang, such as "fad" and "tinpan" (and the "boodle" of the title), ameliorates the faintly disapproving sense of a relationship of slavish imitation, and alerts us to Stead's immediate gravitation to American vernacular speech. Stead starts with a claim about key Australian-American similarities such as constitutional freedom and a colonial past, a shared labour movement and a love of liberty. Rhetorical and material connections between Australia and America are made through energetic descriptions of the fresh and the strong. This prefaces the declaration of decided difference between America and Australia and, by implication, America and Europe:

> Here, where the love of money is brutally outspoken and crassly advertised, no illusions are offered to the workers: they see quite plainly, through numerous scandals (no libel or private-property copyright law) that it is all a scramble for boodle and nothing else.[36]

This insight about America's relationship to money drives Stead's American novels, which anatomise the scramble for boodle, the alienation this produces and the reifications of many kinds upon which it depends. "Boodle" derives from a Dutch word meaning property in the loose sense of "the whole lot of stuff" or the whole estate. The whole "boodle" relates to another archaic usage denoting a collection or bundle – "kit and caboodle." It is a slang word that probably came into American usage in New York, given its Dutch origins (like "luck," another Dutch gambling term). The word also connotes corrupt handling, counterfeit and fraud; it has a gambling usage meaning "pile" or quantity of money on a gaming table. In America, Stead asserts, money is loved in overt ways, without even a European web of illusions to obscure the ferocious reality of capital relations. American workers *see* the fight for class survival, Stead claims; she declares that American workers know and accept that they are alienated by the American Dream. Ideology cannot soften this blow, but rather accentuates class conflict as a scramble and a Darwinian struggle. Money is a religion and wealth is worshipped: "this acute worship of mammon is something marvellous, incredible as the golden halls of Babylon." This "blatant money-religion of your cities" and "worship of wealth and desire of acquisitions" has alienated both liberals and artists.[37] Again, New York is

---

35 Stead, "It Is All a Scramble for Boodle", 22–3.
36 Stead, "It Is All a Scramble for Boodle", 23.
37 Stead, "It Is All a Scramble for Boodle", 23.

in pride of place in these descriptions, this time by Stead's phrasing: the "golden halls of Babylon" echoes the way in which many Europeans described the polyglot and monumentally modern city in their travels during the 1930s. New York as a hubristic market city, full of exchange of all kinds but dominated by a singular belief in money and dreams of wealth, appears fully arrayed in Chapters Four and Five on the New York trilogy.

Stead's American novels provide a kind of realist anthropology of the American Dream, what Lauren Berlant has called a "realist account of fantasy", or an unsentimental anatomy of the ways in which "the political and the social are floated by complex and historically specific affective investments".[38] How relationships and characters are defined in relation to capital is a fundamental aspect of Stead's American novels as they undertake a linked study of the contradictions of capital and power shaped by access to credit, inheritance and property. Domestic incarceration and economic dependency are the hidden realities of gendered experience in *The Man Who Loved Children*. The fleshing out of the circulation of capital and desire is a particular hallmark of her writing about New York City. The portrait of the difficulty of lasting American radicalism in the face of identities so defined by free market ideologies is the work of *I'm Dying Laughing*. As ever, Stead aims her imaginative insight at the question of the human in the economic system; her focus on character is the focus on the unwieldy and often asymmetrical ways in which personalities embody, negotiate or survive ideologies and economies. Gender and desire are both forces that consistently flout, resist or confuse the rational discourses and structures of economics and science.

The critical fortunes of Stead's work became entangled in dominant anti-communist views about literary merit established in the late 1940s by the powerful New York Intellectuals, New Critics and others.[39] The antinomy between realism and modernism was newly narrated as a binary contestation mapped across Cold War struggle. Set against Soviet socialist realism that emerged during the Popular Front years, post-war critics established American modernism as evidence of truly American aesthetic power and innovation. This rehearsal of a recognisable realism-modernism antinomy as a dogmatic Stalinist-authentic American dyad meant that a dynamic body of American left-wing realisms was lost to sight. To reiterate Shulman's point here was that it was: "a left avant-garde that has been obscured by the prestige of high modernism – particularly as interpreted by Clement Greenberg and other *Partisan Review* critics in the decade before and during the crucial period of canon formation after World War II".[40] After its

---

38 Earl McCabe, "Depressive Realism: An Interview with Lauren Berlant," *Hypocrite Reader* 5 (2011), http://hypocritereader.com/5/depressive-realism.
39 Fiona Morrison, "'A Vermeer in the Hayloft': Christina Stead, Unjust Neglect and Transnational Improprieties of Place and Kind", *Australian Literary Studies* 31, no. 6 (2016), https://bit.ly/2LzzDlw
40 Shulman, *The Power of Political Art*, 6–7.

anti-Stalinist rebirth in 1937, the *Partisan Review* (alone of the Left periodicals), was cast as an exception to the dogmatism, reductionism and unthinking adherence to the party-line so evident, it claimed, in its competition at the *New Masses*. It was through the powerful agency of the *Partisan Review* that modernism also retained a confusing association with the Left, which further complicated any general ability to distinguish Left experimental realism retrospectively. In fact, as Chris Vials argues, "the *New Masses* editors rejected neither modernism nor formal experimentation".[41] Shulman, Vials and feminist critics such as Barbara Foley argue that the surveys of the 1930s so often transmitted standard post-war judgements about socialist realism and "the polemics of Stalinism and anti-Stalinism" that it became unthinking. In particular, Shulman identifies the lost significance of the "vanguard critique of the middle class", which "probed relatively unexplored areas of American experience" and produced "vital experiments in form and language, sometimes modernist, more often within the conventions of realism-naturalism".[42] Stead owns a powerful place in the roll call of vanguard critique of the middle class in America and she worked with an avant-garde realism in its pursuit.

If the sense of the radical 1930s that emerged during the anti-communist 1950s created a serious and persistent blind spot around many important and experimental radical writers, this was particularly the case for women writers. For Stead, since she was not American, not a modernist and not allied to the *Partisan Review* and was, instead, a fellow traveller, a political writer, a woman, an experimental realist, an Australian, and connected to *New Masses*, the fate of invisibility seems structurally inevitable, in retrospect. Nevertheless, if Stead was lost to sight in Cold War America, it was also in America and by Americans that her critical fortunes were first supported and then eventually recovered. Stead found and continued to find in New York powerful publishers, critics and readers who championed her work.[43]

Joe Cleary's recent essay about realisms from the periphery of Eurocentric modernism is worth considering in relation to this configuration of experimental realism, gender and transnationality as a literary blind spot. Cleary notes the continued importance of realist concepts such as class consciousness, social totality

---

41 Vials, *Realism for the Masses*, xxxiii.
42 Shulman, *The Power of Political Art*, 7. Other significant sources include Geraldine Murphy, "Romancing the Center: Cold War Politics and Classic American Literature," *Poetics Today* 9, no. 4 (1988), 737–41; Paula Rabinowitz, *Labor and Desire: Women's Revolutionary Fiction in Depression America* (Chapel Hill: University of North Carolina Press, 1991); Janet Galligani Casey, ed. *The Novel and the American Left: Critical Essays on Depression-Era Fiction* (Iowa City: University of Iowa Press, 2004).
43 Fiona Morrison, "An American Introduction: Perfect Readers, Unread Books and Christina Stead's *The Man Who Loved Children*", in *Republics of Letters: Literary Communities in Australia* ed. Robert Dixon and Peter Kirkpatrick (Sydney: Sydney University Press), 127–136; David Carter and Roger Osborne, *Australian Books and Authors in the American Marketplace 1840s–1940s* (Sydney: Sydney University Press, 2018), 271–312.

and historical transition in writing from the global peripheries (where we might see the genesis of Stead's *Seven Poor Men of Sydney*), and argues that an expanded global scale offers a way to revise the realism-modernism opposition that has meant that Stead has been hard to position and therefore hard to "read". Stead's work of the 1930s and 1940s offers substantial strength to Cleary's argument that we need to unpick the realism-modernism antinomy. According to Cleary, "the Cold War simplified and calcified the realism-versus-modernism polemics", and it therefore seems entirely possible that, as with a number of writers on the Left, Stead wanted to "radicalise realism, but not in a modernist manner". To return to Cleary's opening provocation: "we need, but lack, comprehensive theories and historical atlases of twentieth century realism".[44]

Stead's published work moved back and forth along a spectrum of realism and avant-garde experiment until 1935 (mapped from Sydney to Paris and the international Popular Front and then America), though she retained the intensities and visionary totalities arising from her Australian milieu and her engagement with politics and avant-garde forms in interwar Europe. After 1935, Stead was committed to realism more than modernism, but she was still fearless in her incorporation of elements that produced a vivid sense of presence, intensity, drive and will. Lauren Goodlad summarises rather well the kind of realism I am attributing to Stead as she arrived in New York in 1935:

> Although realism enunciates itself as a mode of representation conducive to epistemological work – what Jameson, in a more auspicious formulation, has called the task of *"seeing things, [and] finding out things, that have not been registered before"* – there is, we contend, no reason to suppose that this representational affinity shuts down the creation of compellingly innovative forms, style or techniques.[45]

It is another indicator of the timeliness of this monograph on Stead that a seemingly custom-made description of her realism – that includes a registration of active, critical, ethnographic drivers as well as acknowledging radical innovation and hybrid form – should emerge from transnational considerations of the peripheries of the world system that are sensitive to the world totalities of capitalism.

In 1974, Stead delivered this description of her American sojourn after almost thirty years away: "the Thirties was a terrific convulsion in the U.S.A., and the whole of society was in a ferment, nobody really knew which way the society was going. Oh, it was a terrific epoch, very thrilling."[46] This book will assess Stead's American work

---

44 Joe Cleary, "Realism after Modernism and the Literary World-System," *Modern Language Quarterly* 73, no. 3 (2012), 262.
45 Lauren Goodlad, "Introduction: Worlding Realisms Now." *Novel* 1 August 2016 49, no. 2, 184. Goodlad is citing Fredric Jameson, "Realism and Utopia in *The Wire*." *Criticism* 52, no. 3 (2010): 359-372. My emphasis.

as an interconnected set of episodes that respond to this scene of convulsion. Chapter One traces the key influences on Stead's politics and aesthetics, fleshing out the kind of transnational literary realism that she brought to America in 1935. I start with her origins in Antipodean modernity and work my way westward in an expansive figure intended to echo the expansiveness of her experimental realism. Stead's first American novel, *The Man Who Loved Children*, is addressed in Chapters Two and Three, where claims about the genre of domestic fiction and gendered power will be elaborated. Questions of patriarchal domination in Chapter Two will be answered with forms of feminine resistance and revolution in Chapter Three.

Stead's account of certain neighbourhoods and milieux in New York City before, during and after World War II comprise an under-read Australian and transnational engagement with this unique world metropolis at a key emergent moment in modernity (1935–46). In this capitalist hub, the circulation of stories and commodities, and the restlessness of economic survival and libidinal progress, are the facets of urban experience thematised by Stead through her rendition of the New York *picara* (*Letty Fox: Her Luck*), the post-war dilettante (*The People with the Dogs*) and the wartime financier-libertine (*A Little Tea, A Little Chat*). Chapters Four and Five deliver readings of Stead's New York trilogy through various iterations of the picaresque character and picaresque narrative structure, with a particular attention for the ways in which gender interacts with both market forces and alienation are negotiated.

I'm Dying Laughing is the subject of Chapter Six. The female clown as humourist and political writer stands at the centre of this enormous posthumous novel, one that addresses American national identity and American radical identity with force and originality. This chapter will investigate the inflationary figure of contradiction and its related crises as a Hegelian Marxist figure central to Marxist economics and political economy. Contradiction is the centrepiece around which Stead choreographs her meditation on the failure of the American radical Left in a very turbulent period. The mixed genres of tragicomedy and chronicle amplify and extend the anatomy of contradiction traced by this novel, raising questions about history, generationality and the very possibility of a form of homegrown American tragedy.

---

46   Anne Whitehead, "An Interview with Christina Stead", *Australian Literary Studies* 6, no. 3 (1974), 244.

1
Christina Stead's Westward Expansion: Totality, Avant-Garde Realism and the American Folk

This chapter constructs a contextual field for reading Christina Stead's American fiction by exploring the significant layers of Stead's politics and aesthetics during her impressive westward mobility in the years from 1928, which culminated in her arrival in Boston in July 1935. Her journey from Sydney to London and Paris, and thence to New York, was a journey of evolving and sharpening political and aesthetic focus. The figure of "westward expansion", so familiar from American pioneer rhetoric, organises this historicised reading of Stead's American novels. Stead's work can best be understood as arising from a specifically Australian bedrock, gathering syncretic force through westward movement across the Indian and then the Atlantic Oceans and into Europe, and on to the east and west coasts of the United States. This contextual field includes biographical and bibliographic detail, which, though interesting in its own right, is driven by the need to secure a clear literary premise that supports the larger argument made in this book – that Stead arrived in the United States as a committed, if experimental and deeply original, mid-century realist. We can identify her American sequence as a series of realist novels that work restlessly and intelligently with different genres in response to the prompts to critique offered by the matter of America.

The Man Who Loved Children (1940), *Letty Fox: Her Luck* (1944), *A Little Tea, A Little Chat* (1948), *The People with the Dogs* (1950) and *I'm Dying Laughing* (1986; initially drafted in the late 1940s and early to mid 1950s) display a specific kind of realism that responds to the matter of America.[1] Stead arrived in America in 1935 with a newly re-focused realist aesthetic that responded to Popular Front debates about politics and literature as well as particular provocations from American

---

1 Although *House of All Nations* was influenced by the fact that some of its drafting was undertaken in New York, and for American publishers (drafted 1936–37; published 1938), this chapter will only touch on it as it relates to Stead's American realism. For similar reasons I will only refer in passing to *For Love Alone* (1945), which was also influenced by its American context of production and reception.

politics and American literary genealogies. We can see some of this realist focus when we look at the difference between *The Beauties and the Furies* (set in early 1934, finished before the Paris Congress in mid-1935 but published in April 1936) and *House of All Nations* (drafted in 1935–36 after the main Left writers' congresses and published in 1938). However, her realism retained the traces of the aesthetic sediments that were a direct corollary of her physical movement at a seminal time in her writing life. Although it is in some sense a critical realism, married to functions of critique and indebted to an ambient sense of the work of critical theory of the 1930s, it is also a realism that is disturbed and extended by a background in formations of marvellous intensities from Australian, surrealist and avant-garde influences.

When Stead left Sydney in May 1928, she carried with her an already strong and resonant base for the writing to come, established through a family enthusiasm for the Australian vernacular classics and her own dedication to European (mainly French) realism and avant-garde theatre; a reading that she grafted onto a youthful love for European fairy tales and their miniature versions of the gothic mode.[2] In addition, as Hazel Rowley and Michael Ackland report, the young provincial woman had a developing politics of her own, grounded in the iconoclastic (socialist and culturally nationalist) politics of her father's household. Extramural engagement with psychology and sociology at the University of Sydney in the early 1920s added substance and texture to these politics. Some of the originality and power of Stead's realism is also indebted to her autodidactic passion for philosophers that she had loved as an adolescent, such as Nietzsche. To this she added Bergson and psychologists such as Adler, who were being read and discussed in University circles in the 1920s.[3]

Oceanic Totality and the "Sea of Story"

In 1964, the Saint Lucian poet, Derek Walcott published *The Castaway and Other Poems*. Already known as a poet of the sea, this volume announced Walcott's adoption of the Crusoe figure as an optic for his representation of worldly movement, colonial history and an ambivalent relationship to his own island home in the Caribbean. Five years later, Christina Stead published an essay in *Kenyon Review* that made a cognate move. In this essay she secured her origins as an Australian writer,[4] but this was founded in her origin as a "sea-woman". National identity and the sea were conflated, which, in the ambiguous geography of

---

2   Margaret Harris, "Christina Stead's Earliest Publications", *Australian Literary Studies* 31, no. 6 (2016), 1–10.
3   See the differing accounts of early political exposure in Hazel Rowley, *Christina Stead: A Biography* (Port Melbourne: Minerva, 1994) and Michael Ackland, *Christina Stead and the Socialist Heritage* (New York: Cambria Press, 2016).
4   Christina Stead, "England", *Kenyon Review* 30, no. 4 (1968) 444.

Australia's position as the only island continent, picked up the island logic of the sea while ignoring the land logic of the continent. Her formulation of Australia's position as an island in the "water hemisphere"[5], and her own position as a coastal dweller of this island, allowed her to conflate continent with its antipode, the ocean, as cognate countries of which she had natural citizenship. This move to unify land and sea indexes her thinking about the sea as the ideal figure of unity and the material basis for her almost involuntary mobility. Movement was not volitional for Stead; sea-worthiness and ocean-going adventures were simply inevitable as a birthright. This was an account of a national and writerly origin that she promulgated throughout interviews in the 1970s, until her death in early 1983.

Stead's perspective on her nation and region was formed through proximity to the ocean, and the Pacific Ocean in particular. The oceanic saturates her aesthetic vision in the form of an emphasis on totality (epic scale), materiality (including economic life) and the vitality of incessant movement. The ocean was a point of genesis for the worldly realism that Stead brought to and further developed in America. Later prose influences arose from, or were sympathetic with, her early formation alongside the marine world, including surrealist formulations of the marvellous, realist commitments to the texture of matter and Lukács' priority for life and the epic vision of the whole. Thus, Stead's originality as a realist of world standing is founded on the oceanic aesthetics developed in Australia and extended throughout her travelling life.

Stead mobilises the argument that her proximity to the sea was dominated by her ceaseless rhythms of the working sea. The economic life of the sea was evident in the aleatory circulation of capital from colonial periphery to imperial centre through the constant traffic of harbour shipping. Industrial strikes by ferry and dock workers, the tenuous life of the Sydney Harbour fishermen, and the involvement of her father with the public sector management of New South Wales Fisheries, introduced her to the politics of the sea, and this was another layer of oceanic influence.[6] David George Stead had written at least four books on Australian fish and crustaceans by the time she was six, and Stead's upbringing in the house of this charismatic and self-taught naturalist meant that she was keenly aware of the dimensions and importance of her natural environment. Even though Sydney existed as a key outpost on the colonial/imperial periphery, there was little doubt in Stead's mind that for scale, originality and richness of natural

---

5   Christina Stead, *For Love Alone* (1945; Sydney: Angus & Robertson), 1966, 1.
6   In an interview with Anne Whitehead, Stead identified a strong connection between her international politics and the politics of her youth: "I'd like to point out that the Australian legend is very radical … Australia is a Labor commonwealth." She goes on to cite Marcus Clarke, and then Henry Lawson and Banjo Paterson as key influences on the Bush tradition, as well as the grim stories of the pioneering white explorers. She also notes that, aged fifteen, "all the sorrows of Europe and the revolutions of Europe were known to us, or anybody who cared to learn." Anne Whitehead, "An Interview with Christina Stead", *Australian Literary Studies* 6, no. 3 (1974), 240.

environment, Australia was redoubtably significant. The vital materiality and scale of Australian flora, fauna and landscape are elements in her writing that Stead herself foregrounded under the sign of the sea-woman story she was to tell about her upbringing and eventual expatriation.[7] With a strong impression of vital totality at a young age, Stead's eventual American realism was the recognition of one panorama from the point of view of another, though the hemispheres were different and the mapping of colonial experience was provocatively asymmetrical.

After her return to Australia in the 1970s, when she was being interviewed more frequently, Stead deployed the sea-woman identity as an intriguing way to deal with questions about the reasons for her expatriation to Europe in 1928. She robustly declared her central premise: to be Australian was to be already a citizen of the sea. Her conflation of national identity and the geographical identity of the island continent allowed her to argue that there was no especial volition to going abroad; she had an automatic dual citizenship to sea and nation that generated a symbiotic relationship between a marine identity and an Australian one. An Australian could and would, of course, travel in the country of the sea as a rightful citizen, familiar as they were with the experience of a nation and a continent as a unity that required no passports or negotiation of national borders:

> And the sea – we were all closely connected with the sea. It was part of our lives. Now the sea is a continent with no passports; it's a country in itself. We felt we belonged to the sea. It wasn't a question of leaving Australia, nothing to do with that at all.[8]

Here Stead postulates a relation that has become much more familiar in the recent oceanic turn: that the ocean is a figure of connection rather than division, and that, as Margaret Cohen has suggested, the "marine transoceanic undercuts the focus on nation".[9] From the point of view of Stead's American realism, the sea granted an *a priori* sense of worldliness through figures of connection and expanse, multiple citizenship and an appreciation of the movement of capital. The most important

---

7   Christina Stead to Stanley Burnshaw, 10 June 1965. In *A Web of Friendship: Selected Letters 1928–1973*, ed. R.G. Geering (Pymble, NSW: Angus & Robertson, 1992), 172. Stead was referring to possible titles for the short story collection with the working title of the *The Dianas* (which then became *The Puzzleheaded Girl*) and *The Restless Wave* was another possibility. Stead relates to Burnshaw that she liked the original quotation from Fiona McLeod's *Sea-Magic and Running Water*: "And Manannan heard the man say: / *I will give you love and home and peace* /The sea-woman listened to that and said: / *And I will bring you the homelessness of the / sea and the peace of the restless wave and / love like the wandering wind.*" Stead comments that, "being a sea-woman, it appealed to me."
8   Christina Stead and Rodney Wetherell, "Interview with Christina Stead," *Australian Literary Studies*, 9, no. 4, (1980), 432. https://doi.org/10.20314/als.f6039f695d.
9   Margaret Cohen, *The Novel and the Sea* (Princeton, NJ: Princeton University Press, 2012), 658.

aesthetic contribution of the sea to Stead's origins as a writer, however, was the immersive sense of connective totality.

The original symbiosis between Stead and the sea was first a question of specific location. From Lydham Hall, the sandstone family home high on the ridge in the Sydney suburb of Bexley: "you could see between the heads of Botany Bay – Cape Banks, Cape Solander – and most days which were clear you could see straight through to the Blue Mountains".[10] After 1917, when the large Stead family moved in straitened circumstances to Pacific Street, Watson's Bay (still a fisherman's hamlet on a harbour bay close to the Sydney Heads) she lived only 500 metres from the harbour shore and her affiliation with the ocean intensified. To Graeme Kinross-Smith, she recalled the physical world of Watsons Bay as almost entirely marine: "We swam year round except for two or three of the winter months".[11] The sense of submergence affected the family home, too:

> and in big storms the spray from the Gap used to come right on the roof of our house. It's so close to the ocean. And all the ocean liners, and other ships, mercantile ships and so on, came right in front of our house. The pilot ship was always there, anchored there, and they used to stay there for quarantine. We saw all the ships that came into the harbour, it was very thrilling. And this was the reason why going abroad seemed so natural, because these ships were always in and out, in and out.[12]

This intimacy with the ocean is detailed in the opening pages of *Seven Poor Men of Sydney* as part of Stead's inaugurating vision of 1920s Sydney as an emergent economic centre; the repeated focus on the ships themselves indicates Stead's keen interest in the movement of people and goods as the capital base of Sydney's provincial development. To Anne Whitehead, Stead claimed: "the sea was in a sense my country, and I knew that".[13] All the extensive journeys of her nomadic life, save the repatriating ones in the late 1960s and early 1970s, were by sea. Stead exhibited a lifelong inclination to associate women in modernity with sea-going vessels, which, in a range of different contexts, configured femininity as mobile, adventurous, piratical and malleable, possessed of freight or cargo, or looking for it. In Stead's novels women, like ships, were consciously involved in various kinds of trade – sexual, economic and transnational – as part of a larger effort to manage female survival.

The late interviews repeat and amplify material that first appeared in a contribution Stead made to "The International Symposium on the Short Story" in the *Kenyon Review* more than ten years earlier, in 1968. This short essay, "Ocean

---

10 Quoted in Stead and Wetherell, "Interview with Christina Stead", 436.
11 Quoted in Graeme Kinross-Smith, "Christina Stead: A Profile", *Westerly*, 1, (1976), 69.
12 Quoted in Stead and Wetherell, "Interview with Christina Stead", 436–7.
13 Quoted in Whitehead, "An Interview with Christina Stead", 235.

of Story", was one that Ron Geering used as the opening to his edition of Stead's uncollected stories of the same name, in 1985. Stead's oceanic sense of Australia is traced back to her earliest memories and is inextricably linked to storytelling. She relates how, as a young child of two, her "bed was made up on a large packing case in which were my father's specimens, a naturalist's toys, things from the oceans around us and from the north, Indonesia, China, Japan".[14] Stories proliferated during these night-time occasions of the bedtime tale, when the young Stead was arranged for sleep atop the luggage from her father's marine travels, and the tales of adventure were generated by the exotic objects stored in the cases underneath her. Her father would ask: "'What is in the packing case?' I would tell and, what I forgot, he told" (5). Stead's account of her own storytelling foregrounds her father and his synonymousness with Cook and Banks, rolling together the original master storyteller with the European-invader origins of the island continent.[15] It is the father's voice that generated the "sonorous envelope" of childhood stories; he tested her memory and provided an apprenticeship in storytelling, ocean lore and sea adventure. This voice, and the ocean which it evoked, were the two key elements of Stead's earliest "surround sound" of conscious impressions, coordinates that ordinarily reference the maternal body and its rhythms.

Stead's formidable memory held details about the writer's early instincts that were to be honed and expressed during her writing life : "when he went away, and I wasn't asleep yet, the room would begin to talk to me when I was drowsy, you know. That's, I suppose, how it all started".[16] To Rodney Wetherell, she recalled that:

---

14 Christina Stead, *Ocean of Story: The Uncollected Stories of Christina Stead*, ed. R.G. Geering (Ringwood: Penguin, 1986), 4. All subsequent references are to this edition and appear in parentheses in the text.

15 Stead's later interviews repeat the citation of her father as original storyteller-scientist of the sea world, and herself as the apprentice who would go on to be the family storyteller to her step-sister and brothers, with the sea as her imaginative muse. This is an account of vocation that builds throughout the 1970s. To Anne Whitehead in 1974, she said that: "I have a feeling of the great outback because my father was a naturalist and, in my very early years, when I was a baby, he told me stories of the whole coastline and the history of Australia, the animals" (230). Speaking to Kay Keavney in 1976 she recalled that "he taught her the names of fish and other animals … and made her recite them to him before she went to bed" perched atop "a packing case containing biological specimens – skeletons, fossils, shells which would fill her dreams". Kay Keavney, "Ranked with the Immortals: Christina Stead", *The Australian Women's Weekly*, 17 November 1976, 71–72. To Wetherell: "he was a young scientist then, and he loved Australia. And the things I heard as I went to sleep were all about … the geography – the seashores – the wildlife". Stead and Wetherell, "Interview with Christina Stead", 435.

16 She repeats these details about the talking and complaining furniture that emerged in her father's absence to John Beston in 1975 (and to Graeme Kinross-Smith in 1976), adding, "oddly, there's something in Grimm like that" (93). By the time Stead told this version of her writer's origin story to Wetherell in 1980, themes of oppression, inclusion of the hazy state between waking and sleeping and glimpses of a great natural sense of drama and personality have emerged. This suggests that the critical reception of her work was perhaps beginning to make its way into her own account of her origin as a writer. John B. Beston,

things would begin talking to me, probably because I was being talked to. Everything was having a conversation around me. The wardrobe, and the cupboard and the bed, the big double bed was there, in which he was alone by the door, and the bit of mat – it wasn't a carpet – they were having conversations with each other.

Stead muses about these conversations: "this was a sort of dramatic instinct, you know".[17] When her father left the room, the young Stead went on to imagine voices of her own; to dramatise the furniture's silent lives by giving them specific characters and setting them in dialogue with one another, thus vitalising the scene through conflict, personality and presence. Stead's earliest storytelling instincts, in her own retelling, were about the immersive drama of the individual conveyed through speech.

Stead writes that her apprenticeship in a thousand and one nights of sea stories occurred between the ages of two and four and a half: "… it went on and on, night after night for more than two years" (5). This was the time after the death of Stead's mother but before her father re-married and many step-siblings appeared. Emerging from this period, she took up her father's mantle and became the family teller of tales, though she told "different stories", starting with European fairy tales and then "made up her own":

By five years I used to sing them to sleep and rock them to sleep; and when they were very little and later on I used to tell them stories, talk them to sleep, just as my father had done, except I told different stories. They were mostly out of Grimm and Hans Andersen. I was always fond of those two and still am, and later on I made up some of my own, and that's how it all started.[18]

Stead's account of her origin as a writer rests explicitly on the Arabian storytelling structure of *One Thousand and One Nights* and, before that, the older compendium from the Indian tradition – the *Kathasaritsagara* (*The Ocean of the Streams of Stories*). Stead references this directly: "I was born into the ocean of story, or on its shores" (4). The *Kathasaritsgara* enabled the *One Thousand and One Nights*, and, in time, *The Canterbury Tales,* which, in turn, influenced Stead's early collection of frame tales, *The Salzburg Tales* (1934). The native treasury of story is glossed by Stead as an inexhaustible anthology, like the ocean itself. The ocean becomes Stead's great figure for the scale of human generativity showcased in huge collections of tales:

"An Interview with Christina Stead", *World Literature in English* 15, no. 1 (1976), 93; Whitehead, "An Interview with Christina Stead", 242.
17 Quoted in Stead and Wetherell, "Interview with Christina Stead", 435.
18 Quoted in "Stead and Wetherell, "Interview with Christina Stead", 444.

> But there it was, the ocean of story, starting out in the drops, drops of hill-dew, or sweat on the mountain's brow, running down, joining trickles from the rocks ... broadening and sounding deep and moving in its fullness toward the ocean of story. (10)

For Stead, the ocean was a figure of totality, an interconnected whole made up of multiplicities of life and matter. The human capacity for story is a key expression of the fullness of this totality: "How can anyone store up this vast natural treasury? It is inexhaustible ... There is always a free and fresh supply" (11). The inexhaustible scale of the natural world was the backdrop for her father's stories, which habitually demonstrated "an interest in men and nature, *a feeling that all were equal,* the extinct monster, the coral insect, the black man and us, the birds and the fish; and another curious feeling still with me, of terrestrial eternity, a sun that never set" (5, my emphasis).

As the native of a huge island continent, valued for its scope of life and vital difference, Stead named herself a native of the even greater sea, and called on "the magnitude of the starry distances and our infinitesimal life" (6) as the scene of her earliest awareness of both nation and of story. Infinitude, or totality, was a feeling that was intensely alive for Stead in the late 1960s as she recalled her earliest scenes of artistic vocation. The sense of the life of the whole is crucial to Stead's aesthetics and she was focused during her early and mid-career stages on finding or developing what Donna Jones has called, in her masterful study of vitalism, "modes of perception through which life as it actually is can be known or intuited".[19]

I want to propose, therefore, that Christina Stead's vision of her origin as a writing subject is s related to the importance of immersion. Her sense of her own emergence into consciousness and aesthetic awareness is characterised by a vision of totality figured as immersion, giving us a double structure of immersing and emerging. The island-dwelling and harbourside porosity of the young Stead, described most beautifully in the marine scenes that dominate the first half of *For Love Alone* (1944), was accompanied by an early sense of the equally immersive power of storytelling. Good stories made things vitally present. Powerful stories conjured the vital materialities of desire, sensation and personality. In Stead's life, this power had been first intuited in the 'surround sound' of the voice of her father as he spoke about the ocean, near the ocean and on the ocean, in the form of the packing cases that were her bed. Ocean, story and speech are all key elements involved in Stead's immersive aesthetics. There is a significance to these qualities of totality and immersion that is picked up in another context by Brigid Rooney in her essay, "Christina Stead's 'Kelly File': Politics, Possession and the writing of *Cotter's England*", where she elaborates an argument about Stead and her approach to the composition of character as a kind of possession. Rooney

---

19 Donna Jones, *The Racial Discourses of Life Philosophy: Négritude, Vitalism and Modernity* (New York: Columbia University Press, 2010), 5.

argues that the "notion of 'possession'" is "a doubled and spectral dynamic" that is integral to Stead's "creative modus operandi". She suggests that "on the one hand this involves the writer in taking possession by means of naturalist observation and classification, and on the other hand it entails being possessed."[20] I would argue that the drive to possess and be possessed speaks to the pleasures and propulsions of immersion, which, in turn, frame Stead's commitment to the vitality of *energeia*; the unflagging and often wayward drive to make rhetorical or artistic experience as immediate as possible. The fraught yet productive desire for immersion is anchored in the original Antipodean scene of marine and vocal immersion dominated by the Captain Cook-father figure, the original touchstone of vocal immediacy or *enargeia*. The interplay between the ambivalent pleasures of immersion and vociferous orality in so many of Stead's key characters emerges in the context of a surrealist aesthetics of sensation and automaticity in Stead's early works. Later, it emerges in the vocal architectures of political hypocrisy and heedless domination. The danger of being swallowed up and the desire to be just so consumed propel the fictions of Stead's appetitive characters from at least *The House of All Nations*. The thematics of a luxuriously expressive yet deeply threatening orality also describes something of the experience of reading her work from the late 1930s until the end of her career. This drive toward total inhabitation speaks to the mechanisms and pleasures of immersion, driven by Stead's desire for the vitality of *enargeia*, the rhetorical drive to make material present, even engulfing for the reader. Rooney proposes that Stead herself desired engulfment, and in her late interviews, Stead stages this desire in the original scenes of the marine and vocative immersions of storytelling. Though the interplay between the ambivalent pleasures of engulfment and the vociferous orality modulates across the American sequence, it doesn't, in fact, trend entirely toward an increasingly dark vision that tracks and parallels the defeat of the Left in America. It is Stead's major postwar work, *Cotter's England*, which signals the late-career trend toward a thematics of engulfment (sexual and vocal) without pleasure.

Provincial Vitality

Stead's insight into the plenitude and scale of her Australian origins is central to the story she reiterates about her origin as a writer of panoramic marvels. Ivor Indyk's work on the provincial imagination is relevant here, since his thinking on the provincial artist as encyclopaedist connects with Stead's affinity for totality and her later encyclopaedic vision of America. In his 2008 study of Les Murray and Murray Bail, Indyk argues that, contrary to generally accepted ideas of provincialism as synonymous with insularity, expansiveness was more in evidence:

---

20 Rooney, Brigid. "Christina Stead's 'Kelly File': Politics, Possession and the Writing of *Cotters' England*." *Australian Literary Studies* 31, no. 6 (2016), 3.

The expansive tendency is integral to the provincial stance, which is used to looking within its world and beyond it at the same time. The common understanding of wonder, as not just an attentive state, but also one which is absorbed by the immensity of the perspective, or the implications, opined by the detail, which has captured its attention.[21]

The provincial prodigy was liable to "mystical apprehensions of presence", open to indicators of immanence and a vision of the plenitude of things.[22] This expansive sense of wonder – a grasp of dimension and perspective and an attentive and absorbed capacity for detail – is displayed throughout Stead's work, but perhaps the most famous examples are the "Sea People" prologue of *For Love Alone* and Kol Blount's closing sea eulogy in *Seven Poor Men of Sydney*. Her receptiveness to the marvellous was more generally anticipated by her childhood fondness for fairy tales and then the gothic mode; it continued during her Paris years as part of her engagement with Surrealism.[23]

The provincial Australian writer, on Indyk's argument, was also well equipped to respond to and deploy apprehensions of the panoramic and the vital. As her oceanic commentary suggests, Stead's work is informed by the desire for and interest in vitality, scale and presence. In the early 1970s, she remembered her young adulthood interest in vitalism in these terms:

> The only thing I liked about Australia at that time was a magazine brought out by the Lindsays and their friends called *Vision*; it was a quarterly, a sort of de-luxe affair, you know, it was very thrilling ... At home we had Steele Rudd, I read that, and Lawson and Banjo Paterson, all that sort of thing. I liked that.[24]

The Lindsays, avowedly anti-modernist, believed in a vitality that lay at the heart of a down-under renaissance offering an aesthetic alternative to decadent and worn-out Europe and its introspective modernist forms. It is Bergson, then, through the Lindsays, that we must see as perhaps the most profound and underrated influence on Stead's vision of the rich and specific liveliness of the Australian island-continent, its waters and its people. If the Lindsays' vitalist publications were seminal for the young provincial prodigy, so too were the works of the nationalist Bush tradition and the vernacular comic energies of Steele Rudd.

The provincial writer with whose work Stead had the most contact was Balzac. As Stead said of her high school years: "I fell overboard for Balzac ... I read all the French books in the Municipal Library in Sydney and Balzac was one of my main discoveries".[25] In a pair of letters in June 1942 to Bill Blake when he was

---

21 Ivor Indyk, "Provincialism and Encyclopaedism", *Island* 127 (2011), 84.
22 Indyk, "Provincialism and Encyclopaedism", 84.
23 Harris, "Christina Stead's Earliest Publications".
24 Quoted in Whitehead, "An Interview with Christina Stead", 233.

in Hollywood and she was in New York, Stead puts Balzac at the centre of her inspiration (and her love for Blake): "Old Balzac, I suppose, is one of my masters. I think more or less like him. The next day she added: "Balzac is the one writer I feel as a man – every word he writes seems to be spoken in my ear. I can really see that man, I know him and understand him, as a man ... He was very like you as a personality, no question".[26] Her preference for compendious forms – such as large treasuries or compendiums of tales and Balzac's own vast anatomy – reveals the shared encyclopaedic drive towards the complete account. Christopher Prendergast sees Balzac's contribution to the tradition of classic realism as the attempt to show man and society in their "completeness".[27] For both Stead and Balzac, this drive to the whole necessitated an endless negotiation with the form of the realist novel. Balzac's *La Comédie Humaine* comprises a network of realist novels that offers an anatomy of French provincial life. This anatomy exposes the *habitus* of the provincial middle-class in the kind of detail and with a kind of honesty to which sociologists and ethnographers could only aspire. As Adorno comments in his essay on Balzac in *Notes to Literature II*: "Balzac's prose does not yield to realities but rather stares them in the face until they become transparent down to their horrors".[28] The unflinching commitment to look hard and record what he saw led Balzac to teeming excess and unmanageablity, but also to an unparalleled portrait in his own time of politics, sex and money. Balzac and Stead's prose "open up what society and the novel of manners repress, to stage a kind of explosive upthrust of that which is ordinarily kept down under control".[29] Peter Brooks asserts that the goal of Balzac's imagination was to find: "the latent intensities of life. This takes him beyond the bounds of the 'realism', for which he became famous, into another space, a more occult realm where the real is trumped by the nearly surreal".[30] This maps Stead's trajectory very precisely, both in her attraction to Surrealism and in the ways that it remained as a disturbance in her realist work throughout her life.

Surrealist Revolutions and the Intensity of Speech

The matter of America arose in Stead's life in a very substantial way when she arrived in England in 1928. St Louis-born, New York-raised Wilhelm Blech (whom

---

25 Quoted in Stead and Wetherell, "Interview with Christina Stead", 446.
26 Stead to Blake, June 16, 1942, in *Dearest Munx: The Letters of Christina Stead and William J. Blake* ed. Margaret Harris (Carlton, Vic.: Miegunyah, 2005), 225, 231.
27 Christopher Prendergast, *Balzac: Fiction and Melodrama* (London: Hodder and Stoughton, 1978), 153.
28 Theodor Adorno, *Notes to Literature II*, ed. Rolf Tiedemann, trans. Shierry Weber Nicholson (New York: Columbia University Press, 1991), 132.
29 Peter Brooks, "Introduction", *The Human Comedy: Selected Stories by Honore de Balzac* ed. Peter Brooks, (New York: New York Review Books, 2014), xxi.
30 Brooks, "Introduction", *The Human Comedy*, vii.

I will now refer to as William or Bill Blake, as he called himself from 1938) was the man with whom Stead began a forty-year relationship in the very first week of her arrival in London, though he was her employer in the first instance. Bill Blake was a most curious and contradictory thing, an American Marxist businessman, working for the most part in banking, commodity trading and speculative investment; his most stable income over the next twenty years derived from his capacity for shrewd research into equities and commodities, from which he advised bankers and other kinds of financial speculators.[31] He therefore worked at the unstable end of capitalism – the one most associated with gambling – and was often on the move in pursuit of this work. Stead and Blake then lived a joint life of intense mobility. In many ways, travelling mobility became their *habitus* – a kind of restless position to which their correspondence attests. Together they represent a fascinating mixture of priorities and commitments: theories of economic behaviour and history, accounts of political economy and the primacy of the imagination in both political responsiveness and the aesthetics of the novel. As mobile citizens of the world, the hub of Left ideology was the basis of the modes of critique they engaged wherever they took up residence in London, Paris and New York.

It is hard to underestimate the significance of the Paris years (1929–34) on Stead's American novels, which, including her short commentary on America, are mediated by a sense of a European (especially French and Soviet) political and cultural point of view. Living on the Left Bank, Stead and Blake worked with American bankers and financiers during the day and socialised with the margins of the American expatriate artistic and political communities at night.[32] The heyday of the Lost Generation was past, but there was in its wake a strengthening of political and aesthetic purpose on the Left in reaction to the rise of fascism in Europe. Although Stead continued her formidable program of reading in English, it is possible she was more influenced by French Surrealism at this moment than has generally been claimed.[33] Critics are inclined to see James Joyce as the great

---

31 This research was published as William Blake, *Elements of Marxist Economic Theory and its Criticisms* (New York: Cordon, 1940) and the shorter version was William Blake, *An American Looks at Karl Marx* (New York: Cordon, 1939). Blake had been radicalised as a child growing up in the Lower East Side of Manhattan, watching the iron chains of poverty, illness and oppression in the Jewish ghetto. Blake was a bright young man who had to leave school to support the family as a runner on Wall Street. It was there he taught himself Marxist economics and this autodidactic commitment cemented his allegiance to the Bolshevik cause that he first supported at the end of World War I (and later the Soviet experiment) and never wavered. He always felt that the only resistance to fascism was through commitment to an economic theory that understood, and offered a systematic way of thinking about, the vagaries of capital.
32 Rowley, *Christina Stead*, 231.
33 The key exceptions here are Robin Dizard in her PhD thesis, "Changing the Subject: The Early Novels of Christina Stead" (University of Massachusetts, 1984) and Paul Giles in his chapter on Stead in *Antipodean America: Australasia and the Constitution of US Literature* (Oxford: Oxford University Press, 2013).

influence on Stead in her Paris years, but the French language avant-garde exerted an even greater pull, especially as so many of the remaining American artists in Paris were involved in Surrealist circles. There were several points of intersection between the American expatriate circles in which Stead and Blake moved during their Paris sojourn, and the predominantly American circle who powered the long-running experimental literary quarterly, *transition*. Political art, innovative aesthetics and the work of translation were at least three points of common interest for both these circles on the Left Bank, with an especial interest in a wide definition of experimental work with language.

Seven Poor Men of Sydney (composed 1928–31), *The Salzburg Tales* (composed 1932–33) and to a lesser extent, *The Beauties and the Furies* (composed 1934–35), show the influence of Surrealism in Stead's repertoire of dreams and waking visions, Dalí-esque symbolism and renditions of Gothic nightmare and her interest in the motion capture of specific desire and habitus through the speaking voice. Of Stead's early work, Barnard Eldershaw wrote a rather wonderful description that frames her avant-garde engagement beautifully, though she (they) did not mean to be exactly complimentary:

> It is not fantasy in the world of fantasy, but fantasy in a world of reality and reality in a world of fantasy. The Historical mingles with the imaginary, the real with the unreal in bewildering confusion, and the author behaves as if both worlds, or all worlds, were of the same value.[34]

For a realist, who was constantly stretching her prose muscles in order to convey the chaos, vitality and flux of life, fantasy and dream could prove powerfully true to life, and an invaluable aesthetic tool in its pursuit. As Walter Benjamin commented in his famous 1929 essay on Surrealism: "… at the time when it broke over its founders as an inspiring dream wave, it seemed the most integral, conclusive, absolute of movements. Everything with which it came into contact was integrated".[35] Surrealism was of the greatest interest to Stead at this time in Paris because of this precise point about integration: this was an avant-garde practice in which the forces of imagination and desire were seen as integral to revolutionary politics. As Jeremy MacClancy argues:

> In their desire to smash the shackles of an authoritarian rationality, the surrealists sought to liberate minds by using any method they could imagine to dislocate conventional reason: automatic writing, highlighting overlooked

---

34 M. Barnard Eldershaw, *Essays in Australian Fiction* (Melbourne: Melbourne University Press, 1938), 165–66.
35 Walter Benjamin, "Surrealism: The Last Snapshot of the European Intelligentsia", in *Reflections: Essays, Aphorisms, Autobiographical Writings*, ed. Peter Demetz (1978; New York: Schocken, 1986), 178.

moments when the unconscious erupted into the apparently quotidian, lauding the logic of dreams, and producing poems, texts, pictures, and other artistic items, in any medium, which furthered their aims.[36]

Through reading and writing, Stead had mounted a guerrilla resistance to the hegemony of reason and science in her family home in the forms outlined by MacClancy. Finally, in Paris, her value for imagination and desire was connected productively to the political in the Surrealist context. As Benjamin so elegantly argued, the original and best wish of the Surrealist movement was "to win the energies of intoxication for the revolution", and I would suggest that this very possibility had a tremendous resonance with Stead, who, since she was a child, had mightily contested the preternatural dominance of science with the significance of the imagination.[37]

The Surrealist category of the automatic was one of the most important influences on Stead's fiction. In 1922 a group of artists and writers led by André Breton began to conduct a series of experiments into what Breton called "psychic automatism". This involved writing, speaking, or drawing in a state avoiding "any control exercised by reason [and] exempt from any aesthetic or moral concern". In his first "Manifesto of Surrealism" (1924), Breton proclaimed that "surrealism is based on the belief in the superiority of certain forms of previously neglected associations, in the omnipotence of dreams, in the disinterested play of thought".[38] Automatic discourse raised the possibility of a textual production almost without authorship – a kind of dictation taken while entranced. This could mean working in a dream state or transcribing a waking dream, but for Stead, the automatic was significant because of the impact it had on the way in which she rendered external speech as though it arrived unfiltered and unchecked from the mind. Always dramatic and vital, speech was the strange meeting point between individual psychology and personal materiality. It was the engine of Stead's representation of psychology and character from the outside. Without access to the inside, as it were, because she did not use stream of consciousness, Stead's work with speech is persistently experimental. It was a crucial element in her aesthetics, since speech made her fictional personalities present and vital, despite the strange impossibility of just such a thing. The inexhaustible voice, the convulsive voice, the obsessive and unstoppable voice, are key aspects of Stead's writing. The storehouse of the folkloric and the poetic, the vernacular and the comic, the remembered, manufactured and wilful speech revealed the motive forces of will and desire. Stead's rendition of

---

36 Jeremy MacClancy, "Surrealism and Anthropology", *Oxford Bibliographies*, https://doi.org/10.1093/obo/9780199766567-0140.
37 Benjamin, "Surrealism: The Last Snapshot of the European Intelligentsia", 189.
38 André Breton, "Manifesto of Surrealism" (1924) in *Manifestoes of Surrealism*, trans. Richard Seaver and Helen R. Lane (Ann Arbor: University of Michigan Press, 1969), 26.

speech in her Paris novels reminds us of Benjamin's summation of Surrealism – that it was a "profane illumination, a materialistic anthropological inspiration".[39]

Although Popular Front aesthetics caused Stead to pull back from early Surrealist and avant-garde experiment, there is a latent intensity and restless experimentation in her American realism that is focused on and expressed through speech and the speaking subject. In the decade that Stead spent in America, her experiments with speech dramatised and defined her startling anatomy of American characters and social relations. A disruptive intensity and almost overwhelming mass of speech is marked in *House of All Nations* (1935–36), and this alliance of near automatic speaking and the gigantic character that emerges in this novel is also evident in Sam Pollit in *The Man Who Loved Children*, Letty Fox in *Letty Fox: Her Luck,* Robbie Grant in *A Little Tea, A Little Chat* and Emily Wilkes in *I'm Dying Laughing*. These politically imposing figures gained their gargantuan proportions through often incontinent and overwhelming speech, though, in the case of Letty and Emily, this incontinence was also connected to a complex comic vitality that seemed to be as much admired as reviled.

Popular Front Aesthetics and the Transnational Realist Scalpel

The Popular Front created a clear demarcation in Stead's work between her first three books, which display a realism strongly influenced by avant-garde and European milieux, and her emerging mid-career works, which carried the vitality of an earlier experimental mode but became more obviously committed to realism. Although the Comintern began to emerge from an isolationist period and mobilise the idea of a broad coalition to combat the rising threat of fascism from late 1933, Popular Front was a term first used in October 1934, after the Soviet Writers' Congress in August 1934. The Popular Front was integral to survivalist changes in Soviet foreign policy, but it also successfully tapped into a huge will for a united front against fascism. The Popular Front was therefore an intensely international expression of solidarity, and it was integral to Stead's treatment of the realist novel after 1935.

Katerina Clark offers a useful account of the transnational anti-fascist front from 1935 to 1939 in her work on Mikhail Bakhtin and world literature:

> Travel was also central to the culture of the popular front. The anti-fascists of the diaspora, and their fellow travellers from throughout the world, travelled incessantly, both literally, to the interminable conferences – and more figuratively (such as by correspondence or publication). They participated in transnational networks built from multiple attachments.[40]

---

39 Benjamin, "Surrealism: The Last Snapshot of the European Intelligentsia", 179.

Clark calls on James Clifford's work when she suggests that these fellow travellers exemplify "the travelling mode".[41] In line with Clifford, she maintains that fellow travellers of the 1930s represented the "extra-local perspective" and the critical vision that characterised this mode.[42] "The travelling mode" is an apt description of Stead's general expatriate *modus operandi*, and during the Popular Front in particular, when Stead and Blake were fielding turbulent (and hugely ironic) personal experiences of unstable capital in the context of the declining fortunes of the fraudulent American bank, the Traveler's Bank, where they had both worked since early 1929. This capital collapse saw them travel back and forth between Paris and London throughout 1933 and 1934. In their cross-channel exchanges, they were moving as active fellow travellers, involved in heated European debates and discussions about Soviet policy.[43]

Clark's description of the critical vision that accompanies the "extra local perspective" rather uncannily charts Stead's expanding realism during the Popular Front years. Clark notes Bakhtin's major shift away from polyphony in his work on Dostoyevsky in the early 1930s, to the work on folk culture and the figures of the *picaro*, jester and fool during the Popular Front years. Bakhtin introduced these characters as "eccentric, extra-literary figures who have, as it were, infused literature with the traveling mode" and who operate as "prime agents of exposure".[44] This move in aesthetics, powered by both transnational movement and the political need to engage the "folk", emphasises key literary figures and genres that Stead began to deploy during her American years.

The question of the responsibility of the writer also had a new transnational political urgency. The key international Popular Front Writers' Congresses (backed by the Comintern and held in Moscow, August 1934, in New York, April 1935 and in Paris, June–July 1935) addressed themselves to the nexus of writing and politics with extraordinary focus and zeal. Stead read the papers of the Soviet Writers' Congress and the American Writers' Congress, but she was at the Paris Congress as part of the English delegation. The responsibility and the function of the writer was the key concern at the Writers' Congresses, and starting with Moscow's aesthetic platform of socialist realism, the rhetoric of realism was front and centre. In a wave, all three congresses declared realism as the central tenet of Popular Front aesthetic work. Realism was to rise from its torpor as a nineteenth-century mode

---

40 Katerina Clark, "M.M. Bakhtin and 'World Literature'", *Journal of Narrative Theory* 32, no. 3 (2002), 27.
41 Katerina Clark, *Moscow, the Fourth Rome: Stalinism, Cosmopolitanism, and the Evolution of Soviet Culture, 1931–1941* (Cambridge, MA: Harvard University Press, 2011), 152; James Clifford, *Routes: Travel and Translation in the Late Twentieth Century* (Cambridge, MA: Harvard University Press, 1997).
42 Clark, "M.M. Bakhtin and 'World Literature'", 279.
43 Rowley, *Christina Stead*, 331, 345.
44 Clark, "M.M Bakhtin and 'World Literature'", 281, 283.

obsessed with verisimilitude and come into its own as a twentieth-century political powerhouse.

At the Soviet Congress, Andrei Zhadanov, architect of Stalin's Popular Front cultural policy and of socialist realism in particular, faithfully echoed Stalin's instructions to writers: "To be an engineer of human souls meant standing with both feet firmly planted on the basis of real life".[45] Writers were instructed to strive to "depict reality in its revolutionary development", and realism in particular was called upon to organise a necessary focus on material life and what Gorky called "the vital power of the toiling masses".[46] Several writers and novels were mentioned and endorsed by the Congress as models of the kind of realist work needed by the anti-fascist cause. The literary recommendations and endorsements delivered at the Soviet Congress created a literary genealogy that is clearly linked to Lukács' work in the Soviet Union in the early 1930s. It was consequential for Stead's novels written after 1935 and her American sequence because of a clear focus on the literary adventures of rogues, thieves and assassins. The realist Popular Front counter-canon included novels such as *Simplicissimus*, *Lazarillo De Tormes*, *Gil Blas*, and those by Tobias Smollett, Henry Fielding and Guy de Maupassant. Certain kinds of characters were endorsed, including Faust, Baron Von Munchausen, Gargantua and Pantagruel, while other specific authors such as Percy Shelley, Romain Rolland, André Gide, George Bernard Shaw, Theodore Dreiser, Upton Sinclair and André Malraux were supported.[47] Dickens was seen as too sentimental and unable to see below the surface reality of life, but the continued value for Balzac (following Engels) continued apace. Avant-garde and modernist writing was robustly criticised, with specific hostility reserved for James Joyce and Marcel Proust.

News of the Soviet Writers' Congress is most likely to have come to Stead though the direct report of Ralph Fox. Fox was a British communist, literary critic, journalist and linguist who was at the Marx-Engels Institute in Moscow at the same time as Lukács in 1931. Fox's work of Marxist literary criticism, *The Novel and the People* (written in 1936; published posthumously in 1937), registers the Popular Front platform articulated at the Soviet Writers' Congress in 1934, but elaborates a more nuanced sense of Lukács' wider literary criticism as it stood apart from the Soviet Congress declarations. *The Novel and the People* is so indebted to Lukács that it actually reads as a loose translation of Lukács' literary criticism for an Anglophone audience. It was a deeply influential work for Stead's fiction

---

45 Andrei Zhadanov, "Soviet Literature: The Richest in Ideas, The Most Advanced Literature", in *Soviet Writers' Congress 1934: The Debate on Socialist Realism and Modernism in the Soviet Union* (London: Lawrence and Wishart, 1977), 21.
46 Maxim Gorky, "Soviet Literature", in *Soviet Writers' Congress 1934*, 27.
47 Maxim Gorky, Karl Radek, Nikolai Bukharin, Andrey Zhadanov et al., *Soviet Writers' Congress 1934*.

from its posthumous publication in 1937, though *House of All Nations* (also drafted 1935–36), shows Fox's more general literary and political influence.

In June 1935, Stead and Fox attended the International Writers' Congress for the Defense of Culture as part of the English delegation. Stead's development of the kind of anatomy that makes up her American sequence was informed by the discussions about the responsibility of the revolutionary artist she had witnessed in Paris. Stead wrote a report about the Paris Congress, which was published as "The Writers' Take Sides" in *Left Review* in July 1935. Here she claimed that the role of the author in Popular Front struggle was to "enter the political arena, take lessons from workmen and use their pen as the scalpel lifting the living tissues, cutting through the morbid tissues, of the social anatomy".[48] The formulation of the pen as a scalpel gave Stead a sharp image around which to collect her ideas about the critical obligations of her fiction in Popular Front and other revolutionary contexts. Stead's anatomy of America was powered by a scalpel sense that the work of fiction must expose the contradictions and crisis in the social body. The difference between *The Beauties and the Furies* (1936) and *House of All Nations* (1938) indicates this greater swing toward critique and away from a more heavily symbolic or expressionist modes of writing.

Though he had been a figure of great, if shadowy, influence during the international round of Writers' congresses, Lukács found socialist realism tendentious – it was a literature of agitation that lacked the subtlety of the great works of the European bourgeois realists. In his essay of 1938, "Realism in the Balance", Lukács instead praised contemporary realists such as Thomas Mann, whose grasp of history and social totality was much more politically essential. Mann's "critical realism" mounted a critique of the capital system from a democratic point of view – a point of view sympathetic to socialism but outside it. This was the aesthetic form necessary for the cause of revolution:

> If literature is a particular form by means of which objective reality is reflected, then it becomes of crucial importance for it to grasp that reality as it truly is, and not merely to confine itself to reproducing whatever manifests itself immediately and on the surface.[49]

We can see here that Lukács' choice of realism as the only effective revolutionary form rests on his argument about its capacity to convey a truthful social totality. He argued that a fragmented, and thus temporary or superficial, purchase on socio-political reality meant that hidden social forces could not be revealed in modernist literary texts. The fact that capitalism formed a unitary and pervasive

---

48   Christina Stead, "The Writers Take Sides", *Left Review* 1, no. 2 (1935), 454.
49   György Lukács, "Realism in the Balance", in Ernst Bloch, Theodor Adorno, Walter Benjamin, Bertolt Brecht and György Lukács, *Aesthetics and Politics* (London: Verso, 1977), 39.

whole remained hidden in these works. Mann's critical realism and Stead's critical realism had the essential capacity to reveal the contradictions and points of crisis and alienation inherent to capitalist modernity. Stead's American sequence engages this project with particular force, although this trajectory is obvious in her great banking novel, *House of All Nations*, based on Stead's early days in Paris, working with American banking and financiers.

Daniel Hartley has argued that, for Lukács, realism was actually less a particular form and more an embodiment of an "epic aspiration towards totality"; a kind of categorical imperative complicated by the loss of social and aesthetic integration that Lukcas associated with the alienations of modernity.[50] Following this logic, Hartley suggests that realism (and particularly critical realism) could and did contain and broker compendious relationships with multiple modes and forms to which it might have been constituitively opposed, including fantasy, the grotesque, parable and allegory. This lack of antinomy between artistic experiment and verisimilitude is precisely what the most compelling realists of the nineteenth and twentieth century achieved, and certainly what Stead achieved. Hartley's formulation, Fox's literary criticism and Stead's literary practice seem to me to erode the entrenched binary opposition between modernism and realism. For Stead, the forms and drives of realism (presence, the truth, vitality, sight) were really inseparable from the drive toward the representation of an intuited whole, seated in the magnetism of vital life. Stead's early oceanic and storytelling experiences with imaginative scale, material plenitude and vitality meant that her aesthetic priorities for realism and the question of totality had always been in play, but the events of 1935 sharpened this focus as she left France and moved into her American sequence.

True to his Lukácsian commitments, Ralph Fox also argued that totality should be the prime driver of the revolutionary realist writer, who should strive to render a "complete picture of modern life" and thus enable readers "to perceive the truth of that life". In Fox's view, there was a "great refusal of present day writers" to "face reality as a whole":

> The novelist cannot write his story of the individual fate unless he also has this steady vision of the whole. He must understand how his final result arises from the individual conflict of his characters, he must in turn understand what are the manifold conditions of lives which have made each of those individuals what she or he is.[51]

Fox also argues that "exclusion of sentiment and analysis" and "failure to see the subjective side of the individual" actually "deprive the novel of imagination and

---

50 Daniel Hartley, "The Concept of Totality in Lukács and Jameson" (draft working paper for the Historical Materialism Conference in London, 2010), 4.
51 Ralph Fox, *The Novel and the People* (London: Lawrence & Wishart, 1937), 8–9.

fantasy".[52] This defence of imagination and fantasy represents an important point of agreement in Stead and Fox's views about writing and about the totality. For both writers, imagination and its capacity to render a total portrait of the individual and her or his society was as important as economic analysis, if not more so. For both, the pursuit of truth was the work of the novel: "the essential warp of the creative artist" was "his fight for the truth of life", and for both writers, imagination was central to this work. Fox's list of the great works of realism includes *Don Quixote*, *Gargantua and Pantagruel*, *Robinson Crusoe*, *The Black and the Red*, *War and Peace*, *A Sentimental Education* and *Wuthering Heights* because they were obviously realist as well as highly imaginative and deeply philosophical commentaries on life.[53]

The New York reality of life under capitalism, replete with its struggles, crises and contradictions, was a ready-made subject for Stead and it prompted from her some of the most important work of her career. The social anatomy became Stead's focus in America, and genre was one of the ways in which she cut through the "morbid tissues" of society to expose oppression, contradiction and alienation. Stead produced this anatomy of America in the spirit of Balzac, though infused with the travelling realism inspired by expatriate mobility. In America, her international movement and her literary orientations solidified into a sustained work of critique. Ostensibly this was a critique of American exceptionalism and provinciality from an outsider's perspective (inflected as an Old World outsider but doubled up as a fellow colonial). It was fundamentally a critique of capitalism, with capitalism working as a synonym for America itself.

American Realism and Folk Talk, 1935

When Stead arrived in New York, there was a welcoming radical community comprised of people from Bill Blake's youth and young adulthood on the Lower East Side. These connections involved the proletarian hero, Mike Gold, who had just been at the Paris Congress with Stead and Fox, American expatriates from the Left Bank years and other groups of people working in the left-wing literary circles. For Stead, the most welcoming community were the secular Jewish socialist circles. She liked their "view of the world, [they were] good talkers, good fun … everyone is expected to tell stories, somebody starts up a story and that starts a new roundabout of stories and the next one tells a story and 'oh that reminds me of' and it goes on and on – all evening, it's wonderful".[54] This sociality of stories is seen as a lifeblood or oxygen supply that sustains and maintains communities in huge cities like New

---

52 Fox, *The Novel and the People*, 56.
53 Fox, *The Novel and the People*, 30.
54 Christina Stead, interviewed by Tom Krause, December 1982, 11. Unpublished interview. Heather Stewart papers in the author's possession.

York, and it is a form of positive circulation that Stead sets against the circulation of commodities and wealth.

In "It Is All a Scramble for Boodle", Stead reported that while America had resources, scale, energy and idealism, it lacked a long-term political program or coherent political philosophy. Without this support, American energy could only be focused on survival and money. Marxist theory could offer the necessary revolutionary program for the American middle classes, and the instabilities and crudity of New World capitalism (in her use of "boodle", Stead implies the vernacular sense of a gangster obsession with money) would be appropriately controlled and directed.[55] Stead suggests that the worship of money had meant that the crucial vanguard of American artists had been alienated: "robbed ... of their natural right – worship of their own country" and had fled abroad. The middle classes were therefore politically rudderless. In addition to having no "system" to guide them, the only interesting theme or stories belonged to the troublesome working classes, whose political work was certainly cut out for them. Stead concludes that the American middle-class artists, possessed of a rich and fertile homeland, should ignore European art and "write and think *in American*, think in the vulgate of valours".[56] It is clear that Stead was already thinking in broad terms about American idiom, comic forms and the critical and cultural reach of the American humourist.[57]

The 1930s were the second Red Decade in America, and the buoyant number of paid-up party members and the kind and level of Left political discussion indicated substantial excitement and purpose on the Left. Alan Wald has written extensively about the American Left in this period, and he coordinates, across his many books, a tremendous account of "the force field of publications, networks of cultural activists and writers' organisations that partly shaped cultural work within the framework of national and international events".[58] It was at this extraordinary time for small press and periodical publishing that Blake and Stead were involved with

---

55 Although a colonial politics of Australian–American primitive socialism might seem like an interesting contrast, Stead does not deploy it. She cites America's great natural wealth, beauty and energy. She makes the point that Australia was built on a radical legend, in contrast to America, and emphasises colonial survival. Australia was also avowedly a labour commonwealth in Stead's eyes, as well as a killing continent – the "frightful outback" was littered with corpses of brave explorers. Quoted in Whitehead, "An Interview with Christina Stead", 230–48.

56 Stead, "It Is All a Scramble for Boodle", 24. One of the characteristics that grants the Vulgate its "valour" is that it is translated from the original languages and not just a translation of a translation. The Vulgate Old Testament is the first Latin version translated directly from the Hebrew rather than from the Greek. The phrase indicates the importance of using a national idiom close to its source. Stead demonstrates her naturalistic commitment to a direct translation of American idiomatic speech in *The Man Who Loved Children*, and it is very evident also in *Letty Fox: Her Luck, A Little Tea, A Little Chat* and *I'm Dying Laughing*.

57 *Babbitt* is a novel by Sinclair Lewis first published in 1922. It is a famous satire of American middle-class society in the 1920s.

the *New Masses*. The other great social and literary forum for Stead and Blake was the New York chapter of the League of American Writers, which had been established at the American Writers' Congress in April 1935. Luminaries of the American Left, and of American writing of the 1930s in general, were involved: Gold, Hicks, Cowley, Herbst, Maltz, Burke, Mann, Steinbeck, Hemingway, Dreiser, Farrell, Hellman, West, Carlos Williams and others. Following the Soviet lead (one in tension with otherwise internationalist commitments) the League supported a nativist tradition of realism, grounded in a history and tradition of home-grown American vernacular writing. Their support of realism and the folk spine of American writing was what the *Partisan Review* camp rather curiously opposed as Stalinist, choosing to identify true American writing with modernism instead.[59] As Geraldine Murphy reports:

> Artists and intellectuals affiliated with Front organisations like the League of American Writers experienced a new sense of belonging to American society, of being part of a common cause. That new-found patriotism in turn fostered critical interest in native literary traditions.[60]

The Left was embracing a specifically American culture of the people, and the folk revival added materials to an expanding picture of the diverse makeup of the United States: cultural ethnographies, folk studies and regionalist interest persisted throughout the 1930s. Constance Rourke, who had declared that folk humour was a fundamental American characteristic in her essential ethnographic work, *American Humour: A Study of National Character* (1931), became a quiet celebrity of the Left.

Ralph Fox had suggested that "the greatest treasure house of expression is to be found in the folk language of any people" and that proverbial language contained a "richness of speech and expression" whose "vitality is being renewed, partly by importation from America".[61] Bill Blake devoted a chapter of his *Understanding the Americans* to the question of the folk. In the chapter "Of Folk-lore, Folk-song, Dances and Fun Generally" he claims, in line with Constance Rourke, that

---

58 Alan Wald, *Exiles from the Future Time: The Forging of the Mid-Twentieth Century Literary Left* (Chapel Hill: University of North Carolina Press, 2002), xiv.
59 Franklin Folsom, *Days of Anger, Days of Hope: A Memoir of the League of American Writers 1937–1942* (Niwot: University Press of Colorado, 1994), 117. It was a professional writers' body, unlike the John Reed clubs, and only published authors could join. It had a permanent secretariat whose job was to hold Congresses every two years (1935, 1937, 1939 and 1941). According to Folsom, the League was interested in the "wider spectrum of American life". Harold Rosenberg wrote after the AWC that there was "a recognition of the unbreakable connection existing between the course and fate of culture and the art of writing and the course and fate of society" Harold Rosenberg, "The American Writer's Congress". *Poetry* 46, no. 4 (1935), 224.
60 Geraldine Murphy, "Romancing the Center: Cold War Politics and Classic American Literature", *Poetics Today* 9, no. 4 (1988), 739.
61 Fox, *The Novel and the People*, 128, 139.

Americans are "exuberant and vital, quick on the uptake" with a "unique brand of jokes".[62]

> The source of American humour was freedom to assail anything, joy at the unveiling of hypocrisy and false dignity, zest in discerning mad inconsequences and using them to illumine reason ... Mark Twain, who began as a roughhouse humourist, Ring Lardner, whose stories are the bitterest fruit humour has ever borne; American humour has been rooted in truth, social truth ... [63]

For Blake, American humour had an incontrovertible politics: these were "authentic old American sources imbued in the twentieth century with a new revolutionary spirit, sign of the pioneer and the harmonic underlay of minorities".[64] For Stead, comedy was often connected to the critical work of social truth and it had the great merit of energetic vitality as well. Stead's first experience of American folk humour had been at home in Sydney, given her father's love of Artemus Ward and Twain. As Rowley reports:

> David Stead liked nothing better than to entertain young children. His own favourite book as a child had been Joel Chandler Harris' tales of Uncle Remus, Tar-Baby and Br'er Rabbit, and he was an adept at Uncle Remus speak ... David Stead's other linguistic model was the American comic writer Artemus Ward.[65]

Stead was immediately struck by the richness of the urban and rural folklore in America, which she recorded in the exuberant but alarming miscellany that is Sam's speech in *The Man Who Loved Children*. In early 1936 in New York, Stead was taking notes from the published papers of the Soviet Writers' Congress, and she noted Russian ideas on folk story, which had always been one of her interests. Eventually, Stead had a related idea about an American folk project and this was later expressed in a 1942 Guggenheim Fellowship application, in which she proposed:

> To collect American legends and contemporary lore from diversified regions in the United States, upon which to base a cycle of stories in the style of *The Canterbury Tales*. This should be a large volume with numerous original,

---

62 William J. Blake, *Understanding the Americans* (London: Frederick Muller, 1954), 105.
63 Blake, *Understanding the Americans*, 106.
64 Blake, *Understanding the Americans*, 109.
65 Rowley, *Christina Stead*, 17. As Stead recalls to Jonah Raskin: "my father loved America: he had the California spirit, the pioneering spirit. He was kind of like Theodore Roosevelt, a great individualist". Jonah Raskin, "Christina Stead in Washington Square", *London Magazine* 9, no. 11 (1970), 74.

imaginative tales. I would go into a few selected areas (small towns or large cities) to collect stories from local scholars and natural bards.[66]

Apart from the hallmark ambition of scale, fascination with ethnography and the short form compendium, Stead's Guggenheim project aligns in interesting ways with Left aesthetic and cultural commitments during the Popular Front years in Europe and America.

American speech was Stead's great act of ethnographic concentration. The ventriloquised American voice in *The Man Who Loved Children* is a miscellany of possible folk variations and all kinds of discursive positions. The folkloric is connected with the virtuosic emphasis on vernacular speech – mixed with elements of the fantastic, grotesque, disproportionate and satirical. Chris Vials argues in his work on mass literature and realism during the Popular Front in America that a focus on ordinary individuals and their vernacular cultures was a rejection of sentimentality in these realist-based epistemologies and complex subjectivities.[67] For Barbara Foley, the vernacular breaks down the dichotomy of realism against modernism. She notes that because of the rigid opposition to modernism, realism is not seen as open to innovation and experimentation, which short changes the vibrant leftist culture that amalgamated high and low, modern and traditional.[68] Literary experiments with vernacular speech were part of this innovation.

In the case of the four protagonists of the four major American works – Sam, Letty, Robbie and Emily – the vocal trope is the most insistent textual force, and it is marked by comic range, folk registers and vernacular experiment. What does this mean, this repeated paradigm of locality, orality and comedy? In all cases, too, the humourist is a key figure, ranging from Sam Pollit's chilling proto-fascist quips and folklore to Emily Wilkes' female Gargantua via Letty Fox's gold-digging Mae West. Letty is a rogue and a gambler, and this intersects with the humourist character through the possibilities of the literary *picara* and trickster. The New York characters are typically gangsters and the regional characters are humourists – the folksy, vernacular, idiolectic Americans (Baltimore, Arkansas) – though this is not an exclusive opposition. Verbal incontinence characterises the speech of the key American characters, with the exception of Edward, who is nonetheless surrounded by and participates in a prodigious generation of oral storytelling. For Stead, American speech was certainly a test of ear and memory, and the bedrock of her negotiation of form and real life, but speech had been her most telling literary signature since at least *The Salzburg Tales*. This takes us further back to Stead's

---

66 Cited in Margaret Harris, "Christina Stead's Human Comedy: The American Sequence", *World Literature Written in English* 32, no. 1 (1992), 43.
67 Chris Vials, *Realism for the Masses: Aesthetics, Popular Front Pluralism and U.S. Culture, 1935–1947* (Jackson: University of Mississippi Press, 2009), xvi.
68 Barbara Foley, *Radical Representations: Politics and Form in US Proletarian Fiction, 1929–1941* (Durham, NC: Duke University Press, 1993).

earliest days as an audience for her father's bedtime stories and her experiments with the specific furniture characters, demarcated through an early use of idiomatic speech.

Domestic fiction, the picaresque, the libertine and the tragi-comic chronicle were the genres of Stead's critical realist anatomy: the American novels offer a mosaic of different modulations among the keys of genre, gender and geography, anchored in different kinds of character on the one hand and addressing key themes in political economy on the other. The first American novel, *The Man Who Loved Children*, works with the form of the domestic novel and is set in the original home ground of the American colonies, Washington, DC and Annapolis, Maryland. The American novels that followed form a trilogy because of their common focus on New York and because they adopt varieties of the picaresque in order to dramatise the way in which desire, capital and storytelling circulated in the metropolis. The challenge of representing New York City is marvellously managed through a form devoted to the deeds of rogues, scoundrels, prostitutes, swindlers and dilettantes, so prominent at the Soviet Congress and in Fox's literary criticism. Modes of urban and rural pastoral frame the family collectivities of Edward Massine's life in *The People with the Dogs*, and offset his dilettante wandering. Emily Wilkes' movement in *I'm Dying Laughing* has hints of the transnational epic and the peregrinations of the female rogue, but these elements support the larger tragi-comic life and times chronicle that structures Stead's account of the woman trickster as failed radical.

With each book and each new genre, Stead moved further and further into her encyclopedic project to cover America – its speech, its regions and its fundamental free market identity. Ultimately America became very much like the characters with which she was most often fixated – troubling, vivacious, seductive, immense in scale and in need of vivisection. Critique was her aim, satire was one of her levers, but it is the dazzling virtuosity of her work with genre and character (as well as political situation) that remains with the reader and makes this set of books so valuable. Read together, *The Man Who Loved Children, Letty Fox: Her Luck, A Little Tea, A Little Chat, The People with the Dogs* and *I'm Dying Laughing* offer evidence of a related group of critical realist texts, characterised by their anatomy of American ideology, an uncompromisingly experimental treatment of speech and an ambition of vision that is particularly remarkable for a world writer, much less a woman writer in these mid-century years. The syncretic layers of Stead's twinned political and aesthetic development delivered a writer to America who was coming into her mid-career power.

2
Fascist Miscellanies and the Allegory of the Domestic Front in *The Man Who Loved Children*

> No matter how intimate the social spaces in which they occur, the affective bonds of sex and family life prove unscalable, even unrealistic.[1]

In *The Novel and the People*, Ralph Fox wrote admiringly of E.M. Forster's capacity to convey the secret history of real experience.[2] Christina Stead's first American novel, *The Man Who Loved Children* (1940), offers just such a history: a dark vision of a domestic sphere, set during the Roosevelt years in Washington, DC, and in and around the Maryland landmarks of colonial America. Where the domestic sphere was presented in the American nineteenth century as the great and inspiring sphere of incipient liberal humanism, maternal reform and sentimental morality, Stead produces an American mid-twentieth century domestic allegory of political domination, humiliation and resistance. Her youthful interest in the "lives of obscure men"[3] develops throughout her American anatomy as a series of secret histories of the domestic sphere, which finally evolves into a sequence of intensely metropolitan tales of sex, marriage, money and politics of ordinary people whose lives are constantly negotiated between public and private spaces.

This chapter will argue that this first novel in Stead's anatomy of America is a work of critical realism that engages and extends the genre of the domestic novel, and through this deployment, offers an allegorical critique of both house and nation. Stead's elaboration of the small scale of the domestic speaks to the large scale of the national and international, rehearsing again her attraction to totalities. This reading deals first with the figure of Mr America as the man about the house, and argues that his domination of the domestic scene offers a critique of New Deal

---

1   Mark McGurl, "Gigantic Realism: The Rise of the Novel and the Comedy of Scale", *Critical Inquiry* 43, no. 2 (2017), 429.
2   An early possible title for *Seven Poor Men of Sydney*.
3   Ralph Fox, *The Novel and the People* (London: Lawrence & Wishart, 1937), 2.

America in various ways. Sam Pollit is associated with the vernacular, but travestied verbal performances of all kinds litter his monologic omnipresence and ironise his association with the democratic associations of vernacular America. Stead sends Sam to British Malaya as part of an American anthropological expedition, and thus dramatises the powerlessness of the petty tyrant when extracted from his small dominion. American imperialism in the Philippines is implied to a certain extent in Sam's Malayan sojourn, though of course British Malaya and Singapore were British colonial entities. Sam returns home unabashed by his lack of success in Southeast Asia, having alienated his colleagues and endangered his job. He cheerfully resumes dominating his house and family with new linguistic raw materials from his time away.

Chapter Three will examine two strands of subaltern resistance to Sam's domestic oppression, which includes trapped but trenchant maternal opposition from within the system on the one hand and daughterly rebellion and eventual revolution on the other. Each strand of resistance is associated with specific textual modes that the domestic novel holds together, albeit uneasily. Undercutting Sam's dominant vernacular mode runs an undercurrent of gothic realism that surrounds the description and registers of Henny Pollit, Sam's semi-incarcerated wife and the beleaguered mother of his many children. Alongside this strand of the domestic Gothic, Stead manages a third formal strand – a female *Künstlerroman* of striking originality. Louisa Pollit, Sam's eldest child, creatively negotiates a series of difficult experiences and confrontations that present an extraordinary rendition of the development of the artist as a young woman. The turbulent home is the space of her difficult apprenticeship as a creative subject. Lauren Berlant's work is suggestive for this reading of the operations and textual forms of male power and female resistance in *The Man Who Loved Children*.[4] Berlant's work on the relationship between fantasies of sentiment and the reality of nation space in America delineates the opposition between the patriarch's phantasmatic and optimistic rhetoric of the sentimental nation and the different, realist account of this fantasy delivered by his wife and daughter, whose suffering and economic precarity are exposed by Stead. These lives are not governed by sentiment or access to hegemonic idealism and are therefore, following Berlant, often ungainly, difficult, awkward, incoherent and uneasy. These elements of experience comprise exactly the secret history of the domestic polis that Stead seeks to reveal.

The First American Novel

Although *House of All Nations* was influenced by the matter of America, *The Man Who Loved Children* is the first in Stead's American sequence proper, and it was

---

4   Lauren Berlant, *The Anatomy of National Fantasy: Hawthorne, Utopia and Everyday Life* (Chicago: University of Chicago Press, 1991).

fully drafted in the United States. Stead had been settled in lower Manhattan for over a year before she started work on the novel in 1937. Directly after landing in Boston but before arriving in Manhattan in 1935, Stead and Blake had taken a trip to the American colonial heartland. This early trip around Baltimore and Maryland alerted Stead to the physical parallels between Sydney and the Delaware-Maryland-Virginia area. Having visited the Georgetown and Annapolis sites, it seems extremely probable that the obvious topographic parallels between Stead's past and her American present provoked productive contemplation about the relationship between the two places. Given the cross-mapping of suburban Sydney and Washington-Annapolis, it seems very likely that the novel was always inspired by both Australian and American materials.

This has been difficult to argue because of the several interviews in Australia in the last decade of her life when Stead claimed that she set the action of *The Man Who Loved Children* in America rather than its proper home in Australia to protect her family from the exposure that the autobiographical material might have entailed. Australian academics who knew Stead in the 1970s concur with this reason for the transposition. Adding to the confusion, Hazel Rowley claimed that Stead moved the action of the novel at the behest of her publisher, Simon & Schuster, since they felt that the Australian setting would not sell. While this is not unlikely, there is no existing correspondence to support this conjecture.[5] Australian critics tend to imply gently that *The Man Who Loved Children* is really an Australian novel, but one operating with a wound that divides the work from its proper autobiographical location. I will suggest in this reading of *The Man Who Loved Children* that the American setting was in fact creative disruption that allowed Stead to work with such speed and relative precision on the difficult material of her childhood.

In an essay for *The Paris Review*, published in 1974 as "A View of the Homestead", Stead referred to her transposition of childhood locales and experiences in Australia to the American setting in a slightly different way. As part of musing about what she would do upon her return to Sydney, she thinks about returning to her childhood homes at Bexley and Watsons Bay. She claims that her reconstruction of Watsons Bay as part of the Chesapeake in *The Man Who Loved Children* means that she does not need to return to the Sydney version; there has been a satisfactory replacement in art, making actual return redundant:

> The other place – "Watsons"? By a magic that I came by, by accident, I was able to transport Watsons noiselessly and as if it were an emulsion or a streak of mist to the Chesapeake; and truly the other place is not there for me anymore; the magician must believe in himself.[6]

---

5 Hazel Rowley, *Christina Stead: A Biography* (Port Melbourne, Vic.: Minerva, 1994), 261.
6 Christina Stead, "A View of the Homestead", *The Paris Review* 57 (1974), 126.

The transnational suturing of childhood experience and adult setting is described as a mystical process of "transport" that was like "magic", part of the writer's art. The noiseless transposition operates like an emulsion or "streak of mist" so appropriate for the watery Chesapeake. This version of translocation as an inspired and effortless crossing of water privileges a more alchemical reading of the meeting of Australian past with the American present in which she found herself in the late 1930s, recalled for an international audience at a key moment of repatriation in the 1970s. There is evidence, therefore, that Stead had several versions of the Australia-America transposition of autobiographical experience that she mobilised in different contexts. As with her earlier statements to Australian interviewers that she never in fact left Australia, she was just a sea-woman destined for oceanic movement, the volitional movement away from Australia is ameliorated more on some occasions than others.

Working from the American side, Louise Yelin enumerates the ways in which *The Man Who Loved Children* was a consciously American novel.[7] She argues that Stead identified herself as an American writer and her novel as part of an American literary tradition by inserting her text explicitly into American cultural debates.[8] The literary references alone provide plenty of clues, with citations of Melville, Whitman, Twain, Ward and Bunyan. Yelin details the significance of the birthplace of the American colonies in Virginia near Annapolis, and the related key moments in American history that belong to Washington, Harpers Ferry and the other original tidewater colonies. At this North-South crossroads, Yelin suggests, is a microcosm of the entire national landscape.[9] The "civil war" lines of North (Pollit-Baltimore) and South (Collyer-Monocacy) that map the Pollit marriage make for a geographical combination that is entirely deliberate.

Yelin's explanation of Stead's representation of America lends support to the idea that this domestic fiction offers a political allegory of America. This allegorical reading of *The Man Who Loved Children* is supported by the work of contemporary critics such as Tara Mendola and Jacques Lezra, who are negotiating the complexities and divisions of postcolonial work on allegory:

---

7   Louise Yelin, "Unsettling Australia: *The Man Who Loved Children* as National Family Romance", in *From the Margins of Empire: Christina Stead, Doris Lessing, Nadine Gordimer* (Ithaca, NY: Cornell University Press, 1998), 17–38.
8   Louise Yelin, "Fifty Years of Reading: A Reception Study of *The Man Who Loved Children*", *Contemporary Literature* 31, no. 4 (1990), 472–98.
9   Harpers Ferry and Annapolis are contested, as is Washington, DC, in their identification as either north or south. The cultural border indicated by the Mason–Dixon line runs through Maryland and Pennsylvania – with Maryland in the south (Maryland was a slave state and the US census lists Maryland and DC as part of the south). In its portrait of the very crossroads of nation, *The Man Who Loved Children* is set both at the national capital and near the origin of the colonial nation as it was first invaded.

We take allegory to have replaced realism as an explicitly, even vulgarly, *political* mode – often to be rejected for just this reason. In the period since the mid-1980s, allegory has become, for the first-world critic, the mode in which the subaltern is permitted, or made, to represent; it is the mode that makes available, to the attentive eye, otherwise obscured social totalities.[10]

Mendola and Lezra's work recuperates what they see as Jameson's ill-fated position on postcolonial allegory, and Fredric Jameson in turn was working through Lukács' strong objection to the allegorical mode.[11] For the purposes of thinking about *The Man Who Loved Children*, allegory emerges from Stead's twin aims of critique and the negotiation of scale. Stead's fiction not only refuses the separate spheres ideology of the nineteenth century; she positively overlays the State, the nation and the home in an echo chamber of allegorical significance. Her novel of domestic life offers an allegorisation of State, whereby the domestic (*domus*) reveals something about the people of the democracy (*demos*). In *Neodomestic American Fiction* (2010), Kristin J. Jacobson argues that in the 1930s in America there was a "feeling of proximity and overlap between discourses of aesthetic and socialist revolution, not least at their convergence point on questions of *modern domesticity*, which had been otherwise associated with white middle-class women's fiction and culture".[12]

The politics that Stead's novel engages are indeed socialist: American exceptionalism, American imperialism and the drive for centrist economic reform during the Depression are targeted. Uncle Sam and Franklin Delano Roosevelt are authoritarian and anti-revolutionary models for the folksy fascist that is Baltimore's Sam Pollit. New Deal economics are referenced through the inexorable arc of Depression-era downward mobility and pressing economic questions of debt and credit. The experience of mothers and children in the unhomely home at the centre of the novel (in the capital of the country) thematises the political situation of a variety of oppressed subjects, including the proletariat and the racial subject. Awkward but insistent parallels with plantation life are implied throughout.

The family unit, so central to bourgeois identity and to the liberal reformist agenda in the Roosevelt years, is portrayed by Stead to be a nightmarish prison house of oppression, interference and fascist authority. The political, economic and national life of America is viewed through the aperture of the Pollit family, with its homespun father-dictator, the vituperative mother-opponent and the children-subjects, with an especially important position given to the resistance fighter-stepdaughter who is faced with the need to engineer revolution from below.

---

10   Tara Mendola and Jacques Lezra, "Introduction: Allegory and Political Representation", *The Yearbook of Comparative Literature* 61 (2015), 3.
11   Fredric Jameson, "Third-World Literature in the Era of Multinational Capitalism" *Social Text*, no. 15, (1986), 65–88. https://doi.org/10.2307/466493.
12   Kristin J. Jacobson, *Neodomestic American Fiction* (Columbus: Ohio State University Press, 2010), 25. My emphasis.

Paula Rabinowitz's work on re-formulations of domestic fiction in American proletarian women's writing (revolutionary writing) in *Labour and Desire* suggests that Stead had read a lot more of this fiction by American radical women than we had thought.[13] Her interventions at the level of genre and theme indicate something more robustly well informed than simply writing back to Margaret Mitchell's *Gone With the Wind* (1936). In *Grotesque Relations,* Susan Edmunds argues that the sentimental novel of domesticity and the American New Deal were new allies in the 1930s, united in the work of economic reform that would save America from the Depression: "If the New Deal crowned a historical process that made the modern sentimental home an omnipresent artefact of everyday life, the modern sentimental home did much the same for the New Deal".[14] Edmunds suggests that works such as Meridel Le Sueur's *The Girl* (1939), Caroline Slade's *The Sterile Sun* (1936), Richard Wright's *Native Son* (1940) and Ann Petry's *The Street* (1946) were domestic novels that resisted this process, and criticised the impact of maternalist and New Deal social welfare programs on the lives of poor Americans. Other radical women writers such as Josephine Herbst, Tillie Olsen, and Djuna Barnes criticised the constraints and hypocrisies of domesticity.[15] These under-examined works were inclined, Edmunds argues, to subject the sentimental domestic sphere to grotesque deformation and therefore "joined Faulkner in making the domestic sphere a locus of major aesthetic experiment".[16] Stead's first American novel knowingly joins these American literary genealogies as Stead writes a novel about the very impossibility of domestic sentimentality by exploring the sentimental man as fascist.

The dominance of Sam in this domestic fiction, rather than the centrality of either the daughter or mother of the house, constructs the domestic front as the equivalent of the provincial politics of the FDR administration, where the public sphere is metaphorised as domestic through fireside chats, homespun plain-talking and a white plantation home subsidised by slave labour as the seat of government. Casting a wider political net, the Pollit name annexes the figure of Harry Pollitt into this story of the benign/malignant father of the house of the state. Harry Pollitt was the General Secretary of the Communist Party of Great Britain – a figure of dominating influence and ruthless tactics who used Stalinist models of the cult of

---

13 Paula Rabinowitz, "The Contradictions of Gender and Genre", in *Labor and Desire: Women's Revolutionary Fiction in Depression America* (Chapel Hill: University of North Carolina Press, 1991), 63–96.
14 Susan Edmunds, *Grotesque Relations: Modernist Domestic Fiction and the US Welfare State* (Oxford: Oxford University Press, 2008), 31.
15 Deborah Nelson's work focuses on women writers who deliberately and systematically eschewed the sentimental, the sympathetic and the cult of sensibility in favour of the clear-eyed and analytic. Deborah Nelson, *Tough Enough: Arbus, Arendt, Didion, McCarthy, Sontag, Weil* (Chicago: University of Chicago Press, 2017). In terms of the American literary context, Yelin notes that other women writers publishing in the United States around 1940 included Willa Cather, Carson McCullers, Zora Neale Hurston, Dorothy Parker and Lillian Hellman. Louise Yelin, "Fifty Years of Reading", 472–498.
16 Edmunds, *Grotesque Relations*, 383.

personality to retain control of the Party for many years. Despite a glowing obituary for Fox, he was behind the savage internal Party reactions to Ralph Fox's book on Lenin. Pollit also works as an ironic homonym. Sam's family name certainly references the polis or ideal city state that grounds early Greek political philosophy. Although this reference to the body politic indicates the allegorical relationship between family and nation at one level, this meaning is challenged by the British regional use of polis to name the police, those who regulate the state.

Man-Child About the House

Sam Pollit is the titular man who loved children. It becomes readily apparent to the reader that his Peter Pan ways, and "king of the kids" modality, actually indicates his great wish to still be a child, though with an adult's power. Following this logic, a more correct appellation for Sam is therefore "the man who loved himself". In the last third of the book, Henny finally sees this truth about Sam: "it seemed to her that (now that the clouds had rolled away) she saw her husband for the first time: she had married a child whose only talent was an air of engaging helplessness by which he got the protection of certain goodhearted people" (Saul Pilgrim, her father).[17] Residing at the confluence of north and south, reverent towards the nation's capital, speaking in support of an idiosyncratic northern liberalism but behaving like a southern autocrat/plantation owner, Sam Pollit stands in for America as a concatenation of regions, accents and positions. He is also that most untrustworthy and protean being, the political hypocrite masquerading as a down-home guy and true patriot. In Sam, Stead dramatises the danger of the man-child and what it means that he is in control of his own estate. Into Sam, Stead rolls the great White Father, Uncle Sam, FDR and the imperialist liberal as bad anthropologist in the Far East. Here she reveals slowly but surely the dangers of the liberal leader as poisonous hypocrite and fake radical.

When we meet Sam, coming home in the dark and stopping to admire his "island in the sky, Tohoga House"(17), we are struck by his attractive vitality of mien and thought, but soon sense his less appealing side, arising from his speculations about the attractive young woman who admires him, his passive spectatorship of the violent altercation between his eldest daughter and second wife, and his grandiose self-regard. Nevertheless, the reader extends to Sam considerable benefit of the doubt, as we are mesmerised by the creativity of the author of "Sunday is a Funday"(22), and the fascinating elasticity of his speech acts. Yet Sam, the seemingly benevolent clown, also turns out to be a fascist and misogynist of quite a creative stripe, who exploits his patriarchal privileges with abandon. He triumphs at the end of the novel, his happy survival endorsed by the

---

17 Christina Stead, *The Man Who Loved Children* (1940; Harmondsworth: Penguin, 1970), 318. All subsequent references are to this edition and appear in parentheses in the text.

homosocial structures that will supply a replacement for his wife and eldest girl as part of the requirement for the female labour upon which his domestic and social dominion rests.

Sam Pollit is the first fully-fledged American that we hear in Stead's American anatomy. We see immediately the exhilarating yet ominous combination of the child-like and destructive, the charming and the malicious:

> "My mind says to me, it says, little glumpy Looloo been seein' things and Looloo's been unhappy too."
> She hung her head.
> What you see in the darkness of the night, Looloo?"
> "Nothing!"
> That ain't much for tuh see. Air you tellin' your poor Sam de troof?"
> "I never lie," she said angrily.
> "No josts [ghosts], no sperrits, no invisible hands, no nuffin?" (20)

Sam sounds like he might be solicitous for Louie's state of mind, but he is engaged in his normal gaslighting of Louie by implying that she might be fantasising again, as her preference for the Gothic might encourage. The qualifier, "your poor Sam", introduces the kind of troubling inversion of father-child hierarchy that Sam so often exploits with all his children:

> Bring up your tea, Looloo-girl: I'm sick, hot head, nedache [headache], dot pagans in my stumjack [got pains in my stomach]: want my little fambly around me this morning. We'll have a corroboree afterwards when I get better. (28, square bracket translations reproduced from the original text)

Stead's capacity to capture Sam's specific idiolect indicates her phenomenal memory and her ethnographic fascination with speech. The prevalent voice in the domestic space is the male vernacular voice, and Stead uncannily channels the Artemus Ward and Uncle Remus stories to which she was exposed as a child. In *The Atlantic Cable*, for example, Artemus Ward sounds like this, and the textual overlap with Sam is striking: "Near can I forgit the surblime speckticul which met my gase as I alited from the Staige with my umbreller and verlise".[18]

Sam Pollit's control of his domestic situation arises from his socially endowed position as patriarch and wage earner, but he maintains this control through a form of domination sourced in his miscellany of voices and this a kind of aural domination. His right of the *seigneur* to access all bodies is exercised as a matter of vocal control. As Steven Connor has argued:

---

18 Artemus Ward (Charles Farrar Browne), "Atlantic Cable Celebrations at Baldinsville", *The Complete Works of Artemus Ward* (Project Gutenberg, November 2004), ebook, n.pag.

Monologists project and fantasise a listener, they are unconscious self-deceivers and are in love with the sound of their own voice. Talk is the monstrous charm – the oral, the engulfing, related to food and drink and appetite. Voice is immediacy, presence, engagement.[19]

The central point about Sam's speech is that his colonial and patriarchal engulfment of others frequently occurs in moments of vernacular free-wheeling, which are meant to connote charm, democracy and comfortable domesticity. The diction of the humourists indicates their democratic language and values, and this does not seem intuitive or trustworthy in the hands of a monologist or demagogue. The genius of Stead's critical portrait of vernacular Sam is that she ironises his register by dramatising his disregulated array of registers, all of which are aimed at maintaining power. His vernacular use is therefore exposed as monologically self-centred, and as manipulative as any of his other speech acts. His vernacular register should or could nicely match his domestic situation, but its excessiveness and continual accumulation alerts his daughter that she is dealing with a hypocrite of awful proportions.

As a tyrannical leader of the body politic, Sam's wonderfully flexible vernacular showcases the deployment of power in quite the opposite vein to democracy, but you have to be listening carefully:

"Procyon the raccoom, Gimlet, the parrot, Didelpha the vixen possum, Cocky-Andy, the sulphur-crested cockatoo, Big-Me the pygmy opposum, not to mention the birds and reptilians ... And fustest, you must write to your poor little Sam ebbly week and tell him how 'tis tuh hum; and second, you myust keepo a record of the birds and hanni-miles wot visit Tohoga House, Tohoga Place that is. No! Momento! Loogoobrious can do that. It will be a good thing for her, keep her mind off of herself, on which onpleasant objeck," he continued (believing that Louie was there), "it is glued at time of speaking. But that is, no doubt, on account of her fai-hairy figuar and her bewchus face." (72–73)

Sam is talking in his childlike idiolect about the animals of Tohoga as well as instructing his children that they must write every day to report on the control they are maintaining over his plantation. He takes the opportunity to denigrate his daughter and earn laughs from his other children.

Sam prodigious use of *ethopoie*, or the impersonation of others' voices, means that he transforms into a kind of vocal farrago in one person: a one-person show of different regional dialects and different high and low registers. Jennifer McDonell reads Sam as a figure of the polyglot who delivers a linguistic anthology of America: "a queer amalgam of the rags and tatters of American history".[20] His discursive

---

19 Steven Connor, *Dumbstruck: A Cultural History of Ventriloquism* (Oxford: Oxford University Press, 2000), 29.

range covers: "saint, bard, president, fisherman, hero, leader, educator, tourist, pastoralist, philanthropist, magician, scientist, comic roles, cuckold, *paterfamilias*".[21] McDonell goes on to provide this wonderful account of Sam's speech world:

> Sam constantly echoes other voices which seem to emanate from elsewhere, from some point distant from the auditor: Mark Twain, Roosevelt, Artemus Ward (who also used an idiosyncratic cipher of ugly and absurd proportions) his children and others. The effect of this ventriloquism is to make Sam a travesty of all the figures he echoes.[22]

Rather than operating as a travesty, Sam Pollit is the collecting point for Stead's encyclopaedic desire to catalogue many Americas in one book. Folk and vernacular America is a strong part of this collection, but Sam is as indiscriminate and engulfing in his linguistic proliferation as he is as a parent. Sam delivers a veritable chorus of discursive modes and speech acts, including seductive baby talk, Scots and Malay dialect, orotund Wordsworthian self-production, the African American spiritual and African American work songs, Mark Twain, Artemus Ward and more. Sam represents a compendium of voices, familiar from *The Salzburg Tales,* but improperly collocated in one man.

This is not just one American, but a miscellany of American voices, rising like a cacophony and revealing a great deal about the childlike but domineering pathology of its source. Constance Rourke's championing of the vitality of American humour is in the background of this work and its vocal renditions, but Stead's mission is to reveal the folksy humourist as a domineering racist, sexist and imperialist. His excessive accumulation gives him away. For the nastiest rendition of bigotry dressed up as humour, it is hard to decide between the racist rendition of the Jewish vaudeville comedian and the sexist "when she walks, she wobbles" piece of mockery:

> "I dunno vitch I vant, a vatch, or a veskit," Sam ignored him, doing one of his favourite imitations, a vaudeville Jew. Little-Sam faded into the house, grumbling.
> "I give you tree per cent," continued Sam. "Vot you want vid a veskit? Vid a veskit I kip my visky [whiskers] from flyin' away in de vind!" The children screamed with laughter. (67)

---

20 Jennifer McDonell, "Christina Stead's *The Man Who Loved Children*", *Southerly* 44, no. 4 (1984), 402.
21 McDonell, "Christina Stead's *The Man Who Loved Children*", 399.
22 McDonell, "Christina Stead's *The Man Who Loved Children*", 375.

2 Fascist Miscellanies and the Allegory of the Domestic Front

Stead makes us think through what it is to exercise will through speech. Sam's tool of oppression is oppressive talk; this is not the regenerative and politically promising polyphony in Bakhtin's vision of the novel in his work on Dostoyevsky. Although plastic, protean and creative, even uplifting in general sonority, it is incontinent and infantile too, which confuses the subject of its domination, often an actual child:

> And I am myself so ill, Looloo-girl, that I can hardly rejoice as I always do at the birth of a child. The great glory of man, the great glory of the flaming forth of new stars, the glory of the expanding universe, which are all expressed in our lives by the mystery, wonder, and tragedy of birth have always thrilled me beyond expression. And here I lie, with bones of jelly. It did for me, Looloo. (277)

Here, Sam characteristically abrogates all prerogatives and speaking positions to himself: transcendent idealist, birth-giving mother and sickly child seeking comfort. Joseph Boone reads *The Man Who Loved Children* as Stead's case study of pathological paternity, where the pathology originates in the unregulated excess and confused gendering of Sam's boundary-crossing, both verbal and physical:

> As its title implies, this is a tale of fatherhood told with a vengeance, tracing in exacerbating and often surreal detail the will to power of Sam Pollit's obsessive attempt to impose his ego on his progeny, to author as well as authorize their very existences.[23]

Even when Sam is excoriating his own wife in a dishonest and manipulative way to his children, he talks like a child and lines up his second daughter to replace his wife:

> Sam's plaintive, bashful question to Little-Womey, "Why is Mothering out all day? Why is the Henny-penny always away from her chicken-lickens now? Don't she want to take her responsibilities any mower? Why, Little-Womey, soon you got to be my wife, I speck".
> "Yes, Taddy," Evie answered, from the porch door …
> They heard Chappy's loud crowing laughs.
> "Daddy said I could be his wife," Evie told Louie, looking up at her confidentially and not sure whether she would laugh and approve. Louie turned her back, and Evie's face fell. (376)

---

23 Joseph Allen Boone, "Of Fathers, Daughters and Theorists of Narrative Desire: At the Crossroads of Myth and Psychoanalysis in *The Man Who Loved Children*", *Contemporary Literature* 31, no. 4 (1990), 512.

Although the vernacular delivery should ironise this extraordinary bit of Freudian manipulation, Evie does not do anything other than confidently believe what she is being told by her father. Only Louie's reaction can give Evie the check she needs about proper boundaries.

As Judith Kegan Gardiner has suggested, Sam's male narcissism is of a very malignant order indeed.[24] We can see that this self-regard is at its epicentre when his young female admirer declares, according to him, "Mr Pollit, I just love to hear you talk!" His response is "that did it," Sam said rapturously, "yes, that did it" (21). As Steven Connor suggests in his work on ventriloquism and the voice, the most intense and intimate kinds of self-relation result in the voice of seduction. Such a voice seduces by conjuring itself up as a precious and fascinating object, or texture, or sensation. The seductive voice of the father is also the voice of the domestic tyrant.

The great parallel for Sam's verbal domination is the famous boiling down of the marlin sequence near the end of the novel. Sam's domination of his house, wife and children has intensified in direct relation to his lack of power in the public sphere at this stage of the novel. This oppression is worked through his ever-present voice and constant presence about the house, and it is metaphorised as the all-engulfing smell of his fish oil experiment that really drives Henny to her death and drives Louie to help her on her way. Sam's voice and its associated power and omnipresence is like the smell of the endlessly boiling fish throughout day and night:

> The effluvia of the fish, all that could be conveyed by air, were seeping again round the house, for the storm was passing away at last, and all that remained was the flickering of the sky, fringes of rainy cloud, and the pools of water underfoot. The water in the creek was lapping high too. *It seemed to Sam that nature was licking at his feet like a slave, like a woman,* that he had read of somewhere, that washed the feet of the man she loved and dried them with her hair. (446)

Everyone else at Spa House is oppressed and revolted by this fish effluvia, and for Henny it is the last straw but one, but Sam is positively re-charged and alight with improper and tell-tale scenes of erotic domination of subaltern subjects. The novel exposes the reality that the family unit is designed to substantiate and support masculine power at the cost of women and children. The patriarch may exercise obliterating kinds of power, no matter what his actual merit or public standing, unchecked by any form of restraint. Any dissidence from his children is met with

---

24 Judith Kegan Gardiner, "Male Narcissism, Capitalism and the Daughter of *The Man Who Loved Children*", in *The Magic Phrase: Critical Essays on Christina Stead*, ed. Margaret Harris (St Lucia: University of Queensland Press, 2000), 149.

rapid and malicious consequences. Sam is, of course, delighted to have a personal chain gang:

> The great project filled him with joy. "With my own labour union, said he to them. "I need nobody; no strikes, no trouble, only the work going up fast."
> "You don't pay anything," Ernie said, disagreeable. (317)

This bastardised version of organised labour is met by Ernie's response about pay, first and foremost, but the parallel between the children and an unprotected workforce is made quite clearly here. A little later in the Spa House experiment, Sam gives himself away as a straight swap for any number of likely fascist leaders from the mid to late 1930s:

> "If I were autocrat of all nations," with "supreme power, the lives of all, the life of the world in my hands," he told them what he would do. For example, he might arrange the killing off of nine tenths of mankind in order to make room for the fit. This would be done by gas attacks on people living ignorant of their fate in selected areas, a type of eugenic concentration camp; they would never know, but be hurled painlessly into eternity, or they would pass into the lethal chamber of time and never feel a pang."
> "But you would keep yourself alive," said Louie, unpleasantly. (364)

At this point, Sam is back from his travels overseas, not one whit more liberal or progressive or worldly, though these are exactly the claims he makes for himself.

Man-Child at Large

To take the allegorical shift in scale between the domestic and the nation one step further, Sam's journey to Malaya extends the allegory of the domestic into the realm of America's imperial amibitions in the world at large. Without access to a captive audience for his constant and miscellaneous verbal assault, Sam has nowhere near the power to which he is accustomed, even though he has the advantage of race. Susan Strehle and Amy Kaplan have both argued that the domestic and the imperial often operate as coextensive categories. In her work on Barbara Kingsolver's *The Poisonwood Bible,* Strehle argues that the private sphere of family relations offers an allegorical critique of patriarchy and of American imperialism by exposing the ineluctable importance of gender exploitation to both projects.[25] Kaplan has argued that Americans used the vernacular and the folksy domestic to create and maintain America's imaginary posture of innocence to obscure its imperial

---

25 Susan Strehle, "Chosen People: American Exceptionalism in Kingsolver's *The Poisonwood Bible*", *Studies in Contemporary Fiction*, 49, no. 4 (2008), 413–29.

aggressions.[26] Judith Yaross Lee concurs, arguing that "vernacular conventions ... deflect attention from America's own imperial enterprises".[27] Stead gives good coordinates for this argument in *The Man Who Loved Children* when she sends Sam to British Malaya, though the colonial relation here is historically with Britain. The strangeness of this aspect of Stead's transposition of action from Australia to America is not really obscured by the emphasis on Sam's role as an anthropologist interested in all possible cultures. Nevertheless, Sam's expedition ensures that the reader sees the relationship between what we witness in the house and its translation to the world. In Malaya, however, Sam wields no power comparable to his domestic control (above and beyond hierarchies of nation, race and gender) and is, on the contrary, a childlike figure among the white adults and a figure of fun among the Chinese and Singaporean communities. Sam's posture of innocence is hideous, but it is also telling in a range of ways: in terms of imperial ambition, in terms of a desire to be exceptional, in terms of the avoidance of the reality of economic suffering on the coat-tails of fudgy idealism. Sam in Malaya is certainly an allegory for America in the world in the late 1930s.

The obvious ironies of Sam's presence and comportment in Malaya appear frequently as moments of bombastic idealism. Here, this discourse is leeched of the power it has had to oppress his family and maintain his position as petty tyrant: "Sam's heart seemed to expand at the contact of so many alien peoples and the generous feeling he called love of man and worship of mankind had grown up like a puffball in Singapore" (214). In the main, Sam seems silly and mostly harmless, a "puffball" in the larger sphere of the world. Sam's woolly liberalism, political naiveté and embarrassing ignorance are dramatised through our access to Naden's view of him. Stripped of the domestic context that feeds and strengthens his vernacular stranglehold on rhetorical power, Sam is thrown back to another favourite discourse of his – liberal idealism:

> His heart was flooded with a blue sea of hope; it was his own experience with the cheerful, good-natured people that made him hope that the progress of friendship between nations would be as easy – it merely required a little good will, such as he had, and the thing would be done in half a day. (219)

---

26 Amy Kaplan, *The Anarchy of Empire in the Making of US Culture* (Cambridge, MA: Harvard University Press, 2005). Kaplan also makes the argument, based on earlier fiction, that the domestic was associated with a language set and topography at the heart of American foreign relations; indeed, from a rhetorical point of view, figurations of the domestic were *essential* to the formulation of international politics as a set of relations. For both critics, the political and the domestic were not only aligned, they were absolutely interpenetrated.

27 Judith Yaross Lee, "The International Twain and American Nationalist Humor: Vernacular Humor as a Post-Colonial Rhetoric", *The Mark Twain Annual*, 6 (2008), 39.

2 Fascist Miscellanies and the Allegory of the Domestic Front

Sam's childlike liberal vision is punctured by Naden's worldly knowledge of the race question in America, and his inevitable awareness of the privileges of whiteness. Even he, though, is struck by the stupidity of Sam's view:

> What can a white man in a country of white men know about anything of that sort? Naden forbore to make further remarks to his superior about dark skins in America, but he thought to himself – this also is a man who – Washington or no Washington – knows nothing about how his own country is run. (215)

This is harrowing in some respects, because the reader can see that the Singaporean man of colour, though required to be servile, has a perspective for which both Henny and Louie must struggle with all their might, and in vain.

When Sam returns home, he effortlessly turns his short time in Malaya into a kind of linguistic imperialism. He uses this to extend his domestic domination, having failed on the world stage and setting in train events that will mean the loss of his job, which will further concentrate his presence at home. Even though we have seen how ridiculous Sam seems on the world stage, in his own castle his imperial power remains undiminished and is set to intensify. He merely absorbs the specificity of the Malay language-set into his own miscellany of seduction and domination: "Everything had to have its Malay name; and already he was beginning to slop over, drown them with his new knowledge, bubbling, gurgling as he poured into them as quickly as possible all he had learned" (288). He has, in true colonial style, undertaken cultural and linguistic trophy acquisition. Here Sam is most like Teddy Roosevelt, with his terrible misogyny and big-game hunting:

> "Little *perempuan Melayu, Singapure punya* sitting under an umbrella selling Eastern candies, black eyes moist as the antelope, oval copper face, full wide lips, my Little-Womey, Little Malay beauty!" and he sang to each of them as he busied himself with them, dressing them up in all the wonderful scarves, sarongs, a Kelantan shawl of woven silk with a body of royal yellow and end of red and orange; a sarong batek made in Java of dyed cotton, blue with center bister and white; a handkerchief of Malay-red silk interwoven with gold thread, the center brocaded in heliotrope and yellow; a blue and gold silk sarong from Trengganu; and beautiful strange clothing that he had picked up wherever he went." (295)

Sam's monologic mania – his cataloguing instinct to touch and control everything in the room – is a part of the vehicle of American imperialism; the goal of transforming the world into oneself by subsuming everything and disallowing all difference. The colonial encounter speaks volumes: the white colonial father who fancies himself a naturalist is completely at sea in diverse political environments and unable to survive the teeming nature he proclaims to love. The natives will defeat him and so will the environment, but he can still reign supreme as the petty despot of his ramshackle home, where neither law nor custom can protect his plantation subjects.

This chapter has suggested that there are three horizons for reading *The Man Who Loved Children*. First, despite an established critical tradition of reading this work through the lens of the transposition of setting from Sydney to Washington, the novel was a work provoked and shaped by the matter of America. Stead's engagement with the painful material of childhood was structured through the creative disruption of her detailed negotiation between Australia and America. Second, the genre that Stead calls into the lists for the teeming life of her characters and her teeming criticisms of New Deal American is that of domestic fiction. The opportunity to mount an allegorical critique of New Deal America is taken up, as is the opportunity to extend revisionist Left-wing accounts of sentimental domestic fiction and the role of the family home. Finally, it is clear that the engine of Sam Pollit's power as petty tyrant is his voice, and this is a critique of charming totalitarian fathers, bad liberal leaders and fascist hypocrites alike. The miscellany of his various registers betokens unthinking domination and his particular hypocrisy is to deploy American vernacular to pacify, provoke and humiliate the small demos of his family. In the following chapter, I examine how this secret history of the downwardly mobile middle-class family looks from the point of view of two female subjects imprisoned in different ways in its complex domestic webs of economic, social and rhetorical power.

3
Debt, Domestic Enclosure and Daughterly Revolution in *The Man Who Loved Children*

Stead's secret history of unsentimental family life anatomises the material experience of mothers and children in the houses of the common petty despot. Stead's domestic allegory of America works with unerring focus on the gendered ground that supports the figure of the local fascist. Feminist political economists came to work much later on the experiences that Stead's novel anatomises, and the argument of this book is that it is precisely the true political economy of the American house that Stead worked to reveal. The material and unsentimental reality of the *domus* lies in class struggle, unpaid labour, galloping debt, prostitution and near slavery. Referencing Engels, Jennifer McDonell has suggested that *The Man Who Loved Children* "also bears the imprint of Marx's powerful analysis of the origin of the family in slavery … for the Romans *famulus* meant domestic slave, and *familia* referred to the total number of slaves belonging to one man".[1]

This chapter continues to investigate Stead's unhomely home as an allegory for the state of the nation. A petty tyrant as seductive fascist is the titular head of the house/plantation who has commandeered all possible speaking positions, both public and private. His second wife and his eldest daughter are left to resist his oppression and they do so in very different ways. Henny's entrenched yet energetic opposition, though doomed, means that she is left with the non-verbal and ineffectively verbal means of delay, denial and delinquency. Famous for her possessions, ditties and tirades, her subjectivity is sequestered in the last refuge of her bedroom, in politically ineffectual affect (rage) and informal and underhand means of survival. She is associated with the Gothic and grotesque as the true litmus test of the failure of the homely home. Her stepdaughter, Louie, also comes

---

1   Jennifer McDonell, "House Arrest: Domestic Space in Christina Stead's Fiction", in Caroline Guerin, Philip Butterss and Amanda Nettlebeck, eds, *Crossing Lines: Formations of Australian Culture: Proceedings of ASAL Adelaide 1995* (1996), 138. Friedrich Engels, *The Origin of the Family: Private Property and the State*, rev. trans. Alec West (1884, New York: International, 1972), 121.

into her own subjectivity as woman and artist through growing and stubborn resistance to her narcissistic father. She repurposes abjection to emerge as the revolting subject and she makes a revolutionary exit at the end. Louie eventually figures out that she will not try to battle her father for control over her own fate on his terms of speech and idealism. Instead, she turns to writing and the authorisations of love and genius.

The Matter of Mothers

At the centre of the Pollit economy (the pol-economy) is the embattled, vigorous and ultimately tragic figure of the mother. Henny Pollit is the lynchpin of Stead's unsentimental portrait of family life during the New Deal in a family whose fortunes are declining. By the end of the novel, with the move to Spa House near Annapolis, the Pollit family is in dire straits, and as their heroic "Gulliver Sam" treats this as a Huckleberry opportunity to retreat to his own private colony of children and try and live off the land rather than compromise himself, his exhausted, compromised and ill-used wife tries every trick in every book of credit, favour-begging and prostitution to keep her children from starvation. She does everything thinkable and then some unthinkable things to ensure their survival, as has been her habit for over a decade. Without her wealthy father's backing and the use of the family name to cadge credit and favour, Henny's situation, by the late 1930s, is very dire indeed.

Henrietta is from a Dutch word meaning power or ruler ("*ric*") of the home ("*heim*"). Though the diminutive and thereby ironic version of the upper-class name is used in this novel, it positions Henny as the genuine economic and moral force in the household. In the war that constitutes her marriage, Henny occupies a complex position of drudge, slave, southern spitfire, survivor, victim, breadwinner and prostitute. This is not Marmee from *Little Women*; it is the anti-Marmee. Henny, as the anti-sentimental mother, reveals to us something deeply hidden and unpalatable about the maternal inside of family life. This is a brave and relentless account of the non-idealised realities of domesticity and the true effect of home economics.

Installing a dark witch at the heart of the American New Deal home (with its freight of bourgeois sentiment and sensibility) is a study of alienation in modernity. I think Stead is interested in looking at alienation in the domestic sphere at the very historical moment of a kind of folksy incarnation of it. It is left to Henny to manage the money of the family, and although she is untrained and ill-prepared for such work (and this is surely a source of criticism as well as part of the unending drama derived from the class struggle at the centre of the marriage), it is also true that Sam's massive hypocrisy lies in claiming everything, sequestering everything, indulging in idealism and producing almost nothing except exploitation. Henny's suffering is connected to her historical entrapment in the economy of the late 1930s and registers the real work of women in her situation – the downwardly mobile middle class of the Great Depression.

In a twin gravitational field that holds for much of the novel, Henny Pollit maintains her vituperative position in opposition to the hypocritical man about the house. The loss of his job and their declining economic fortunes finally erodes her resistance efforts. Sam counsels fiscal virtue: "'We must never think of money or of owning things,' said Sam kindly, bending a rather dewy eye on her"[2]. In response, Henny, who must actually feed the children and keep the house going and live with the gendered double standard, thinks:

> "He lives", said Henny to herself, in her bed, "in a golden cloud floating about over a lot of back alleys he never sees; and I'm a citizen of those back alleys, like a lot of other sick sheep. I'd like to pull the wool off his eyes, but I don't dare. He'd take the children away from me; I'd be branded, hounded – I know his Lordship." (133)

Henny must contend with the contradiction between the fact of her responsibility as the sole practical adult and a congruent lack of formal power. She is trapped in the world of material survival; the world of the mattresses, clothing, cleaning and cooking. She rightly identifies that the political economy of material enslavement is relentlessly gendered:

> He talks about human equality, the rights of man, nothing but that. How about the rights of woman, I'd like to scream at him. It's fine to be a great democrat when you've a slave to rub your boots on. I have to stuff mattresses because we haven't enough money to buy new ones! Look at my hands! ... I'm the heiress: I'm the rich woman who can stop up all the holes and darn all the tatters in her underwear and borrow old coats from her sister and beg old-fashioned jackets from her cousins, and I don't sacrifice at all. It's all on account of me. The whole thing is due to my bad management. (89)

What we see with Henny is different kinds of advancing enclosure. The first is her retreat to her bedroom as a cave of mysterious accumulation and indexes a private world that speaks a different language and holds a different power than that of her political opponent. The second is her identification with the racial subject of slavery, and the third is the advancing trap of indebtedness.

---

2   Christina Stead, *The Man Who Loved Children* (1940; Harmondsworth: Penguin, 1970), 104. All subsequent references are to this edition and appear in parentheses in the text.

Confinement and Accumulation

Even though Sam makes the most noise and the loudest claims, Henny's body, her anachronistic and magical things, and her conflation with the fading Arcadia of her father's house on the hill in Georgetown, make her the centre of Stead's novel. As a stepmother she contributes to the problem of vexed maternity or complicated origin familiar from European fairy tales, but still, as Stead's first American novel opens, Henny holds, knows and inhabits the domestic world as the tried and tested warrior of the battles it has seen:

> She had the calm of frequentation; she belonged to this house and it to her. Though she was a prisoner in it, she possessed it. She and it were her marriage. She was indwelling in every board and stone of it: every fold in the curtains had a meaning (and perhaps they were so folded to hide a darn or stain); every room was a phial of revelation to be poured out some feverish night in the secret laboratories of her decisions, full of living cancers of insult, leprosies of disillusion, abscesses of grudge, gangrene of nevermore, quintan fevers of divorce, and all the proliferating miseries, the running sores and thick scabs, for which (and not for its heavenly joys) the flesh of marriage is so heavily veiled and conventually interned. (5)

This grotesque blazon demonstrates the wonderful and generative darkness of Henny's vision, one that Stead sets in opposition to Sam's hypocritical invocation of goodness and light. Henny's rhetoric of belonging involves incarceration, but it does suggest "indwelling" in her father's house as compensation of a kind: "she and it were her marriage", which triangulates the homosocial system in which Henny was inured as a commodity.

Stead's invocation of this house is virtuosic in its eye for material detail, and a Gothic darkness of vision and related specificities of the material world are worked together in Henny's worldview:

> And at other times, as now, she would sit with her glances hovering around the room, running from dusty molding to torn curtain frill, from a nail under the transom left over from the last Christmas to a worn patch on the oilcloth by the door, threadbare under so many thousand little footsteps, not worrying about them, but, considering each well-known item, almost amiable from familiarity, almost interested, as if considering anew how to fix up these things when fatigue had gone and the tea and rest had put new energy into her. (5)

The obscure meaning of "domestic" as "intimate and familiar" comes into view here. Henny's marriage is situated in the contested ground of struggle and difference within the family home, but in some way Henny really is married to her father's house – she knows it and it knows her, they are "almost amiable from

3 Debt, Domestic Enclosure and Daughterly Revolution

familiarity" (5). We realise, too, that despite her tirades and outbursts of cruelty to Louie (and eventually her favoured Ernie), Henny is constantly and obsessively working at holding the house and the children together with the strength of her body and her hands. Her attention is given over and over to small improvements to her prison, but there is no outside for her. Only small or hidden reforms can be effected, rather than any revolution of the actual domestic system that imprisons her. No matter her visits to Washington or Monocacy, Henny is associated with the inside of the Tohoga house and she is enclosed and trapped by the logic that the domestic extends over women. This scene of incarceration, fight and struggle is the scene of the impasse of women in modern marriage in Stead's secret history. It is for this reason that the domestic scale of a "storm in a teacup" is thought by Henny to be as weighty as civic debate. This is another thread of the allegorical scale of Stead's domestic novel:

> As Henny sat before her teacup and the steam rose from it and the treacherous foam gathered, uncollectible round its edge, the thousand storms of her confined life would rise up before her, thinner illusions on the steam. She did not laugh at the words "a storm in a teacup". Some raucous, cruel words about five cents misspent were as serious in a woman's life as a debate on war appropriations in Congress: all the civil war of ten years roared into their smoky words when they shrieked, maddened, at each other; all the snakes of hate hissed. Cells are covered with the rhymes of the condemned, so was this house with Henny's life sentence, invisible but thick as woven fabric. (5–6)

The reference to civil wars reminds us of the location of the Pollit/Collyer marriage at the troubled intersection of American North and South, as they struggle over issues of territory, money and freedom. The sharpest irony emerges from the fact that the Collyers, though they earned their money from oyster farming, inherit their behaviour and the style of their grand house at Monocacy from the plantation south. The decline of their daughter's economic fortunes originates in a bad marriage, but their debt and then her own debt means that she struggles with the realities of plantation capitalism as the semi-enslaved subject whose exploited labour sustained the suspect edifice in the first place.

"Maternal" was first used as an adjective in French to denote the first or native language, or dialect. The materiality of the mother's domestic world can be found in original and primal compression in her bedroom. This bedroom stands in for the body of the mother, and its association with the maternal body and its mysteries offers a counter to Sam's tyrannical miscellany. One of the axes of resistance to his verbal anthology is Henny's private accumulation of objects. Sam's verbal domination is offered a silent but intensely powerful alternative by the eloquent grammar of Henny's things:

> A musky smell always came from Henrietta's room, a combination of dust, powder, scent, body odours that stirred the children's blood, deep, deep. It had as much attraction for them as Sam's jolly singing, and when they were allowed to, they gathered in Henrietta's room making hay, dashing to the kitchen to get things for her, asking her if she wanted her knitting, her book, tumbling out into the hall and back, until it was as if she had twenty children, their different voices steaming, bubbling and popping, like an irrepressible but inoffensive crater ... But she sometimes let them snuggle into the shawls, old gowns, dirty clothes ready for the wash, and blankets thrown over their great easy chair, hold their small parliament on the flowered green carpet, or look at all the things in her dressing table, and in what they called her *treasure drawers*. All Henny's drawers were treasure drawers. In them were spilled and tossed all sorts of laces, ribbons, gloves, flowers, jabots, belts, and collars, hairpins, powders, buttons, imitation jewels, shoelaces, and – wonder of wonders! – little pots of rouge, bits of mascara, an anathema to Sam, but to them a joyous mystery. Often, as a treat, the children were allowed to *look in the drawers* and they would plunge their hands into this mess of textures and surfaces, with sparkling eyes and rapt faces, feeling, guessing, until their fingers struck something they did not recognize, when their faces would grow serious, surprised, and they would start pulling, until a whole bundle of oddments lay on the floor, and their mother would cry, "Oh, you pest!" (30)

For the children, Henny's hideout offers not just the pleasures of absolute retreat but an alternative world. Their joyful collectivity when they are allowed to visit is registered in a healthy verbosity and pursuit of energetic tasks. The plenitude of the children's group voice is profoundly positive: "their different voices steaming, bubbling and popping, like an irrepressible but inoffensive crater." As a treat, the children can "hold their small parliament" in Henny's room, or sift through the accumulated hoard of treasures that spill out of drawers. This abundance of sensuous texture and smell is the scene of resistance that Henny maintains in her marriage; it is a non-verbal but critical mode of alternative power. The room connotes Henny's fundamental association with the deep and dark mysteries of the maternal body, with its "musky smell" and "body odors that stirred the children's blood, deep, deep ... but she sometimes let them snuggle into the shawls, old gowns, dirty clothes ready for the wash" (30). These accumulated last remnants of wealth and class privilege, and Henny's refuge, are decimated by the family's downward mobility and the symbolic registration of the defeat of the mother and her body.

Henny's bedroom is the private sphere within the private sphere (the inside of the domestic inside) and it is a treasure trove barred successfully to the patriarch, excluding infrequent or forced sexual encounter. Her loss of her cave of delights occurs when they are forced to move to Spa House in Eastport. All these wonderful possessions, which are the remnants of her old life as a southern belle and scion of a wealthy family, are sold to feed the children and service the debts that sustain the family as Sam engages in his Robinson Crusoe experiments in self-sufficiency. With this metonymic richness lost, Henny's final defeat becomes certain:

> No one (and least of all Sam, that know-all and see-all) knew for certain what was in even one of Henrietta's closets and tables. Their mother had locked cabinets with medicines and poisons, locked drawers with letters and ancient coins from Calabria and the south of France, a jewel case, and so on … The little girls were allowed to come in after knocking, and would tiptoe forward, holding their breath, fascinated by Henny's magic. As other times she would be sniffing her smelling salts, or taking aspirin, or mending linen, or reading, always using her eyes which grew darker and more tired every day, always doing things that were private to herself. (31)

Henny's last bastion of self-possession inheres in this magic refuge of texture and smell. The innermost sphere of the domestic world is an alternative bodily miscellany to set against Sam's verbal anthology, and its power is opposed to his because it is a collection of things that the children must read and interpret independently, though they are remnants of a faded and wordless past.

Henny's other mode of compendious resistance is associated with a spirited repertoire of Baltimore folk sayings, recitations, ditties and rhymes that the children beg her to repeat, although these are often reluctantly won from her because the sentimental or pedagogical aspect of their repetition does not interest her. For the children, however, Henny's ritual recitations are another of the many mysteries surrounding their mother and form part of their attachment to her, which proves troublingly unbreakable to their totalitarian father, who can't understand the order of knowledge or its force of connection. They are fond local sayings, but tellingly dark: "A fool for luck, a poor man for children, Eastern shore for hard crabs, and niggers for dogs" and "I have a little house and a mouse couldn't find it and all the men in your town couldn't count the windows in it: what is it?" (3).

Henny's epistemology is made up from her view of the darkly grotesque world in which she lives but which she does not seek to interpret: "the wonderful particular world" (7). For the children "when they went out with her, they saw it: they saw the fish eyes, the crocodile grins, the hair like a birch broom, the mean men crawling with maggots, and the children restless as an eel, that she saw" (7). Henny has no time for sentimentality and sees only the rather grim and squalid nature of life as waste, dirt, unfortunate desires and rotten luck. This association with the grotesque finds significant ballast in her association with figurative economies of darkness and blackness.

Black

In *The Logic of Slavery*, Tim Armstrong argues that slave narratives foreground key instances where "the hidden becomes a category of analysis".[3] The enslavement of the racial body and the occlusion of self-possession, work and voice – the entrapment of debt and the reification evident in the abstraction of the body of the slave to an object of value – are implied in Henny's "blackness". This parallel is irreducibly racist, since the comparison of the downwardly mobile middle-class white woman and the enslaved racial subject implies that both parties have a parity they emphatically do not possess, given Henny's class and whiteness. Nevertheless, Stead collocates woman and blackness in the case of Henny, and adds to this a recurring element in the political economy of the domestic sphere; that women and enslaved people cannot benefit from even the simplest aspects of organised labour. In a later short story, "The Magic Woman and other Stories", Stead writes about the intersection between gender, race and ethnicity in a triple reading of woman, slave and migrant:

> The woman in the home, no status to speak of, no trades-union, yet has the awful power of hunger and suck, givers of life and holds off death, sets out her law, defies their law for our sake; the man's power is evident: the woman's is stranger ... Behind the concept of woman's strangeness is the idea that a woman may do anything: she is below society, not bound by its law, unpredictable; an attribute given to every member of the league of the unfortunate. To make a small payment for their disability, we endow the slave, the woman, the dark-skinned alien with unusual interior vision ... It is perhaps our way of recognising that they are thinking inadmissible thoughts. The angle of seeing is different: it is from underneath, for one thing; not to mention other differences, national, local, personal.[4]

In this rendition of the domestic feminine, the strange otherness of the figure of the mother is partly explained by the fact that she exists outside/underneath social law and is therefore unpredictable and unreadable. With her inadmissible and mysterious thoughts and her perspective from "below", the mother wields tremendous and "awful" power in the realms of intimate survival and its acts of defiance and resistance.

Stead's description of paradoxical subalternity and power frames the mother as a member of a "league of the unfortunate", which includes the "slave" and "the dark-skinned alien" or migrant. All members of this league have, by way of

---

[3] Tim Armstrong, *The Logic of Slavery: Debt, Technology and Pain in American Literature* (Cambridge: Cambridge University Press, 2012), 1.

[4] Christina Stead, "The Magic Woman and Other Stories", *Ocean of Story: The Uncollected Stories of Christina Stead*, ed. R.G. Geering (Ringwood, Vic.: Penguin, 1986), 529–30.

position, an "unusual interior vision". The layering of race, colour and maternity appears repeatedly in *The Man Who Loved Children,* and the work of this book to draw out the matter of America in Stead's American novels makes this set of intersections even more apparent. Stead's allegorisation of Henny as a slave is important, if unwieldy, not least because it points to the dearth of accounts of female slavery by African American women themselves, in this period or later. Stead is also making a strange but powerful connection to Harriet Beecher Stowe's *Uncle Tom's Cabin* (1852) as a crucial reformist domestic fiction in the American tradition.

Henny's alliance with blackness appears in descriptions of how she looks, including expatiations on her sallow skin and black eyes and the kinds of things with which she is associated, such as dark bitter tea and bitter foods. The description of Henny's eyeball is a good example of her tropological "blackness":

> She would look fixedly at her vision and suddenly close her eyes. The child watching (there was always one) would see nothing but the huge eyeball in its glove of flesh, deep-sunk in the wrinkled skullhole, the dark circle round it and the eyebrow far above, as it seemed, while all her skin, unrelieved by brilliant eye, came out in its real shade, burnt olive. She looked formidable in such moments, in her intemperate silence, the bitter set of her discoloured moth with her uneven slender gambler's nose and scornful nostrils, lengthening her sharp oval face, pulling at the dry skinfolds. Then when she opened her eyes, there would shoot out a look of hate, horror, passion, or contempt. (4)

Darkness or blackness indicates that Henny is the Other, that she has a negative worldview, that she is grotesque and that she is not free. Her worldview is fantastically particular and generative, however, and the reader understands that Henny's stories of the grotesque and darker sides of life are also stories that are most likely to be true – detailed, specific and often humorous in the dark ways that they relay information about bodies, desires, improprieties, extortion, manipulation and powerlessness. Not surprisingly, Henny's dark vision plays a key role in Louie's unfolding creative vocation.

Henny's darkness is also figured as torrential and engulfing rage that erupts when Henny is overcome by her domestic struggles. In the terms of classical political contest, Henny is permanently defeated because she is always in the grip of the irrational and the Gothic – there is nowhere for her to move economically, emotionally and argumentatively except backwards. She is always operating, however vituperatively and creatively, within the existing system, and the gendered lineaments of discourse, on top of economic enslavement, spell defeat. Having said this, Henny's irrationality and rage – her rhetorical alignement with the dark witch/hag – actually powers an extraordinary resistance to Sam for an impressive length of time. If the secret history of the house requires a record of the true nature of women's experience in the sentimentalised domestic sphere, then Stead's offers yet another shocking revelation about this secret world of women: they are enraged.

Debt and Foreclosure

The Man Who Loved Children thematises debt as a key element of classical political economy. Debt is another kind of incarceration and enclosure for Henny and it is ultimately fatal for her. Henny's debts rise as the fortunes of the family decline after her father's death. *The Man Who Loved Children* is orchestrated through this rise in debt, which works in parallel with Louie's emergence through and out of the family unit:

> From the moment they came to Spa House, Henny had begun to lose ground in the war. Back she went, step by step; and it seemed that Sam, as poverty closed round them, gained stride by stride. Poverty was a beautiful thing to him, something he was born to and could handle: to her it was something worse than death, degradation and suicide. (319)

For Henny, poverty presents the greatest abjection and must be avoided at all costs. As a result, the novel is full of formulations of credit and debt, saving and spending, prostitution and gambling. Henny is indebted when we meet her, but she has her father's name and backing to assist with this age-old form of genteel economic management. When her father dies and then her husband walks away from paid work on a matter of principle, Henny's debt spirals because she has neither name nor income to draw on to service her promises.

Debt is built on a secret history of human obligation and survival.[5] As a driver of plot, debt has turned out to be a prodigious theme in literature. The debt plot calls to mind *The Merchant of Venice, The Friar's Tale, Moll Flanders, Middlemarch, Crime and Punishment, Vanity Fair, The Cherry Orchard, Great Expectations, Martin Chuzzlewit* and *Little Dorrit*. Debt concerned class, marriage, property, obligation and indenture. Material and non-material things could stand surety for a debt. Since the debt economy could be managed in any number of ways, lending money was linked with erotic relationships and relations of inheritance, with secret benefactors and, so often, infringements of the law. Debts were often secret and so were the terms of repayment. Financial crises arose from debt. When debtors were unable to pay this self-expanding overhead, over-accumulation and crisis would always follow. Henny's debt plot in *The Man Who Loved Children* participates in

---

[5] David Graeber, *Debt: The First 5,000 Years* (Brooklyn: Melville House, 2014); Margaret Atwood, *Payback: Debt and the Shadow Side of Wealth* (Toronto: Anansi, 2008); Benjamin Kunkel, "Forgive Us Our Debts: The History of Debt", *London Review of Books* 34, no. 9 (10 May 2012): 23–29.

the dark end of a subset of debt narratives, which concern female indebtedness, the extension of credit, and the eventual erosion of good standing, financial capacity and selfhood. The very possibility of domestic survival is secured by the secret history of Henny's debts, and her demise (her foreclosure) is predicted by this very common form of economic enclosure.

We learn quite soon of Henny's entrenched money troubles:

> would she get her own family together and arrange a kind of official moratorium with her creditors so that either she could pay them off by economy and reform, or her father or Hassie could be eventually moved to pay them off? (134).

This manipulation of the old forms of credit dependent on family members, social standing and the obligations of credit networks and gentility, has a sharper edge as we realise that Henny views sex with her own husband as one way in which she can manage her pressing credit crisis: "'I'll wring every penny of my debts out of him some way, before he goes; I'll find a way, anyway. I won't suffer,' and a small trickle of courage came back into her veins" (145). Bert Anderson, Sam's colleague in Washington, and a classic bounder, has been a source of financial support, but only in exchange for sex. When Sam is away, Henny's secret economy of indebtedness comes into view as systemic:

> "I was so terribly strapped after Ernie came, I just borrowed right and left – I hadn't the faintest idea how to run a house, and I only had Hazel Moore five months before Samuel quarrelled with her. I blush, even in my own room, when I think I never paid Connie O'Meara the hundred. She must think I'm a cheap chiseler! I'll pay her first." (90)

For Louise Yelin, Henny's pawning, pilfering and borrowing "signify her exploitation" and that she is thereby connected with the proletariat.[6] The allegorical ambitions of Stead's domestic novel are evident in Yelin's assertion about the similarity between the financial entrapment of Henny and the working class, though Stead makes the point that there were labour protections and union actions available to the proletariat that Henny cannot access.

In *Debtor Nation: The History of America in Red Ink*, Louis Hyman demonstrates usury was a growth market in America's 1930s volatile market culture, with the expansion of predatory lending from loan sharks in the context of interwar monetary chaos.[7] One of the many dark moments in Henny's debt plot

---

6   Louise Yelin, *From the Margins of Empire: Christina Stead, Doris Lessing, Nadine Gordimer* (Ithaca, NY: Cornell University Press, 1998), 23.
7   Louis Hyman, *Debtor Nation: The History of America in Red Ink* (Princeton, NJ: Princeton University Press, 2011).

concerns her desperate dealings with the repellent loan shark, Coffin Lomasne. In her effort to feed her family, Henny, who has accepted appalling terms from the usurer, has forfeited on repayments. In response, he lets it be known that Charles Franklin may not be Sam's child, which introduces a final spiral of conflict in Henny's marriage. Lomasne, associated with death, sewage and the upstream section of the Eastport River, is the veritable spectre of economic predation and death:

> As Sam peaceably observed, not even a Johns Hopkins fanatic collecting particularly loathsome antediluvian growth, or a syphilographer, would touch "Coffin" Lomasne with a forty-foot pole. He had two legs, but clearly he crawled on them; he had a backbone, but it was pliant as a willow wand; he had clothes and they were as clean as any boat-builder's on the shore, but these clothes were looser than grave-clothes, had a moral not a corporeal stench quite sensible to the nose, and though "Coffin" Lomasne did not lack flesh, through his long immersion in marshy places and abandoned, despised sumps, it clung to his bones like grave wax. You looked at Lomasne and saw an obsequious, fifty-year-old dead beat, and, as soon as your back was turned, you felt certain that there stood a loathsome ghoul. (340)

Henny's debt and death are anticipated in her contact with this ghoulish figure, and there is a sense in which Henny's death operates as the forfeiture of her life for a debt. Rather than Death as the "debt we owe to nature" as Freud has it, we can see, as Armstrong argues in *The Logic of Slavery*, that "debt necessarily imposes a plot in which redemption and justice are *deferred* – this is the spectre of debt's continuation".[8] Good standing and class position have been the only grounds for the extension of functioning or genteel credit, and with this long gone, as the dealings with Lomasne indicate, there is nowhere for Henny to go since there is only the infinite deferral in the forms of payments that can never be acquitted.

At the nadir of the Spa House poverty, as Gulliver Sam potters about experimenting with his plantation, press-ganging his children and relaxing, Henny has sold everything that moves, from the treasure in her cave of wonders at Tohoga all the way down to old cutlery. Her attempts to secure funding through sexual favours have found decreasing enthusiasm from Bert Anderson since her market value is denuded by the sheer physical impact of raising seven children in poverty: "Mother has had to sell everything she ever owned that she could: I've sold the clothes off my back. I only can't sell this furniture and this carpet because they are too big and he would notice that" (431). Ernie has discovered that Henny had raided his careful savings: she "had smashed everything he had" (406) by changing "his good money for trash money" (405) in his red money-box. This leads into a fearful sequence of domestic abuse by his mother, who belts Ernie until

---

8   Armstrong, *The Logic of Slavery*, 65.

3 Debt, Domestic Enclosure and Daughterly Revolution

he had "fallen to his knees and pleading" (431). Even Louie, the great survivor of ambient domestic violence, goes to school in a terrible state. Henny faints after this thrashing of her son, which represents a limit of betrayal and abuse, and she thereafter has black and hollow eyes and Ernie, who has hung his own survival on this small domestic bank, hangs himself in effigy.

These scenes offer the direst moments of Henny's debt plot, since a deep sympathy and intimacy between mother and son around the importance of capital, which has been carefully built, is utterly betrayed and with it, Ernie's method of surviving the domestic scene: "Ernie and Henny lived in an intimacy of their own, largely built up of calculations, loans and commissions. Ernie understood her need of money; she understood why Ernie should make a profit out of her need" (61). Ernie's obsession with capital has allowed him to survive his domestic milieu because "he had already defined all his relations to the world" (61). Ernie's efforts at capital accumulation add up to a sizable hoard, until his mother steals his money and replaces it with base metals. Ernie's financial miscellany has been destroyed and Henny's economic future is now even more hopeless, having alienated her next best hope of financial aid: "I thought the Big-Mouth would get a job and give you a start and you'd be able to make money for Mother" (403).

The suicide-murder of Henny, which involves Louie's cup of tea (the real "storm in a teacup") laced with arsenic and originally meant for both parents, follows Ernie and the marlin boiling episodes. Henny, like the marlin, has been boiled down over a long period, her integrity and sense of self broken by poverty and the effort to hold off Sam's ineffectual narcissism as she tries to feed the family. The description of the marlin applies to her: "its great eyes were sunken; it looked exhausted from its battle for life. There was a gaping wound in its deepest part" (454). Sam had even started to invade the sleep of her children during the fish boiling sequence and she is less able than ever to protect them from his incursions.

Spa House had become "a dark cavern of horrors and winds perpetually moving and howling" (360). Tellingly, the mother who was the centre of Tohoga House is now absent from the semi-slum that is Spa House because all forms of retreat are denuded: "when Sam was in all day, now, Henny would send a message that she would be out all day" (360). In the outside world, however, Henny can find no port of call either. Sam's move to almost total domination and his increasing energy as his family suffers more and more depredation is now unambiguously tragic rather than comic. The inexorable ending to Henny's debt plot is foretold in many ways, but most of all in her habitual game of Double Patience:

> In five minutes the game was out! Henny forgot the storm and the fish in the copper and looked helplessly at the eight stacks of cards before her, each with a king on top. The game that she had played all her life was finished; she had no more to do: she had no game … She was seized with such violent nausea, such a feeling of the emptiness and aimlessness of the game – thinking that she

might have to go through another fifteen or twenty years before it came out again! (461)

In addition to the prophetic realisation that "she had no game" (461), the final hopeless fights with her husband indicate that Henny has lost the capacity to signify. The bitter eloquence of some of her former Philippic tirades are long gone: "she vomited insults in which the word 'rotten' rose and fell, beating him with it … 'You rotten flesh', she screamed, insane, 'you rotten, rotten thing, you dirty sweaty pig, pig, pig'" (485). Even the younger children intuit that something in the quality of the conflict is different this time: it was "the intensity of the passions this time that stifled them all" (485). Henny's tirades have been reduced to sequences driven by rhythm and repetition, and her capacity to represent herself or her point of view is eroded beyond all reason.

Henny's end presents the reader of *The Man Who Loved Children* with a difficult prospect. To a certain extent, it is a suicide, since the narrative seems to indicate that Henny knows what Louie is holding, and she takes the poisoned cup of tea out of her hands deliberately. She is defeated by her struggle to survive poverty and oppression with the cards so absolutely stacked against her and with no capacity to step outside the cultural or economic logic in which she is encased. She cannot even bear to think of waiting for another game of Double Patience to come out. Having weathered Sam at his most revolting over the fish extraction, having experienced the total colonisation of personal space and sleep and air to breathe, having betrayed her son, the reader sympathises with Henny, and with Louie (the kindly cat-killer and protector of the children) as the agent of Henny's demise. This is a scene of self-destruction and of mother-killing.

The moment of matricide is confronting to read and confronting for the wider meanings of the novel, especially in regards to Louie and the position of women as mothers and daughters in this political economy. Marx translated Jacques Peuchet's essay on suicide written in early nineteenth-century France, an essay in which the suicide of middle-class women had been examined and the importance of gender relations to developing a criticism of society had been noted. For Marx, suicide was one key manifestation of alienation that marked both the public and private sphere.[9] This does not alleviate the grimness of the act of matricide, even if the question of consent is tricky. Louie's involvement with her stepmother's demise might be considered as her moment of revolutionary conviction and pragmatism: she considers that Henny's debt and suffering are too great. As a revolutionary, Louie might see that no small reform will do; escape from the actual system is essential and death is Henny's last option for escape. It might be that as the wealthier partner in the marriage built on class struggle that Henny must be the term that gives way to the exigencies of materialist history. What we do know is

---

9   Heather A. Brown, *Marx on Gender and the Family: A Critical Study* (Chicago: Haymarket Books, 2013), 44–48.

that Louie must also escape, so that she can "repay" her father for the years of humiliation and oppression. This is a very different kind of pledge to a deferred future. She might also escape with her destiny as an exceptional woman secured by the fact that she does not leave with mother, aunt or sister.

Louie's plans for revenge respond to her father's behaviour and not her mother's. Her planned vengeance is a promissory note – a kind of credit – which helps her maintain dignity and agency as she weathers humiliation. It is articulated in her sworn oath that she will "repay" Sam, which she vows after Sam's premeditated beating of Louisa, and the more damaging and malignant claim that they are no different after all: "you can't help it you are myself" (135). Louisa rejects the beating and the malignant rejection of her individuality by swearing, "I will repay … vengeance is mine, I will repay" (133). This makes for a revenge plot that supersedes both debt plot and profit motive. This plot is deferred to the future, when it seems that Louie might become the political woman writer of a book like *The Man Who Loved Children*, which tells the secret history of her domestic life and her father's despotism. Her method of repayment cannot engage the male prerogative of speech, so she turns to writing, as evidenced in her strange compositions:

The desolator desolate
The tyrant overthrown;
The arbiter of other's fate
A suppliant for his own! (278)

The revenge plot is therefore connected with Louie's *Künstlerroman* and her desire to achieve both the freedom and the satisfaction of "paying up" or paying back, a response that was denied to her mother.

The Undomesticated Daughter and the Revolting Subject

The plucky and imaginative heroine's preparation to love and be loved was at the heart of all domestic novels of manners. It was helpful that she was often an avid reader and a teller of tales. Nina Baym's account of the basic plot of the domestic novel of manners is the story of a young girl who is deprived of supports she had rightly or wrongly depended on to sustain her throughout life. She is thus faced with the necessity of winning her own way in the world and the need to develop a strong conviction of her own worth as a result.[10] The symmetry of this account of the domestic novel of manners and the travestied version we see in *The Man Who Loved Children* reinforces Stead's interrogation of the sentimental

---

10 Nina Baym, *Women's Fiction: A Guide to Novels by and about Women in America, 1820–1870* (Urbana: University of Illinois Press, 1992).

forms of domestic fiction. Allied to this interrogation, Stead's critique of American political economy operates through her exposure of its deep realities and roiling contradictions in her secret history of the domestic front. The character of Louie as both revolutionary and writer in the making is part of Stead's emphatic response to the cult of domesticity and all this entailed politically and aesthetically for the daughter and artist in the making.

Louisa is characterised by the complete absence of the usual attributes of the heroines of romance or sensibility:

> She felt a growling, sullen power in herself which was merely darkness to the splendid sunrise that she felt certain would flash in her in a few years. She acknowledged her unwieldiness and unhandiness in this little world ... Louie knew she was the ugly duckling. But when a swan she would never come sailing back into their village pond; she would be somewhere away, unheard of, on the lily-rimmed oceans of the world. (57)

We find in Louise an unaccountably strong sense of destiny and an immovable obstinacy, a mulishness beyond rhyme or reason, which her stepmother appreciates in light of her father's tyranny: "Sam had his remedies, but Henny smiled in pity at his remedies" (34). Louisa is a singularly rebellious girl and Susan K. Martin's account of the influence of *Seven Little Australians* is essential reading on this count.[11] Louie has nothing of renunciation or pathos about her; she is, instead, profoundly resistant, and although she knows all too well both the experience of domination and the labour of domesticity, she remains profoundly undomesticated at the end of the novel.

Given the clarity with which we are led to see Henny and the children as an unpaid and unorganised labour force, vulnerable to fascist seduction and exploitation, a revolutionary in the house is deeply significant, but this is complicated in Louie's case by her needs as an artist. Louie's struggle to survive in the ambit of her narcissistic father and embattled stepmother takes the form of her own self-election as a writer, and this complicates her protection of her siblings. In contrast to all the noise around her, Louie takes to the written word, scaffolded at first by her strange compendium of quotations of great male thinkers and autodidactic reading.

The growing dissidence of her creative work gives form to the forces of her growing adolescent desire and Louie Pollit's *primum mobile* as a writer is eventually expressed as a romantic and erotic prerogative. Her desire is the locomotive of her creativity, and this is completely irrespective of her abject or non-ideal embodiment. Sam, disgusted and titillated by Louisa's maturing physicality and the powerful enigma of her desire, is determined to control her in this very realm:

---

11 Susan K. Martin, "'The Other Seven Little Australians': *The Man Who Loved Children* Reads Ethel Turner", *Australian Literary Studies* 25, no. 3 (2010), 35–48.

3 Debt, Domestic Enclosure and Daughterly Revolution

> He poked and pried into her life, always with a scientific, moral purpose, stealing into her room when she was absent, noting her mottoes on the wall … and investigating her linen, shivering with shame when suggestive words came into her mouth. Her speech, according to his genteel ideas, was too wild, too passionate, too suggestive – not to use the words "passionate" or "passional", which she was fond of. (322)

Passion connotes the powerful agency into which Louie taps. Productive authorship and pleasurable agency are derived from the possession of a love object to persuade. The subject position of the lover rather than the loved raises Louie above the kind of abject position she commonly occupies in her father's company, and teaches her to resist it. The kind of abjection with which we associate Louie at Tohoga makes a return quite late in the novel, as events at Spa House slowly spiral to their tragic conclusion. Stead is, as always, unafraid of the extremity of Louie's physical and verbal abjection:

> "I don't know what to do. I don't know what to do. I can't bear the daily misery. I can't bear the horror of everyday life." She was bawling brokenly on the tablecloth, her shoulders heaving and her long hair, broken loose, plastered all over her red face messy, no shoes, big and fat, bellowing… She stood at the door, halfway open, and beat on it with her soft half-open fists, crying brokenly, "I can't help it" and weeping endlessly. (396)

As a marginal subject and improper body, Louie still manages to find strategies of resistance to the tyrannies of her traumatic home. If the above scene is anything to go by, there is overdue work on Louie's creative capacities and political resistance in her role as a maker of theatre. Imogen Tyler's recent book, *Revolting Subjects: Social Abjection and Resistance in Neoliberal Britain*, investigates aspects of marginality, social exclusion and injustice created by neoliberal ideologies of selfhood, and she is most interested in various political and aesthetic strategies that are crucial for resistance to this kind of subjectification. She identifies the "revolting subject" as a key figure of resistance; an abject or subaltern figure whose marginal status the subject themselves seeks to rewrite and recreate. What if, Tyler asks, the status of the abject offers a powerful form of resistance?[12] In the larger global environment, these abject subjects may be more widely understood in the categories of those whom industrial imperialism systematically overlooks: slaves, prostitutes, the colonised, the domestic and the unemployed. These are Louie's people, it seems:

> She felt at home with them, she was eccentric, ugly and awkward, and they were quite evidently in their lives, eccentric, ugly and awkward. Sam had a

---

12   Imogen Tyler, *Revolting Subjects: Social Abjection and Resistance in Neoliberal Britain* (London: Zed Books, 2013), 34.

voice, *she had an ear,* and these struggling poor people, gasping just at the surface of the river, about to sink, had lives. (70, my emphasis)

As a step-mothered and motherless girl, Louie fits quite literally into Tyler's notion of the abject subject as one who is haunted by the original exile from the body of the mother, but even though the connection here is with the eccentric, ugly and awkward, Louie is identified with her ear.

Queer subjectivity, in particular, contests normativity and disarticulates abjection. Tyler's formulation of queer resistance gives a very satisfying interpretive frame to the strange and compelling instances of female pedagogy, female sociality and queer desire that characterise Louisa's apprenticeship as an artist. Louie's set-piece interaction with Nellie, the strange maid who is dismissed at Monocacy, involves a strangely loaded contest around female knowledge of the body and the world, which is articulated as the question "what do you know?" (168). Only thirty pages later, Louie reacts to the loss of a school-friend, Olive, with a lover's grief:

> Something seemed to hit Louie. A new sort of pain, sharp and quick as lighting, tore out of its swaddling clothes of flesh, inside Louie. For a moment, she was conscious only of her wrung bowels and the cause of misery beside her, the dark spindly creature. I can't bear this, something said very audibly inside her … It was like the first stab of an abscess; the sufferer knew it would come back. I can't bear it. She looked at Olive, "Oh, Olive, don't go." (190)

Louie's desire for and celebration of her young female teacher, Miss Aiden, allows her a generative position as adoring and chivalric writer. This queered position and the desiring agency it endows allow her to withstand her father's shaming: "with a sort of sacred horror, he looked aghast at her fat thighs half revealed … 'You'll find your place in the world, Looloo, but whatever we eventually find in that mountain of fat, it isn't going to be a Pavlova'" (113). Louie negotiates her inability to measure up to any ideal of womanhood wielded by her father through her discovery of the transformations of romantic obsession. By the time she has moved to her new high school in Annapolis, and just as things are becoming more and more dire at home, Louie relishes her adoration for Miss Aiden: "Louie became the chief flatterer of Miss Aiden" (332).

In this context, Louie is described rather wonderfully as a "blue-eyed female Caliban" who "made a point of never going to school without a poem or a scene (in a play) in Miss Aiden's honour" (333). In homage to the fixed object of her passion, the grotesquerie of a female Caliban is transformed by the prerogative to love:

> Louie had formed a magnificent project, The Aiden Cycle. The Aiden Cycle would consist of a poem of every conceivable form and also every conceivable meter in the English language, each and every one, of course, in honor of Miss Aiden. Part of the Aiden cycle was to be The Sonnets, dedicated to The Onlie

Begetter, a little thing which would occupy by a brief time in that life that was entirely for Aiden ... Learn *Paradise Lost* by heart. Why? She did not know really: it was a spectacular way of celebrating Aiden. (332)

With a decided sense that this homage was a form of gendered resistance of an altogether difficult and notorious kind, "Sam decided that all Louie's homework must be done in the family dining room, under the eye of one and all" (333). The inspiration that Miss Aiden offers as an object of queer desire supports Tyler's hypothesis that abjection can be rewritten as a form of political and aesthetic resistance: "Mooning and moping over Miss Aiden till the entire family of Pollits thought the child was queer, while Hassie told Henny, 'she must early look out for a husband for her, or else some accident would happen to the great overgrown child'" (369). If Sam's excessive miscellanies represent domination and Henny's excessive accumulation of faded treasures represents resistance and refuge, then Louisa's Aiden miscellany represents revolution: "'I love, I love, I only know about love', cried Louie madly, bursting into tears" (467). Her plays also supply pieces for her assemblage of self-declaration, desire and resistance.

Louie is a riveting example of the revolting subject. Abjection defines Louie in her domestic economy – both mother and father despair of her unconventional and uncompromising selfhood – but from and through this abjection, she achieves both aesthetic and political goals:

But Louie, dragging herself by main force out of those frightful sloughs of despondency and doubt and uncleanness which seemed to be sucking her down, with amorous muddy lips, saw hours of lightning, when the universe split from heaven to hell and in the chasm writhed the delirium of glory, the saturnalia of which explained her world to her: she would stand on the beach watching the tall dry grass which stood in the moistest part of the shore and suddenly she would think. (325)

Despite the ironic exaggeration of this sequence of adolescent insight, Louie's position as the abject subject associated with the "muddy lips" and "uncleanness" of despondency and doubt is nevertheless connected with insight and genuine thought. She is a visionary and a survivor of the house of horrors as well.

Revolutionary Exit

After Louie's involvement with her stepmother's fate, she steps into a double maternal absence of lost mother and lost stepmother; she is set to enter the world as a self-made woman, self-possessed and self-redeemed. The return of her aunt to fill her mother's shoes has meant that she is free to leave the house and the state, and set off alone for the revolutionary arcadia of Harpers Ferry:

> Taking some food out of the ice box (she was always hungry), she ran out of the house and in no time was screened by the trees and bushes of the avenue. She smiled, felt light as a dolphin undulating through the waves, one of those beautiful, large, sleek marine mammals that plunged and wallowed, with their clever eyes. As she crossed the bridge (looking back and seeing none of the Naval Academy as yet on their little beach, or scrambling down the sodden bluff) she heaved a great breath. How different everything looked, like the morning of the world. (512)

Louisa disinherits her natural father from her new and necessary genealogy and sets up a new line comprised of heretics, rebels, Christians and puritans on her Baken side. Jennifer McDonell reminds us that Harpers Ferry connotes freedom and justice, willpower and high romantic rebellion, the Bible and John Bunyan, conscientious dissent and the early struggle for slavery.[13] This is heroic and idealistic America. The geography of Louie's final destination indicates, as McDonell surmises, a daughterly declaration of independence that announces a third American Revolution, following on John Brown's second and Thomas Jefferson's first:

> All to her, in this land, all, with the meeting of the waters, and the Southern sun pouring over the hills and their burning silky heads, John Brown's Fort, the starry nights, skirlings downhill on skates from this haunted and embattled siege rock, the quiet, deserted streets, the frank worries about the death of the town and its real estate, made the Harpers Ferry of her summers a sort of revelation to Louie: the placid high-minded heavens of Pollitry were rolled up and there was a landscape to the far end of the sky – an antique, fertile, yeoman's country, where, in the shelter of other customs and tribal foods, people believing themselves to be the children of God stuck to their occupations, gave praise, and accompanied their humblest deeds with the thunder of mystic song. (155–56)

As the first of the novels in her anatomy of America, I have argued that in *The Man Who Loved Children* Stead constructed a political allegory for the panoramic nation through domestic fiction. The political allegory that the domestic novel offers speaks to the national scale through Sam as domestic vernacularist and petty imperialist, and Henny's incarceration as enslaved white woman and household debtor in New Deal economic dysfunction. Louie offers a vision of the adolescent girl as artist-rebel and proto-revolutionary, whose final steps are toward American revolutionary homelands. The next target of Stead's ambition was New York City. Stead was interested in representing experiences of this iconoclastic city from the

---

13 Jennifer McDonell, "Christina Stead's *The Man Who Loved Children*", *Southerly* 44, no. 4 (1984), 394–413.

3 Debt, Domestic Enclosure and Daughterly Revolution

late 1920s, through to the post-war era. *Letty Fox: Her Luck*, *A Little Tea, A Little Chat* and *The People with the Dogs* were not to be allegorical works about New York City; they were to be material, episodic and accretive, and for this she needed another family of genres altogether – the picaresque.

4

The New York Love Market and the Picara Fortunata in *Letty Fox: Her Luck*

> The thing about New York that no one seems to have noticed but which is absolutely striking is that they all do tell tales.[1]

In "It Is All a Scramble for Boodle", Christina Stead identified the "brutally outspoken and crassly advertised" importance of money in America. She expressed an emphatic horror about the way in which this ideological characteristic saturated even the world of romantic relationships:

> Everything is expressed in terms of money; [I am] shocked by women's pages where the money value of divorce, security value of a suitor, and advice concerning a reluctant alimony payer are discussed, and where women are told that when they have lost their husband's love, they have nothing to rely on but the coercion of alimony, where the money value of children is discussed … Nowhere else is human love discussed in terms of the stock market.[2]

As early as 1935, Stead had noticed that in America, the realms of romance, courtship and marriage were dominated by a rhetoric of money and the market. Love, like the free market, was a game for speculators, gamblers and gougers. Building on this insight, Stead made aspects of reification the centre of her critique of capital in the New York trilogy. Stead's portrait of American metropolitan modernity through her three New York modulations of the picaresque narrative takes the reader into the urban byways of commerce and exchange of all kinds. The city panorama delivered by Stead's mobile stories and storytellers is expansive and compendious enough to reflect both city life and the energy of the market culture that dominated it. Commodities, people and stories circulate in fascinating ways in

---

1   Barry Hill, "Christina Stead at 80 Says Love is her Religion", *Age*, 17 July 1982, 2.
2   Christina Stead, "It Is All a Scramble for Boodle: Christina Stead Sums Up America", *Australian Book Review* 141, no. 6 (1992), 23.

the financial capital of the United States, where capital and desire move together in such protean formations.

Stead's New York *picaras* and *picaros* have strong American antecedents, which Stead knew well. As Jackson Lears reports, young colonial America was a federation of states seemingly dedicated to the function and success of colonial capital at various unregulated new cities and frontiers, and therefore America in general had a particularly strong picaresque tradition from the beginning. If we follow De Tocqueville, we might see American society as a vast lottery, redolent with market instability and associated regimes of gambling. Discourses of Providence were at hand to legitimate and organise contingency and luck in one's pursuit of the American Dream, but the confidence man was also a devotee of Fortune. American rogues, *picaros* and *picaras* all subscribed to fortune as they grappled in their resilient ways with the delinquency and narrative blundering that dramatised the dark underside of the culture of luck.[3]

Since arriving in New York in 1935, Stead had trained her novelist's eyes and ears on the street level of the capital of Capital. In the years during World War II and just after she published three novels that offer a shrewd set of experiments with the genre of the rogue's progress, contoured by gender and three different thematic elements from political economy specifically connected to speculation and gambling. These included a portrait of the marriage game as a hard-core capital market in *Letty Fox: Her Luck,* a portrait of financial piracy and gangster speculation during wartime in New York in *A Little Tea, A Little Chat,* and finally the ambivalent consequences of the ownership of Manhattan property and an old upstate utopia after the war in *The People with the Dogs*. The following two chapters will explore the ways in which the picaresque genre represented the economic and libidinal energies of New York before and after World War II. The picaresque is the literary genre *par excellence* for relaying stories of wayward libidinal, commodity and money economies, and Stead's account of the individual in the city of New York in this period is a familiar account of survival through energy and sharp wits, as well as bleak examples of human alienation. Economic figures of circulating capital, commodity fetishism and the property market all inform the key American inflections of picaresque gold-diggers, femmes fatales, rapacious libertines and propertied dilettantes.

In a letter to Thistle Harris in 1939, Stead refers to ideas for future projects. She writes about two she currently has in mind: "an American Karamazov's story, and a female picaresque".[4] The reference to Dostoyevsky's last novel may be deliberately provocative, given it is a story of patricide, and Thistle was her stepmother. The rich and complicated Russian family, however, directs us to the work Stead finally produced as *The People with the Dogs* and Stead's framing of the project as

---

3   Jackson Lears, *Something for Nothing: Luck in America* (New York: Penguin, 2003).
4   Christina Stead to Thistle Harris, 7 July 1939. In *A Web of Friendship: Selected Letters 1928–1973*, ed. R.G. Geering (Pymble, NSW: Angus & Robertson, 1992), 91.

4 The New York Love Market

American is interesting. The "female picaresque" may well have been in Stead's sights because she found a suitably compelling subject in the form of Ruth Blech, Bill Blake's daughter, about whom she was making notes as early as 1937.

This chapter focuses on the New York *picara* as young woman on the make in a tough marriage and job market dominated by capricious market forces. Letty Fox's ebullient movement through the social vistas of Manhattan allows Stead to manifest her next great critique of women in American urban modernity – the travestied and alienated playing of what I will call the marriage game in the love market. Letty is associated with trickster and gold-digger figures familiar in classic Hollywood cinema at the time. The next chapter will examine Letty's male counterparts – the very differently styled *picaro*s that deliver complementary views of mobility and capital relations in Manhattan towards the end of the war and early post-war years. Picaresque modes of circulation and episodic scenes of capital desire are familiar, but each of the *picaro* stories delivers contrasting and complementary accounts – from the darkest kind of capital reification to a gentler critique of commitment to old utopias founded on inherited property.

"Baghdad on the Hudson"

What is obvious from the opening of *Letty Fox: Her Luck* is the strong shift in setting from suburban Georgetown and semi-rural Annapolis to the thrumming hub of America's quintessential city of New York. We have left Louie's "walk around the world", starting at historic Harpers Ferry, the meeting point of the Shenandoah and Potomac Rivers, and have ended up in some of the most famous metropolitan streets in modernity. In contrast to Louie's vision of an undulating dolphin as she leaves Eastport Creek behind her, Letty's vivacious first-person opening delivers an account of a flighty departure from a rented room in the Village, down to street level, to consider her rental, sexual and financial options. *A Little Tea, A Little Chat* and *The People with the Dogs* also open with New York street geographies and meditations on real estate. Stead's treatment of New York City was focussed on Manhattan and often only a small section of the Lower East Side near Union Square and Greenwich Village, with occasional forays into the Upper East Side. This was an area of Manhattan she knew very well, having made her home in a few apartments in this area during her New York sojourn.

In the 1930s, bank failures, industrial meltdowns, curbside apple sellers and bread lines for impoverished New Yorkers became the norm.[5] New York produced huge contradictions: city assistance schemes and massive building projects, nightclubs side by side with gangster cartels and showgirls, racial tensions in

---

5   Thomas Kessler, "Fiorello LaGuardia and the Challenge of Democratic Planning", in *The Landscape of Modernity: Essays on New York City 1900–1940,* eds. David Ward and Olivier Zunz (New York: Russell Sage Foundation, 1992), 315–29.

Harlem alongside a flowering of art and music. For Sabrina Fuchs Abrams, New York is actually a "study in contradictions", starting with the fact that is seems almost unique in urban history yet also dependent on the powerful ubiquity of the American Dream.[6]

In his 1954 publication, *Understanding the Americans,* for the London publisher, Frederick Muller, Bill Blake referred to New York as "Baghdad on the Subway", while Stead called New York "Baghdad on the Hudson".[7] They both cite O. Henry's fond names for New York. A native of North Carolina, O. Henry (William Sidney Porter) is associated, rather appropriately, with many witty short stories detailing the life of ordinary people in New York settings from the point of view of an outsider. Porter, like Stead, loved *One Thousand and One Nights* and in another uncanny similarity he is often talked about as the American Guy De Maupassant, a writer for whom Stead had the most powerful regard. O. Henry's approach to New York through many short stories speaks to the inspiring panorama of the metropolis, and this is an aspect of the city Stead was determined to capture too, but in very different ways.

O. Henry thought that New York resembled Baghdad because it was like the marvellous city of Scheherazade's story cycle. The comparison produces an unabashedly orientalist image of the bazaar town where money, commodities, sex and stories endlessly and energetically circulate. Stead would also compare New York with Naples and Venice, again with the emphasis on the busy, the mercantile and the cutthroat politics. These are all port cities, characterised by brio, dirt and "scramble", and an inventiveness associated with hubs of racial mixture. Blake describes New Yorkers as "exuberant and vital, quick on the uptake", constantly "storytelling and swapping stories", telling "yarns, tall stories, smutty stories, limericks, inconsequential but enchanting nonsense tales" and exhibiting a "unique brand of jokes".[8] As the early twentieth-century immigrant city *par excellence*, New York was the site of heterogeneity and diversity, of hustle and bustle, of confidence men and shady ladies. One of the mechanisms that held the multicultural experiment together in the New York system was the persistent and fervent ideology that one was free, through economic effort, to make something of oneself – to rise.

The structure of capital circulation was perfect for the vision Stead had of New York as driven by appetites for capital, sex and stories. Stead's New York ethnography is focused through central figures whose walking and talking embody the circulation of capital and desire:

---

6   Sabrina Fuchs Abrams, "Introduction", in *Literature of New York*, ed. Sabrina Fuchs Abrams (Newcastle upon Tyne: Cambridge Scholars Publishing, 2009), 1.
7   Hill, "Christina Stead at 80 Says Love is her Religion", *Age*, 2.
8   William Blake, *Understanding the Americans* (London: Frederick Muller, 1954), 103.

Cultures of circulation are created and animated by the cultural forms that circulate through them, including – critically – the abstract nature of the forms that underwrite and propel the process of circulation itself. The circulation of such forms – whether the novels and newspapers of the imagined community or the equity-based derivatives and currency swaps of the modern market – always presupposes the existence of their respective interpretive communities, with their own forms of interpretation and evaluation.[9]

Writing, desire, appetite, talking, walking, stories, scamming: Stead's New York picaresques represent multiple kinds of circulation, starting with capital and moving through cognate economies of sex and story exchange. Jean-François Lyotard's work, *Libidinal Economy* (1974) is usefully provocative in its insistence that every economy is libidinal and that the force of libido exceeds and contorts the circuits of capital rather than the reverse. Particularly in the shape of speech and the strong investments of certain kinds of voice, the intense aleatoric energy associated with libido seems to flood the economic system with affective intensity.[10]

This affective intensity, as well as the intensity of commodity life and activity during the war years, meant that though the novel of manners was the genre that Henry James and Edith Wharton had adopted to investigate Manhattan life and social structures, Stead needed something much more capacious and raucous to map and catalogue the Manhattan she knew in the 1930s and 1940s. Inventories of the features of the picaresque indicate how precisely the genre is deployed by Stead in the 1940s to control and shape the mass of detail of New York City. Among theorists of the picaresque from the critical heyday of work on the eighteenth-century picaresque, a penchant for lists of features emerged, and some of these describe Stead's mid-century New York narratives very well. Ulrich Wicks' identification of panoramic structure, Sisyphean rhythms and elements of fortune and adversity clearly applies, as does Claudio Guillen's interest in the fact that expedience and cunning outweigh good conduct, even though the outsider or parvenu is trying to thrive and rise.[11] As Rowland Sherrill has argued about more recent picaresque narratives, one of the critical aspects of the *picara* or *picaro* is her or his capacity to bear witness to scale:

> Along with those attributes of protagonist, plot, unity, and tone, an element of the expressive structure of the classic picaresque narrative has to do with social stock-taking. By virtue of the socially marginal character of the *picaro* or

---

9   Benjamin Lee and Edward LiPuma, "Culture of Circulation: The Imaginations of Modernity", *Public Culture* 14, no. 1 (2002), 192.
10 Jean-François Lyotard, *Libidinal Economy*, trans. Iain Hamilton Grant, (1974; London: Bloomsbury 2004).
11 Ulrich Wicks, *Picaresque Narrative, Picaresque Fiction: A Theory and Research Guide* (New York: Greenwood Press, 1989); Claudio Guillen, *The Anatomies of Roguery: A Comparative Study in the Origins and the Nature of Picaresque Literature* (New York: Garland, 1987).

picara, his or her ingenuous demeanour, and a fair degree of literary license, the figure easily (or impishly) trespasses social boundaries, thus serving as a catalyst, or a "lens" for one of the major purposes of the old picaresque narratives – namely, running the social gamut of the culture in question … the *picaro* or *picara* provided a literary device for virtually unlimited access to the social scene.[12]

The picaresque was, for Stead, a key genre in her American anatomy as a vehicle for critique: of capital, of pseudo-radical behaviours, racketeering, prostitution and political hypocrisy. For all the seductive energy generated by the schemes to survive and thrive there was unrelenting corruption and scheming to be recorded. As a genre of social stocktaking, the literary licence afforded by the picaresque has to do with unwieldy plots and unlimited access to the social and material world. As half-outsiders and marginal characters, the *picara/picaro* is self-reliant and mobile (rather like Stead herself) and enjoyed access to the social panorama of his or her time.[13]

The topoi of female survival and female ambition are central to the New York trilogy. New York City could certainly boast some tough broads and witty working girls at this particular historical moment. Cinema was a crucial platform for these characters, but in the world of letters, Anita Loos and Dorothy Parker immediately come to mind. In *Letty Fox: Her Luck,* the framing questions of American radical politics complicate and extend these gendered topoi. The anti-sentimental picaresque allowed Stead to experiment with New York speech and to anatomise various American dilemmas as she saw them: a materialistic and weak middle-class obsessed with easy success, the irritant of fake radicalism in the New York Left and the irresistible rise and rise of gangster capitalism. In terms of her synoptic interest in reification, *Letty Fox: Her Luck* provides an extraordinary demonstration of the way in which sexual relations are discussed as a matter of the market rather than romance. The synonyms for women who are working the marriage market are striking, and they are enumerated below as tourist, gangster, gold-digger, prostitute and libertine. Property is a key element of these discussions about romantic prospects. The solution to this reification is a better system, meaning a knowledge of a political theory (Marxism) that would provide an awareness of one's own alienation and the tools with which to mount a struggle against it.

---

12   Rowland A. Sherrill, *Road-Book America: Contemporary Culture and the New Picaresque* (Urbana: University of Illinois Press, 2000), 3.
13   A good introduction to the *picara* is Julio Rodriguez-Luis, "*Picaras*: The Modal Approach to the Picaresque", *Comparative Literature* 31, no. 1 (1979), 32–46. Rodriguez-Luis and others point out the significance of the early Ubeda text *La Picara Justina* (1605) as the first example of a *picara* narrative. The *picara*'s story was always focused on questions of the body, sexuality, marriage and unfaithfulness. The female rogue generally deployed what power resided in her sexual attractiveness and vulnerability.

"The Girl was New York City"

Stead's critique of the American scene through the focal character of the New York Girl found its shape in the traditional picaresque chronotope of the encounter and the modern chronotope of the urban jungle.[14] The heterotopia of New York was a world in which the young middle-class *picara* was a girl with an office job. With the ultimate prize of marriage in mind, this girl could try her hand at confidence games, gambling, and trickster exploitation, since it was a contingent world of unregulated capitalism and the culture of fluctuation, chance and fortune that it represented.

Stead claimed that Letty was based on "a New York girl I knew very well" and "the girl was New York City".[15] Letty Fox was based on the daughter of Stead's life partner, Bill Blake. Letty is talkative, worldly, practical, mobile, inventive and promiscuous. She is an extraordinary vernacular force, synthesising the gold-digging, wisecracking dame of American cinema and the earlier *picaras* of Spanish and English literature. One of the most significant aspects of Letty's "luck" is surely this vernacular ebullience and witty inventiveness. Her indefatigable first-person energy connects Letty back to Sam Pollit in Stead's sequence of gigantic American characters who overwhelm us with their creativity, appetites and loquacity.

When we meet Letty, she is twenty-four, working hard in wartime New York, living in a hotel, having a doomed affair with the morally suspect Dutchman Cornelis de Groot and deciding that marriage, rather than endless piratical affairs, is the only safe berth for a girl such as herself. Since arriving in New York, Letty's life has been a study in motion, but her footloose mobility and urban freedom have delivered neither romantic prosperity nor practical advantage. Letty claims that "there was no end to what I needed", a comic registration of her insatiable desires. Her confession offers an energetic, often-hilarious rendition of the vicissitudes of sexual, economic and professional markets without much reflection, since she is too busy:

> One hot night last spring, after waiting fruitlessly for a call from my then lover, with whom I had quarrelled the same afternoon, and finding one of my black moods on me, I flung out of my lonely room on the ninth floor (unlucky number) in a hotel in lower Fifth Avenue and rushed into the streets of the Village, feeling bad. My first thought was, at any cost, to get company for the evening. In general, things were bad with me; I was in low water financially and had nothing but married men as companions. My debts were nearly six hundred dollars, not counting my taxes in arrears. I had already visited the

---

14 Mikhail M. Bakhtin, "Forms of Time and of the Chronotope in the Novel", in *The Dialogic Imagination: Four Essays*, ed. Michael Holquist, trans. Caryl Emerson and Michael Holquist (Austin: University of Texas Press, 1981), 84–258.
15 Quoted in Joan Lidoff, *Christina Stead* (New York: Frederick Ungar, 1982), 194–95.

> tax inspector twice and promised to pay in installments when I had money in the bank. I had told him that I was earning my own living, with no resources, separated from my family, and that though my weekly pay was good, that is sixty-five dollars, I needed that and more to live. All this was true. I now had, by good fortune, about seventy dollars in the bank, but this was only because a certain man had given me a handsome present (the only handsome present I ever got, in fact); and this money I badly needed for clothes, for moving, and for petty cash.[16]

Letty's specific bad mood at the outset relates to another "fruitless" love affair because it is unprofitable. Letty's energetic mobility ("flung", "rushed", "quarrelled") is matched by her urgent desire to turn a fiscal and sexual trick and paradoxically "get company for the evening" but "at any cost". Company means that she can swing into action about her penurious state and she may indeed advance her position through sex. Financial "low water" and "married men as lovers" are connected, and with some dissatisfaction. Marriage is clearly the only financially prudent game to play; it is the long game, the game which guarantees a "start in life, meaning a start of at least some seeming respectability from which all economic deals could be brokered.

In foregrounding Letty's inventories (rhetorically reminiscent of Henny's treasure trove), Stead explores what it means for a young woman, even a young radical, to outfit herself as a commodity and a player on the marriage market. The textual equivalent of accumulation is enacted by these inventories, and the pressure is on to profit from the capital invested, otherwise economic crisis will ensue:

> I needed at least two hundred and fifty dollars for a new coat. My fur coat, got from my mother, and my dinner dress, got from my grandmother, were things of the past and things with a past, mere rags and too well known to all my friends. There was no end to what I needed. My twenty-fourth birthday was just gone, and I had spent two hours this same evening ruminating upon all my love affairs which had sunk ingloriously into the past, along with my shrunken and worn outfits. Most of these affairs had been promising enough. Why had they failed? (Or I failed?) Partly, because my men, at least during the war years, had been flighty, spoiled officers in the armed services, in and out of town, looking for a good-timer by the night, the week, or the month; and if not these young officers, then my escorts were floaters of another sort, middle-aged, married civilians, journalists, economic advisers, representatives of foreign governments or my own bosses, office managers, chiefs, owners. But my failure was, too, because I had no apartment to which to take them. How easy for them to find it inconvenient to visit me at my hotel, or for me to visit

---

16 Christina Stead, *Letty Fox: Her Luck* (1946; Sydney: Angus & Robertson, 1974), 3. All subsequent references are to this edition and appear in parentheses in the text.

them at theirs when they were dubious or cool. It seemed to me that night that a room of my own was what I principally lacked. (3)

Letty's audit enumerates the accoutrements she requires for the season. Then there is a man audit, with men sorted by their profession, until Letty alights on the idea that her romantic/capital life is a failure because she does not have "a room of her own". Some of Stead's comic bite can be seen in this ironic reference to Virginia Woolf; "a room of my own" refers to the sexual availability that will increase Letty's chances in the marriage game. If she is lucky, the room may lead to marriage, suggesting that women must sell themselves in order to be respectable. She has assessed with cool-headed judgement the merits of older or younger men with whom to have affairs and declares quite candidly that "I was never fond of money, except to spend, and never went with a man for his money. My supreme idea was always to get married and join organised society" (3).

Though Letty is engaging in informal agreements with men about the exchange of sex for money, this is neutralised as a kind of tourism: "A 'tourist' papa called me, a tourist to men, that is. I reckoned I knew enough about life to write a real book of a girl's life" (15). This "real book" joins the secret history of *The Man Who Loved Children* in undertaking the critical exposition of social relations under capital. In her picaresque mode as a "man tourist" about town, Letty relates an intensely material first-person account of the world that she continually observes with great interest, detailing social conditions and revealing associated folly, hypocrisy and cruelty, including her own. Narrative action is driven by Letty's appetitive need for the next assignation or affair in her pursuit of survival and the eventual stability she thinks she needs. It often seems that the addictive rhythm of turning tricks for this working girl is hard to break. This is the logic of gangster capitalism and the logic of New York street life. Letty reports that her more refined and intellectual sister, Jacky, arraigns her for this, and exchanges the tourist figure for a more telling contemporary criminal possibility: "'You're a gangster, a gun moll,' she would say; and I did not like this from her, beginning to be afraid that I might end up with the riffraff" (52). It is apposite that what Letty fears from this insult relates to class position and fiscal prospects rather than sexual, economic, territorial or sisterly impropriety.

Gold-digger

This period of American cultural output produced a version of femininity where threatening female autonomy was most positively read under the sign of trickster behaviour. The female trickster was involved in acts of survival and self-definition, especially in the socio-sexual marketplace to which their gender, American ideology and capital markets shackled them. As Lori Landay suggests:

> By transgressing the cultural delimiters of the women's sphere – domesticity, sentimentalism, repression of the body, suppression the mind – the female trickster violates the boundaries between men's and women's spheres and enters into the new country of the public sphere – participating in an anti-domestic and anti-sentimental tradition in American women's culture.[17]

In her easy movement around the streets and around the world of work, Letty has entered (trickster fashion) into the public sphere with not a whiff of domestic sentiment. This is a lovely articulation of one of Stead's great interests: "the cultural delimiters of the women's sphere". Letty's city adventures and Teresa's international romantic heroine are both options that lie before Louie at the end of *The Man Who Loved Children*.

The trickster woman encompasses a spectrum of gender possibilities, ranging from the irrepressible comic nature of the madcap and screwball in cinema and television to the controlled calculation of the confidence woman. Landay is most interested in her great test figure of Mae West, and Letty certainly seems to have many of Mae West's best characteristics of down-to-earth readings of men and sexuality, of making do and making a living. Letty says energetically to the mildly hopeless Solander Fox:

> "Papa, I'm a beast and a brute, but you've no idea – I can't always depend on men to pay my bills; I do the best I can – I do as well as anyone." "Gold-digger!" said Solander. "But if you don't give me any pocket money, I have to gold-dig," I said. (252)

Letty is an able economist of urban sexual relations, and this was the speculative reality of the marriage market for girls in New York during the 1930s and 1940s. In "doing the best" she could, without male financial backing, Letty feels she must hedge the financial and sexual markets: "I did not pay any of my debts; I contracted others, for I saw the possibility of paying them all at some time or other" (255). This approach informs Letty's view that "I felt I must marry in order to get my own property" (9) and that she must offer sex (a commodity) in order to secure a marriage (contract).

For Letty, to be a libertine is the best path to acquiring her great prize, which is marriage to a middle-class man of means:

> I saw quite well the path I was setting out upon, "the path of libertinage," said my father; and this was one of the rare moments when I caught hold of my own tail and saw what I looked like to others. But for persons of my sort, it isn't a thing one can do. We proceed from great folly to giant error and hope for a

---

17 Lori Landay, *Madcaps, Screwballs and Con Women: The Female Trickster in American Culture* (Philadelphia: University of Pennsylvania Press, 1998), 26.

> great stroke of luck. Also, we sometimes get it. We are not the kind to toe the line and keep our distances. One day, it's a famine; the next, a feast. We see little difference, we suffer in the one, and enjoy the other in a great boisterousness. I prefer it! Do me something, as they say. (353)

Libertinage and gangster capitalism led on to the deepening amoralities of sexual racketeering during the war from which Letty tries, without much luck, to secure an advantage. The extent to which promiscuity might be a source of feminine freedom is undermined by the contradiction that Stead acknowledges about Letty's experience – that she "finds promiscuity necessary in search for security" or, put another way, prostitution of various kinds is necessary in a woman's search for stability and position in a society which sees sex and money as indistinguishable currencies. Letty's promiscuity is neither celebrated nor condemned; it is criticised as an immature and unsystematic response to the "great shame" of women. Maturity (sexual and political) involved discipline, theoretical structure and focus, rather like the maturity attributed to Persia, Solander Fox's mistress, another libidinal woman, but one who lives with great discipline outside social norms. She is also, unsurprisingly, an authentic radical and self-supporting woman. In line with the narrative positioning of Persia as a brave and enigmatic proponent of free love, the most significant condemnations from Stead in *Letty Fox: Her Luck* were not of female promiscuity but of infantile and non-systematic (non-theoretical) reactions to marital entrapment and inertia. *Letty Fox: Her Luck* produces a critique of middle-class women and the marriage-divorce racket, which reveals the American private life as saturated with capitalist hypocrisy and free market ideologies.

The disordered crossing of the sexual and the fiscal is clear when Amos, Letty's summer-camp lover, tries to recuperate the costs of the termination Letty undergoes after the end of their affair. The family looting of Grandma Fox's possessions after her death is also indicative of bankrupt and perverse social and familial relations. Although Letty claims that "anything I have I owe to myself alone" (391), over the course of the novel, her inheritance from Grandfather Morgan is hedged, negotiated, held over, bartered and finally just improperly used up:

> On my twenty-fifth birthday I was to get the thousand dollars that Grandfather Morgan left for me; and, more than that, everyone has always felt that Father owed me for the shares of Standard Oil of New Jersey that were given to me when I was born and were later sold to pay for my medical and school expenses. I supposed that I would get this money when I actually got married; but on account of my vagaries in love, my family had been holding out on me; not so much giving me the forbidding frown, as secretly and tranquilly exercising their economic advantage over me; so that I felt I must marry in order to get my own property, even though I am long past my majority. My own standpoint was different. I felt that if I had the money I would attract a

husband in a short time. I attracted men enough; the difficulty was that I could not keep them. (12)

The "vagaries in love" seem to indicate a disappointing lack of success (seen by Stead as a peculiarly American obsession), and the family ("holding out on me") is seen to manipulate the Morgan inheritance for economic rather than moral discipline. Letty continues to account for herself as an asset whose time is running out ("I am long past my majority") and for whom longevity and future returns are questionable: "I could not keep them [men]".

The Morgan inheritance is required because Letty feels that she has to buy a husband herself in order to "join organised society": "... if I had the money I would attract a husband in a short time" (12). This is a reversal of the direction of the romance plot, of course, with Letty providing her own dowry through a manipulation of the terms of her own inheritance. The problem of "keeping" men is related to Letty's energetic insatiability, but also to her ongoing lack of stability. The focus on Letty's economics at the outset of the novel is also the point at which we end – she must "marry in order to get her own property" and of course she marries the equally libertine Bill Van Week, the disaffected son of a millionaire, who is inevitably disinherited the minute they agree to marry (as survivors and comrades) and Letty is found to be carrying his child.

The idea of Letty as a kind of prostitute is somewhat the point, of course, but Letty does, in fact, earn her own living and pay her own rent most of the time because of her huge capacity for work. In this vector of her life there is no hedging: "I could work twelve hours a day. Free, now, at night, I worked hard. I typed manuscripts for publishers, did easy literary jobs, and wrote my letters" (360). Letty's hard work is next connected to her amazing facility at writing advertising copy. Copy writing was always going to be Letty's *métier*, with its association with verbal plasticity, mass production, the machinic and the promiscuously indiscriminate:

> I was astonished at first at my facility in this line [writing copy]; but then I realized I was well-set-up and a well-oiled machine suited to any of the lively arts of the day. Hadn't I tried the epic poem at school, the detective novel, when the radical journals started to consider them a people's art (or the opium of the people – they didn't make up their minds), a French satiric and indecorous play (Les Loups-Phoques), imitations of Verlaine, Baudelaire, and Laforgue, when it suited me; and could I not turn my pen to anything, editorials, pageants, and arguments full of slogans as a plum pudding of raisins! Yes, I was much fitted to live in my own age; a great gift. (412)

Tremendous facility, with an especial talent for comic writing, was also an attribute of Ruth McKenney in *I'm Dying Laughing*, who also squandered her considerable talent and lost sight of worthwhile work in pursuit of money. Letty's comment that her facility and empty sloganeering meant that she was "fitted to live in my own age" pinpoints the *picara*'s capacity to survive, but not necessarily to thrive.

Luck and the Love Market

In *Letty Fox: Her Luck*, Stead fleshes out her initial amazement that love relations were talked about as though they were matters of the market. Letty's romance market descriptors have included tourist, gangster, gold-digger, brute, libertine, prostitute and hustler. The New York City love market, full of alienated confidence players, was, fundamentally, an unstable mechanism. As with Moll Flanders' "fortunes and misfortunes", Letty's destiny on the love market means she must cope with "her luck". "Luck" came into English from Dutch as a gambling term in the late fifteenth century, a boom time in England for roguery, vagrancy and waywardness and their attendant literatures. The implication of this provenance suits Stead's vernacular American context very well.[18] In Stead's post-Depression anatomy of America, luck carries the penumbra of the market and associated ideas of providence operate as justifications of market instability. Luck/chance is cognate with predictably unstable capital and Stead presents capitalism as a form of gambling that produces cycles of impoverishment and suffering. In the context of boom-and-bust capitalism, Letty is styled as a happy gambler – more specifically, a female swindler – playing the marriage game, hedging her bets, staking on her family money and goodwill, hoping to get lucky and ultimately presenting an allegory of individual behaviour in market culture (her luck rather than collective luck). She talks about luck, uses dice-game and financial market jargon to discuss relationships (arbitrage, gouging), and even visits a fortune-teller. Unknown to her, but thoroughly revealed in her ribald confession, Letty's desires, prospects, behaviours and preferences operate within and are perverted by the American capitalist political economy. The further irony of her well-meaning but faint-hearted radicalism is thus rendered all the more acute.

Stead's use of luck highlights the episodic and contingent events that make up the life of her anti-heroine, but also provides a rhetorical focal point for her critique of sex and politics. Luck is a word at the heart of the novel's purpose as well as its action. Etymologically related to enticement and synonymous with chance or fortune, the idea of luck as cognate with Fortuna summons the capricious goddess and her wayward wheel of fortune to mind. Luck, by its very nature, is unstable, and it operates, unsurprisingly, on several semiotic and rhetorical footings in the novel

---

18   The American picaresque is sourced in Alexis de Tocqueville's travel writing and associated with Washington Irving, *Knickerbocker's History of New York* (1809); Herman Melville, *The Confidence-Man: His Masquerade* (1857); Mark Twain, *The Adventures of Huckleberry Finn* (1884), *The Gilded Age: A Tale of Today* (1873), and *Innocents Abroad* (1869), and J. W. Johnson, *Autobiography of an Ex-Colored Man* (1912).

for the purposes of persuasion, justification and thematisation. Luck is thematised as a range of positives and negatives in economic, sexual and industrial spheres. Throughout the novel, good luck relates to instances and claims of success, vitality, action, impressive powers of persuasion and good timing, while bad luck relates to the happenstance lack of power or money, bad timing, superficial powers of reflection and sexual or marital unattractiveness (or both). It is significant that Letty's particular commentary on luck ranges from complaining about the vagaries of fortune to asserting that she was really a self-made and self-reliant woman after all. This is hilariously self-deluded, if we take into account all the lying, swindling, manipulating and betrayal at Letty's hands, but it does represent an important contradiction to the vacillating sense of power and powerlessness that afflicted the libidinal girl in twentieth-century urban modernity. In this sense, one of the meanings of luck-as-contingency may be that an energetic and hardworking young woman wants to be the author of her own life, desire and texts, but her capacity to do this in male homosocial and political economies is subject to ongoing variation and deformation. Letty proudly claims that "I always had a great adaptability, was a regular chameleon" (27), indicating both that she was the perfect capitalist and the perfect fraudulent radical, though there is a telling sense of the emptiness and serial redundancy implied here as well.

According to Jackson Lears, American culture has a profound reverence for luck. In *Something for Nothing: Luck in America* (2003), Lears argues that gambling is an American ritual, and he points out that this is surprising given the dominance of national accounts of Protestant mastery, perseverance, industry and disciplined achievement. The culture of merit should trump contingency every time, suggests Lears, but the addiction to rags-to-riches stories and their associated fetishisation of risk belies the hegemonic account of national prudence and control.[19] In *Letty Fox: Her Luck*, luck and having an eye for the main chance are synonymous with extremely attractive energy – the "bounce" Letty attributes to herself: "I felt, in my rather strident way, that my life was my luck. I could make the best of it" (198). Letty's mother, Mathilde, has no luck (life or energy) and is associated with deathliness and the supine negotiations of alimony and unemployment. Her restless daughter is the self-made individual of great vitality, familiar from Stead's best novels, and she joins a list of Stead's prolix, corrupt, manipulative and attractive characters who also seem to personify the forces of capitalism in her mid-century works: Robbie Grant, Jules Bertillon and Ruth McKenny.

"The Error of Feminine Riot"

Late in *Letty Fox: Her Luck*, Letty disagrees vehemently with her left-wing neighbours, the Fords, on both personal and political matters. Exasperated with

---

19   Lears, *Something for Nothing*, 4.

their permissive parenting and weak political commitment, she claims that: "radicalism is the opium of the middle class. Meanwhile, they're stealing your shirt ... You are all crazy with money troubles" (465). Letty goes on to argue that the frenzy of capitalism produces no systematic thinking and no commitment:

> I'm sick of fake radicalism and fake education. You've got no theory at all for one or the other ... "It's all empiricism and parent-flattery, there's no theory," said I. "But a system can't exist without some thought behind it. The thought is just what I say, you've got to strip yourself of every cent you have, to immolate yourself before capitalism. It's a frenzy they've got you into ..." (465–66)

The theory that is missing that would free the Fords (guilty of the decadent perversions of psychoanalysis) is the systematic way of thinking about freeing themselves of the shackles of capital (that is, theoretical Marxism). A page later, Letty confesses that "about my personal life, I had no theory" (467) and we understand that this is the profound source of her troubles, too, since the sexual and the economic are so thoroughly implicated in Stead's anatomy of American social relations. Both the sexual and financial realms suffer from the dilemmas of American capitalism: weak value systems, unsatisfied desires, cyclical instability, addictive speculation and the alienation of affection. And still no proper reading of Marx.

In talking about *Letty Fox: Her Luck*, and in particular defending it from accusations of obscenity in Australia, Stead pointed out that it was clearly rather more about the "error of feminine riot" than a celebration of it:

> Everyone in the USA understood perfectly that she showed the error of feminine riot! What end was before her [Letty] but deterioration, a miserable middle age, desperate abandon, or total acquiescence with conformity? This was understood by the US press from left to right.[20]

In 1946, Stead further commented that the "sordid mess" that Letty Fox and Teresa Hawkins try to negotiate is how to get "a start in life" (get married) without resorting to fanatical virginity or endless promiscuity. She is quoted in 1946 as saying: "really, I am a Puritan. I am not opposed to free love – and I don't mean wantonness – but I believe there should be some discipline in behaviour".[21] The word "discipline" here makes the double reading of sex and politics quite explicit. Rebellious sexuality is read by Stead as a symptom of a radically alienated social system absolutely dominated by free market thinking. This kind of sexual life is not revolutionary; for that possibility, the enigmatic Persia was the model.

---

20   Christina Stead to Walter Stone, 24 March 1958. *A Web of Friendship*, 172.
21   Quoted in Theo Moody, "'I really am a Puritan', Christina Stead says." *Daily Telegraph* 25 October 1946, 23–24.

For Stead, sex and politics turn out to be alienated aspects of Letty's life, though Stead dramatised her political hypocrisy as related to her sexual libertinage. Letty has some fairly reasonable radical credentials for a New Yorker who loves to tell stories and isn't too strong on reflection:

> There were many nights when I slept only three hours – home-work, meetings, chewing the rag after meetings, accidental conversations on street corners, restaurants, bars, and Greenwich Village cellars where young people lived; giving out leaflets and rushing to bookshops to get new publications; work on the school magazine, selling the *Daily Worker*, or leaflets, organizing rallies. I had time for it all, and school, too. That was the effect of love and expectation upon me. I suppose it would be upon everyone. Fulfillment is the secret of energy, not self-sacrifice; at least for my type. (266)

The racket of duping men under the demands of surviving the wartime marriage market was represented by Stead as the work of the *picara* in *Letty Fox: Her Luck*. This literary equivalent of the cinematic gold-digger metamorphosed into quite a different woman in Stead's second New York novel – the *femme fatale* of *film noir* and Robbie Grant's *bête noir*, Barbara Downs. Alienation and commodity fetishism remain key points of critique in Stead's first New York novel, but it was *A Little Tea, A Little Chat* that presented a vision of what Lukács argued (in *History and Class Consciousness* in 1923) was the pathological condition of capitalism – the fragmentations and misrecognitions of alienated life. *A Little Tea, A Little Chat* picks up the portrait of alienation and moves into considering reification as a radically alienated state of continuous emptiness, prompting restless acquisition of commodities that the subject thinks will paper over their fundamental vacancy and unsatisfiable desire. In this work, the *picaro* moves from being a likable rogue with redeeming qualities of energy and *élan*, into an irredeemable gangster capitalist – what Srinivas Aravamudan called the "grand criminal".[22] As Moll Flanders understood, it was possible to be shifty in a new country when the capacity to exploit the contradictions of free market society made roguish survival a viable prospect. This survival seemed eminently preferable to sentimental captivity or domestic incarceration. The spectrum of gendered freedom and constraint changed in the 1940s as the representations of female freedom shaded from the screwball, madcap and gold-digger into the *noir femme fatale* in films such as *The Awful Truth* (1937) and *The Lady Eve* (1941).[23]

As one might expect, Letty's luck is extremely variable in the end; she is gulled and exploited quite as much as she attempts the same. She has survived, however,

---

22 Srinivas Aravamudan, "Subjects/Sovereigns/Rogues", *Eighteenth-Century Studies*, 40, no. 3 (2007), 460.
23 Landay, *Madcaps, Screwballs and Con Women*, 37.

and is still energetically and ambitiously on the move, the perfect economic subject and working girl:

> I respect not only my present position, but also all the efforts I made, in every direction, to get here. I was not always honest, but I had grit, pretty much; what else is there to it? The principal thing is, I got a start in life; and it's from now on. I have freight, I cast off, the journey has begun. (602)

Letty is often unprincipled and acts in extraordinarily bad faith, but she is resilient, she loves life, she can survive chaos, she is a creature of urban and commercial ebbs and flows. Nevertheless, unchecked freedom – political or sexual – is not possible for Letty. As she settles down, so too does her world; the buoyant progressivism of the 1930s gives way under the pressure of war, the radicals fall into line "with an ungraceful bump", with "everyone turning into a model citizen" and giving up "iconoclasm" (544). Yet there is reason for hope on the matter of sexual, financial and political freedom: "we girls can only go on getting freer. But not by gangsterism, don't you see?" (304). Gangster capital run amok is the harrowing subject of *A Little Tea, A Little Chat*, which we will see in the next chapter.

Letty's misfortune is to be beholden to Fortune's contingencies, since she does not apply a theoretical system that would stop the capitalist wheel of chance and its distorting effects on both personal desires and political economy. This chapter has examined the *picara* as the girl who "was New York City" in the 1930s and 1940s. The complex totalities of Manhattan life are mapped by Stead through the adventures of her energetic *picara* and here the questions of gender, marriage, the body and capital have been all-important. Letty Fox negotiates the mind-boggling marriage market in New York with spirit, though she is helped by her lack of self-reflection or integrity. In this market she circulates freely, bumped along by contingency and market forces, unable to connect in a human way with many people, including her family and her sister. Stead's exposition of this love market/love racket was meant to be disturbing, though broadly comic. It reveals a parallel economy of quasi-prostitution as young New York girls try to find an advantageous mate. The next chapter examines two complementary portraits of male rogues, with quite different narrative materials. The later picaresque in *The People with the Dogs* is beginning to show signs of being overtaken by the pastoral form and the double genre of tragicomic chronicle that defines *I'm Dying Laughing*.

5
Men, Mobility and Capital Relations in *A Little Tea, A Little Chat* and *The People with the Dogs*

> On the unbounded oceans of American life its millions of mariners are equipped with a sensitive compass that sees them through storm and stress. The name of this magic instrument is "the Dow-Jones Average".[1]

> Writers search in vain for the picture of the great business man … Dreiser alone has tried to picture the career of such a man, but in general the artist has shied away from him as from the devil – the villain.[2]

For William Blake, son of immigrant Jewish-European parents and self-taught economist, American life was an "unbounded ocean" where the Dow Jones average was the compass that steered citizens through "stress and storm". The implication of the degree to which capital was synonymous with American life is striking. The reverberation of the maritime metaphor between Stead and Blake's work is similarly striking. Stead had framed young women's negotiation of the marriage market and related divorce racketeering in terms of shipping as early as drafting in the early 1940s (Letty as a doughty tug, for example). In the early 1950s Blake's portrait of American citizens, penned during his years in England and designed for English travellers and general readers, was as mariners who steered the city streets of urban modernity using an instrument that measured the state of financial capital first and foremost.

The New York trilogy, of which *Letty Fox: Her Luck* was the opening salvo, dramatises the impact of this super-saturation of intimate relations by the structure of capital relations. *A Little Tea, A Little Chat* and *The People with the Dogs* offer further and different meditations on this theme, carrying forward Stead's ongoing experiment with speech and genre in different but connected ways. From the

---

1   William J. Blake, *Understanding the Americans* (London: Frederick Muller, 1954), 7.
2   Ralph Fox, *The Novel and the People* (London: Lawrence & Wishart, 1937), 94–95.

immersive reading experience of Letty's episodic and encyclopaedic first person, Stead moves to the experience of men, and this necessitates a switch to third person. *A Little Tea, A Little Chat* offers a formidable experiment with third person as Stead works to approximate the dramatic monologue in novel form. The People with the Dogs displays a less galvanised use of third person, and the question of the theatre arises as a matter of citation and homage rather than performance. And from the dystopian rendition of the frenzied ways in which the alienations of money and sex overlapped and interacted in the late wars years in New York, *The People with the Dogs* formulates a milder post-war critique of utopian thinking and the potential inertias lying in wait for the owners of the means of production, even if they come from good left-wing and anarchist stock.

In the second and third novels of her New York trilogy, Christina Stead retailed stories of two men as very different navigators of the streets of New York. While these men and their worlds are strongly connected through Stead's account of mobile masculinity on the streets of Manhattan, both central characters display connections with Sam Pollit and Emily Wilkes. The differences in these two portraits of masculinity are tied to the different time frames in which they were written and set (war vs post-war, Manhattan vs Europe), and are certainly tied to the inevitable real life models with which Stead always worked. They also represent two distinct but complementary variations on the mid-century New York *picaros* as libertine and dilettante respectively, which rather radically anticipates both Saul Bellow and Philip Roth (though follows Dreiser).[3] Stead's commitment to working from real life characters, and (for the most part) the conditions of the historical present in which she was writing, meant constantly evolving work with genre, so Stead delivers these two mid-century rogues as libertine and dilettante respectively. Stead's fascination with theatre, and her dabbling with collaborative writing for theatre in her later New York years, is another element of real life that connects and distinguishes these two novels. Although *A Little Tea, A Little Chat* does present an excess of speech and sexual conquest so disregulated that it connotes absolute alienation, it is worth keeping in mind that there is a dark vitality here still that eludes the dark masterpiece of the 1950s, *Cotter's England*. It is another element of Stead's quiet but intense engagement with the theatre in this period – this time Chekhov – that suffuses *The People with the Dogs*, and through Edward Massine's amateur theatrical dabbling we can see aspects of Manhattan theatre life of the period.

In her early days in New York, Stead wrote that "N.Y. was in some respect a living revelation to me".[4] Her descriptions of her first impression of Manhattan date from the same time: "the vision of uptown and Wall Street main ranges main ranges, miles of vertical glass, the endless viaducts, ribs against the sky, gas and oil

---

3 Theodore Dreiser, *The Financier* (1914; New York: Penguin, 2008).
4 Christina Stead to Florence James, 13 August 1936. Florence James Papers, State Library of New South Wales, ML MSS 5877/14.

tanks ... The skyscrapers are, *en masse*, beautiful beyond expectation".[5] Skyscrapers are allied to sublime mountain ranges (canyons feature later as well) and the shapes of modernity are also to be seen in the vertical glass and viaducts that look like "ribs against the sky". Though Stead was familiar with the workings of the port city from her own Sydney adolescence, what she registers here is scale and sublimity. This is not a saturated or porous landscape; it is a vertical and monumental testament to the industrial and the modern. Stead's response was like that of many of the Europeans whose love affair with New York began in the Roaring Twenties and was founded on their romance with the new, the modern and the mechanised. In the *New Literary History of America* section on "1935", Sarah Whiting's comments in her chapter, "The Skyscraper", that:

> If Americans tended to read Manhattan from the interior – the office, the department store, even the interiorized street canyons – Europeans could not help but read the city as an object, first glimpsed from an offshore steamer arriving in the port of New York ... several Europeans during this period saw in New York the possibility of a new kind of monumentality, one that was freed of Europe's mantle of history.[6]

Although Stead's first view of New York seems European, it becomes clear that her reading is also an Antipodean one. She does not, as a fellow colonial, associate New York with freedom from history and a celebration of the unfettered and progressively modern. She sees instead that commodity consumerism and the rhetoric of the free market dominated New York and New Yorkers, which takes us again to "Boodle" and the inveterate "scramble" for money, an insight drafted in the mid 1930s. The New York war years (1942–1945) were altogether another test of economic man and woman, and this is uniquely registered in Stead's darkest and in some ways most outrageously prodigious realist experiment since *House of All Nations* (1938).

The darkest of Stead's fictions about alienation under capitalism is *A Little Tea, A Little Chat*. In a letter to Nettie Palmer in December 1950, Stead referred to *A Little Tea, A Little Chat* in this way: "I think it's very good: but I recognise it's not very 'nice'. It's merely true. Too bad. (New York City in wartime – everyone was *not* rolling bandages.)"[7] Written in war-torn Europe in the mid to late 1940s, when

---

5   Christina Stead, "It Is All a Scramble for Boodle: Christina Stead sums up America", *Australian Book Review* 141, no. 6 (1992), 22.
6   Whiting suggests that the scale of New York, which the European intellectuals perceived as liberating (and we have seen that Stead was no stranger to scale), was seen by many American writers as alien "in comparison to an idealized pastoral." Cited in *A New Literary History of America*, eds. Greil Marcus and Werner Sollors, (Cambridge, MA: Harvard University Press, 2009), 689.
7   Christina Stead to Nettie Palmer, 5 December 1950. In *A Web of Friendship: Selected Letters 1928-1973*, ed. R.G. Geering (Pymble, NSW: Angus & Robertson), 121.

she was living on relatively little and moving rather a lot, Stead's true story of New York is a financier-libertine's story of a blackly comic kind. David Malouf, who thoroughly admires the novel as one of Stead's best (he agrees with her), hears and sees the ludicrous energy and monstrous deeds of Robbie Grant in the context of Jacobean City comedy which devoted itself to the degrading and material drives surrounding urban life as the collocating point for perversions of exchange in the form of sex and money. Malouf calls this the "cannibal game". Malouf identifies a dark view of America at the heart of Stead's American works, though this "horrible and marvellous" panorama was, if we turn to Stead, just an account of what actually happened, based on someone she knew well.[8] Stead's claim for this dark vision of New York City during the war years is that it was true life. Financial speculators had become outright gamblers and treasonous criminals, betting against markets affected by the war and hedging their financial and sexual bets with women who are either destroyed by these amoral predators, or who prevail as noir *femme fatale* victors in the market games of cat and mouse.

The People with the Dogs was composed in distinct brackets of time in Manhattan during the period from the late 1930s and then again in 1945, before being finished in Europe in 1948. Perhaps because of its source material, its probing and inquiring alliance with the theatre and Chekhovian sensibilities in particular, this novel presents a much more affectionate portrait of New York than *A Little Tea, A Little Chat*. *The People with the Dogs* fits into the larger New York theme of circulation through its incessant walking, storytelling and rich familial Manhattan networks. Its membership in Stead's critical realist project emerges through its portrait of the pacifying effects of property ownership, as well as its meditation on the escapist fantasies of pastoral utopia. The charming Chekhovian dilettante at the heart of *The People with the Dogs* is Edward Massine, and for him the possession of properties in town and a famous old commune in the countryside of upstate New York removes the need for meaningful work, with the consequences of developmental arrest and artistic inertia. There is plenty of physical movement among a substantial network of friends and family in Manhattan and between his brownstones on the Lower East Side and the collective family retreat in the Catskills. There is plenty of bustling action with the community of beloved dogs in this extended family, but no maturity.

The People with the Dogs is a novel of the post-war period, when the main economic challenge is the housing shortage. Stead takes up this particular element of political economy and places a marooned dilettante rather than an insatiable libertine at the centre of the action. Edward Massine's lucky possession of the means of production through inheritance has removed the goad of survival or the strange pleasures of the speculator's capital safari. His life after the war is rich with family, pets, friends, amateur theatre communities, and the flow and swell of

---

8   David Malouf, "Stead Is Best at Egotistical Monsters", *Sydney Morning Herald,* 17 July 1982, 36.

storytelling in the Manhattan he loves so well. His challenge is not the excess energy and restlessness of a capitalist so rapacious he might have no actual interiority; his is the opposite problem, of lassitude, ennui and wasted talent. Nevertheless, the inveterate storytelling that saturates the extended Massine family also makes it seem as though Stead's New York is really built of constant elaborations and exchanges of verbal production of all kinds. Capital is not the only significant element of New York life that circulates with infinite plasticity, as Stead's record of everyday folklore, novels in the making and theatre collaborations indicates.

Letty Fox's New York City, scene of female libertinage and amoral manoeuvres amidst the unstable forces of the marriage market, was still a record of the excitement and commitment of a radical milieu, however undisciplined. This was New York of the mid to late 1930s, Letty's majority coinciding with the height of radical commitment in the Village and other parts of Manhattan. As the war continued into the mid 1940s and as the radical project continued to lose velocity and support, American market forces became more predatory and less regulated. Investors, armament barons and property speculators bet against military outcomes (positive or negative) and benefitted. The financial scene of New York had become a Darwinian jungle, operating according to market logic and gangster strength. Where human relationships were only tested by prostitution and exploitation in Letty's confession, here, in *A Little Tea, A Little Chat,* they seem perfectly inhuman. Whenever Robbie Grant avows Left politics, we know that political revolution is as unlikely as a shred of genuine romantic feeling.

The Great Game of Women and Commodities in *A Little Tea, A Little Chat*

Stead undertook early drafting of *A Little Tea, A Little Chat* under the title "The Blondine" in the mid 1930s. She returned to the work in earnest in 1946–47, after she had handed over *Letty Fox: Her Luck* to the publishers in 1945. She spent one year in New York and one year in Europe working on *A Little Tea, A Little Chat,* which then lines up with a similarly nomadic circumstance of composition that produced the other novel about finance, the *House of All Nations,* though the optimism of the 1930s can be felt in the earlier book in its ebullience. Both, of course, deal with finance and the grand criminal; both were closely modelled on extraordinary individuals whom Stead knew well. Robbie Grant is based on Blake's long-time business associate and boss, Alf Hurst, and, like Hurst, is a Scottish-Jewish businessman of Herculean energy and appallingly low moral sense. He seems like a custom-built gangster/commodities trader: "This man, husky, tall, fair, with fine blue eyes, a square-set fleshy nose of extraordinary size, and a powerful chin, gave her one sharp glance and turned away".[9] This is Stead's answer

---

9   Christina Stead, *A Little Tea, A Little Chat* (1948; London: Virago, 1981), 10–11. All subsequent references are to this edition and appear in parentheses in the text.

to Dreiser's *The Financier* (1912) and *The Titan* (1914), and a nastier cousin of her character, Jules Bertillon, in *House of all Nations* (1938).

A Little Tea, A Little Chat presents the appetitive movement and the episodic lure and gull (bait and switch) that structure the great picaresque narratives from both the European and English traditions. Stead's portrait of Robbie Grant as the master shark and amoral libertine in the shark pool of New York speculative investment captures the confidence-man of the nineteenth century and crosses him with the New York gangster to produce the mid-century rogue as urban super-capitalist. His economic relations are corrupt and, mirroring and extending this corruption, so too are his sexual relations. Here, the possibilities of the reifying effects of capitalism postulated by Lukács and others are dramatised with critical realist focus. Even the scene of the "tea and chat" – the scene of seduction – is not connected to pleasure: it is a mechanical continuation of market conquest and an expression of constant movement as a flight from interiority, thought or conscience.

Barbara Downs ("the Blondine") is also an uncanny portrait of the ambitious prostitute and gold-digger who has Robbie Grant's number and winds up beating him at his own game. Stead examines avarice and lust as they are aligned and complicated as pure market forces, and, like Balzac, she understood that ever-expanding capitalism always needs the energy of particular individuals to continue to thrive. In this urban ethnography she inventories people, places, networks, amounts of money, swindles, pay-offs and bribes down to the last detail.

In order to find a genre best able to capture from the outside the predator as New York businessman, Stead calls in the libertine novel from the French *Ancien Regime* as a cousin of the picaresque. *A Little Tea, A Little Chat* is not a confession and the key textual influence is Dostoyevsky's *The Gambler* (1866), which relays an account of erotic obsession, feverish with desire for money, status and economic pursuit. In American cultural genealogies, *A Little Tea, A Little Chat* lies somewhere between Herman Melville's *The Confidence Men* (1857) and Oliver Stone's *Wall Street* (1987). Although lack of sexual restraint was the libertine's most titillating characteristic, for writers like Diderot the libertine narrative was one geared to erotic subversion; for Stendahl it was an opportunity to investigate human nature and social organisation. The hero (and much less often the heroine), who was often a cowardly rogue and a scoundrel, was allowed to follow his inclinations unrestricted and unconfined as an investigation of liberty. This meant that the story of rolling seduction was typically anti-heroic and anti-sentimental and therefore deeply disinterested in sensibility or manners. As with the *picaro*, therefore, the freedom and mobility of the dissolute rake was a narrative well placed to offer a critique of social relations.

If Letty's libertinage is seen as a direct correlation of her economic and social position in the marriage market (and the market as such), so too is Robbie Grant's. His habitual disregard of moral law is just unfettered economic behaviour and it turns out that he is almost as alienated by it as the women he exploits:

> He had little pleasure out of his own real hobby, libertinage; and he gave none. Women fell away from him, but he did not know why; and he retained only the venal. He had little to muse upon. Few women he knew wrote letters, and most of these contained requests for money, put in some roundabout or clumsy form. He kept what he got, and would conceal them, for further meditation, in various places: in the bottom of the dustcovers over his many suits; some were in his collarbox, some in his hatboxes, some under the paper lining of the drawers. Every time there was a question of moving, or of sending clothes to the cleaners, he had some interesting hours, during which he would lock the door of his apartment while he went over everything looking for *the private matters* he might have *caché*. (24–25, author's emphasis)

The solipsistic lack of pleasure or thought, the idea of erotic encounter as a hobby or relaxing distraction and the paranoid retention of the venal letters related to these encounters are both horrendous to contemplate, and darkly comic. As a man of no introspection, the idea that he archives his private matters in a locked hatbox that stands in for his cranium is blackly comic:

> When he was alone again, he got the old-fashioned leather hatbox, the locked one, which had been all night on top of the wardrobe, and put it on the polished oval table in the center of the room. He looked at it several times and pulled at the lock. He spread out all his keys on the table, about thirty-five in all, and after sorting out about eleven smaller ones, he began to try them systematically. He was going through them a second time, with a serious, contented air, when the hotel desk telephoned him to ask if a lady could come up. (284)

The fussy delight in systematically trying to find the right key for the documents that control his life but have been displaced from his head is at once terrible and amusing. His "serious contented air" suggests that actually this hide and seek game is his favourite pastime – this is where he experiences actual pleasure. The secrecy of his actions is ironised by the hilarious intimacy and domesticity of suit dustcovers, collarbox, hatboxes and drawer linings.

The Blondine

The pattern of hide-and-seek capitalism dominates Robbie Grant's solipsistic world. The cat and mouse game of bait and switch fascinates both Grant and Barbara Downs. The cut-throat game of competitive capital also controls Grant's homosocial world, with "friends" like Flack the analyst, Hoag the Fixer, his disappointing son and heir and a host of male competitors (real and imagined). But without the layer of alienated sexual contact and enigmatic danger, Robbie does not find it nearly as satisfying to participate. Unlike the other marriage pairs in Stead's fiction, Grant and Downs do not present a central contradiction or a portrait of opposites. They are alarmingly alike, though the Blondine must play the game differently because of gender. As the *femme fatale* of the piece, it is a game that Barbara Downs wins conclusively. She wins because she is, in fact, a representation of money itself – the bottled blonde as ultimate counterfeit allurement:

> Barbara Downs naturally did not appear to herself as an adventuress, as Grant did not appear to himself as a lecher. Barbara, for example, believed that she was in the center of a kind of exchange of values: she was the broker. She knew a few laws, enough for her purpose, and for the rest she put nothing on paper, but her name to a marriage certificate. Her society was full of women like herself, who made connections, put people in the way of things, mentioned names, made love in the routine of business, and in return, received money in cash. All that she met could be paid for and was: she was therefore only a dealer. She surely believed that everything was for sale. (194)

Barbara's own position in the game is not clear to her, and this lack of insight is common in the *picara* and *picaro* narratives. She thinks of herself in completely inhuman and therefore reified terms: "she was in the center of a kind of exchange of values: she was the broker". Her commodity is her body and her unsentimental willingness to barter it makes her a player in which only men are interested: she "made love in the routine of business". This is not prostitution to Downs, since in her own mind she is just a neutral dealer in a world in which everything is for sale. She embodies the logic of capital and gives no thought to freedom.

The Blondine becomes Robbie Grant's fatal obsession because this "dangerous 'ooman" presents as a synonym for money itself, dressed up as an enigmatic adventuress and experienced prostitute. Robbie Grant's assignations reveal that despite all his endless, winding lies and self-deception about radical politics and needing to find the right woman, his restless predation and insatiable swindling amounts to an embroilment in capital deals that are fated to destroy him in the end. As Grant says about himself: "The rest of the time, I'm either making money or looking for the right woman" (65). For a man who can never let an investment go, Barbara Downs presents to Robbie an inexorable lure. For a man for whom there is no subjectivity but pursuit – the relentless movement of circulating capital – she is the perfect addiction. She is inexhaustible in her enigmatic attraction and the lack of happiness she will bring. David Flack – Robbie's friend and equities analyst – understands that there is no distinction between Grant's relentless pursuit of different women and his capital speculation: "Your schemes on the side are like speculation in blondes" (68). Robbie Grant persists with the distinction between investment and women but, as a speculator who made his early fortune in the grain exchange, he inexorably betrays his reified perspective when discussing the matter of wheat: "No, no – I'm honest. I'm looking for that little patch of wheat, I want an oasis" (68).

When Peter Hoag first sees Barbara Downs, he immediately notes her magnetic capacity to attract and hold the attention of his homosocial gang of commodity speculators. The sense of her as "a woman used to men" implies her habitual prostitution, but there is also her combination of calculating eyes and animality. He senses her ambiguity: she can be used but she is also a predator. The famous cinematic stills of noir *femmes fatales* like Barbara Stanwyck come to mind, with Barbara's blonde hair and catlike face, peculiarly like a mask: "for a second, a strange, flat face with cat-eyes and pointed cat-lips floated before his eyes; then he saw it was Mrs. Kent." When Peter Hoag is introduced to Mrs Kent, "all that he saw about her excited his business instinct" (9). Hoag, used to reading the market for commodities that will interest his male associates, senses immediately her availability, as well as the exciting ambiguity at the borderline between animal and human:

> They sat next to a large mirror. The light fell on her head. The restaurant was beginning to fill with well-fed, hungry, energetic, successful men. All looked at her. She was a woman used to men. Her cheeks were full, the chin noticeable, the facial bones large and high, smooth. Her eyes were narrow, oval, violet, with a darker outer rim. The eyes were set level with the face and a little close together, and her front face appeared flattish. She had a full mouth with a protruding lower lip. Only a slight heaviness round the jawbones and a disappointed expression, a light fold from nose to mouth, showed that she was past her youth. Her eyes and hair were the extraordinary features of her head. The eyes were calculating but resplendent. Her smooth hair left the forehead bare but grew into lanugo round the temples and neck; and the empty temples were also animal. (4)

As a woman of indeterminate country and a shady past, she was not an unusual figure in immigrant hardscrabble Manhattan. Barbara Downs is somewhat vampiric in her "haunting" of "some little bars" and degraded too, washing "in the back room" and sleeping with any available man (8). This survivalist program seems quite natural to Downs: "I'm used to holding my own with men. I can manage. I just need some introductions" (9).

Barbara Kent/Downs is not just an ex-showgirl and small-time prostitute; she is not just the gangster's moll or noir ornament. She is a cunning, though entirely alienated, player of the sex and money game. Most of all, she is a cipher for money itself. The elusive nature of her history, the mysteriousness of her previous relationships and the possibility that she might be a spy obsesses Robbie Grant. He is sexually obsessed but he is also focussed by the capital game that he lives and breathes; he may have outlaid money that he cannot recoup, and he might have lost out in the larger competitive economy of homosocial bartering of women. Downs rejects maternity (she may or may not have her mother with her); she is nebulous, impenetrable and endlessly plastic, critical to scenes of exchange but hard to pin down, endlessly exchanged but functionally elusive in terms of long-range value. She is both medium and means of homosocial connection, but she is unstable.

This white Russian of indeterminate origin may be described as a cat, in homage to the general *femme fatale* triple threat of ambiguity, blonde attractiveness and danger, but it is her description as wheat and honey – the emphasis on her blondness – that is most interesting here:

> One day he saw her sitting with her naked back turned toward him and her thick long hair coiling over one shoulder. She turned to him. He saw the light on her skin, how fair it was. He thought of this all day and night and called her to himself "The Blondine." Next day he found her lying on her side, all her fair skin exposed, her hair in its loop at the nape of the neck, her arm curved round the neck of a toy Angora cat she always had on her pillow and took to bed with her. She had once had a cat like that, deaf, she said, which slept all day and mewed all night. She preferred this one. The woman, the cat, the pillows, and the expanse of linen moved him. "The Blondine," he said to himself, "how she is wasting herself." (28–29)

Robbie Grant's first thought at the sight of this exquisite example of the Western ideals of female beauty of the period – blonde, white-skinned, curvaceous, luxurious – is that it should be monetised. She should not be wasted. Marilyn Monroe comes to mind here, whose progression to *the* blonde (she was a blondine, too) commenced in 1946, aged twenty. Some of Monroe's tragedy is evident in Barbara's display. The alienation of the subject whose only value is as an object seems evident in Barbara's infantile preference for the stuffed white angora cat instead of the real one, which required human care and patience.

Wheat was a valuable global commodity: Blake and Hurst had been running a grain exchange when Stead met them in her first week in London, and Hurst had intermittently kept his grain business going well into the 1940s, including scoping for business in wheat and other commodities in Canada during the war. In Barbara, with all her expensive turbulence and titillating trouble, Grant sees the commodity in which he has made much of his money as a commodities trader:

> "I saw ripe wheat there, ripe wheat of wheat height; the sun was setting and it changed its shade in the broad sun and the setting sun, like very blond hair – it was yellow, not shining sometimes, and shining and weaving and braided, all in order and brushed, moving in all directions like when she bends her head and neck, softness – in all directions ... That splitted rock is dry but sweet down where the water runs – it reminded me of myself; and that bit of acre with the wheat reminded me of the blondine. The two of us and you see they

are real. The blondine is real … it's good luck, she is like grain, like bread too
…" (66–67)

Grant's fantasy of the landscape of wheat and rock is as romantic a speech as he ever manages, which is a deeply awful prospect. In his wheat vision he absolves "the woman" of any taint. She is not only "not all bad"; the counterfeit blonde is "real" and, even better, she is "good luck, she is like grain, like bread too". He reiterates the "wheat is not bad" – meaning spoiled – since it only has "a bit of rust on it". In this pastoral vision of ripe wheat as blonde braided hair, Grant arrives at a vision that unapologetically collocates the object of his erotic interest and his key speculative commodity. The blondine and the wheat are still good – they are a sound bet.

When Grant is close enough to the woman of his dreams, his rapacity and alienation emerge in his inevitable speculator's audit, where the chase and the investment are weighed against each other as an accounting of value:

Grant squirmed and fought with himself, "I spent twenty-four hundred dollars in sterling silver I brought from England, and I ordered a silver dinner service; and she's got a silver frame there. Two hundred and fifty for photographs – she went to the best photographer in town, they made her look like a Du Barry. She's all right as she is, but they made her look better. I'm out a fur coat I got from Goodwin, wholesale, eighteen hundred dollars." (85)

Barbara's astute management of the game she plays with Robbie is blackly comic because the threat of her "clutches" are an especially effective combination of anti-sentimental manipulation of abundance and scarcity of herself as a commodity on the market:

He went on to show that he was glad he was "in her clutches," that he admired her venality, her conspiracies, and admired her and himself for the large sum of money he had spent and the way she made a fool of him. He said complacently, "Yes, she buys me at one corner and sells me at the next! I don't claim she's innocent. But I'm no good either. Birds of a feather." (59)

Barbara's venality, superior cunning and nose for blackmail give her the edge over Robbie Grant. In the end, before she can be pressured out of the game, Barbara reveals that she has evidence that incriminates Robbie. With this document, which he just assumes she will hide in her clothes and valises where he hides his documents, she is solidly in the lead in their cat and mouse game of sex and money:

She said, "Yes, I did, dear; and I have it with me, I kept it for you, you're so careless. I think you need a keeper. I think you hedged yourself out. You want me to look after you. Now, I'm a good housekeeper, and I think you need someone with you, not an old woman, because you're all alone and I know

Alf Goodwin is threatening you. Let's meet for a little chat at the Pandulfo tomorrow." (387)

Barbara is now calling the "tea and chat" shots with Robbie Grant by turning his standard pick up line for new women on its head. This is a sure sign that his capacity to play the market has collapsed. She cites both the pincer movement of the futures market – hedged out – and the ever-present buccaneer threat from former players in the market.

The supremacy of market forces and the triumph of the commodity as the centre of human value means that human experience is reified in the Scoundrel years in New York. This occurs when the commodity form becomes the dominant form of subjectivity itself and creates a fragmentation of human experience. Robbie Grant dramatises a total surrender to drives of speech, sex and acquisition inherent in capitalism. Notions of human connection are completely denuded, so that art, romance, theatre and politics all come to serve the empty husk of fragmented capitalist subjectivity, which becomes its own escalating logic: "My life's so empty, I need her" (132). Edda cries with impatience: "If you would only study something, Robbie; you have nothing to fill that big empty head of yours" (135). The big empty head has been emptied into his hatbox, where his conscience cannot pursue him. His pursuit of the fatal woman is a guaranteed set of never-ending repeated actions in which he never gets the girl, and this is exactly her alienated value for him. The guarantee of emptiness is true for Robbie Grant and Stead reveals that it is true for the Blondine as well:

> The blondine experienced a very strange sensation in her body, as if her heart had leaped, but it was such a long time since she had loved a man that she did not realize what this was. Almost at once, she began thinking furiously of the money the dark agitated creature demanded. (241)

At least for Barbara Downs there has been a tiny moment of unalienated feeling, though she swiftly counteracts this by thinking about money. It is actually unimaginable for Robbie Grant to experience something like a feeling. Since Grant spends all his time on the move or emptying his head into his clothes container, his feelings, as such, can only be captured in the unconscious:

> He had a strange dream at about this time. He dreamed he was walking across muddy fields in wartime. The landscape was dreary: it was winter. He slipped into a mud-wallow and the more he struggled, the deeper he sank, till the slime filled his mouth, ears and nose, and approached his eyes: but he kept on seeing the heaving field. He felt the filth folding him in, in his armpits, round his waist, his limbs. He kept sinking but was not yet submerged. (375)

Despite the comedy of Grant's very literal interpretation of his dream, this mud and slime seems to have a clear correlation to the spiralling effects of corruption and alienation. The mud field offers a revision of the wheat field sequence and anticipates the threatening water of the East River (389). Robbie gets what is coming to him, but it is both threatening and comic. To be literally frightened to death of a man with the name of Hilbertson (another Scottish name) who hailed from Louisiana in the Deep South is to receive an almost ironically mundane end, not to mention a blackly comic one.

The People with the Dogs: Pastoral, Property and Figures of Communality

The People with the Dogs offers another portrait of the circulation of people and of stories, of comedy and of Manhattan masculinity. In Stead's New York panorama, the Massine set of family and urban relations are predicated on various kinds of worn-out utopian possibilities based on radical politics that are only dimly remembered. The idyllic or pastoral tone held and conveyed by the beautiful property in the Catskills and reflecting very loosely the Oneida experiment, coaxes the tone of the beloved New York streets away from reification and roguery and towards vistas of endless summers spent outside Manhattan.[10] The novel reads as a move from darkly comic vitality to tonally complex inertia, from Dreiser to Chekhov and along this spectrum, pastoral and picaresque speak to one another in odd and effective combinations. Conversation rather than monologue indicates the interest in attractive and abundant communality and its complex challenges. The central character, Edward Massine, is deployed precisely because he was someone that Stead knew well and wanted to record, and because of his existence at the centre of a textured and loving family community. The streetwalking in Stead's second portrait of masculinity and capital relations in New York city seems to reference Walter Benjamin's sense of the well-resourced *flâneur* as a man who has time and inclination for "botanising the asphalt", but the post-war setting makes a difference here.[11] Edward is also alive and well, though uneasily placed in the new dawn of post-war America. Where Robbie Grant is all velocity, all display and no content, Edward Massine manifests something very like inertia, despite his leisured movement through the affective map of Massine Manhattan.

The nostalgic and protracted farewell to a fading world is one that we might loosely associate with Chekhov. This has meant that many readings of the novel ague that nostalgia defines the work. On the contrary however, this book produces

---

10 Oneida was a place in the state of New York where John Humphrey Noyes established a utopian communal religious community in 1848. Noyes believed in a kind of socialism that was both religious and sexual, and the community was bound together through complex marriage practices and social structures.

11 Walter Benjamin, *Charles Baudelaire: A Lyric Poet in the Era of High Capitalism* (1973; London: Verso, 1997), 36.

another striking experiment with form to produce a Chekhovian tale of inherited property, static utopia and ineffectual politics. While *The People with the Dogs* is not a nostalgic corrective to *A Little Tea, A Little Chat*, elements of Stead's farewell to New York may appear in the loving materiality of some of her descriptions of the Lower East Side:

> In lower Manhattan, between 17th and 15th Streets, Second Avenue, running north and south, cuts through Stuyvesant Park; and at this point Second Avenue enters upon the old Lower East Side. The island here is broad between the two rivers and heavily trafficked, north-south, east-west. Here, Third Avenue up to 18th Street is still the Old Bowery, with small rented bedrooms and apartments like ratholes, cheap overnight hotels, flophouses, ginmills, fish places, bowling alleys, instant shoe repairers, moneylenders, secondhand clothing stores, struggling cleaning and tailors' places, barber schools, cellars where some old man or woman sells flowers and ice in summer, coal in winter, dance academies up crumbling stairs, accordion and saxophone schools and such businesses as are carried on for very poor people by very poor people and so occupy a very small space in a very old building. It is the last of gaslight New York.[12]

Robbie Grant's gangster capitalism dissipates a little on this soothing tide of detailed urban pastoral in *The People with the Dogs*. The issue in Stead's last work in the New York trilogy is not the relentlessly addictive rhythms of capital; rather it is the mild paralysis and developmental arrest of never quite leaving home, since (if you are young/old Edward) you are as materially enfolded in the Massine houses as you are psychologically folded in the bosom of the family. Edward Massine's relative inaction is nowhere near as repellent as Robbie Grant's entirely alienated relationships with women, family and colleagues, but the novel elaborates a critique of quietist utopian thinking and the ennui that seems to stem from the almost smug privilege of having everything you think you need, as well as a vague notion that you belong to the Left in a kind of inherited and anarchistic way.

Edward Massine participates in Stead's American anatomy as the more communal and therefore more human face of New York. He is a man connected to family and to distinct neighbourhoods since birth. Like the male dilettante wanderers of the nineteenth century he is well-resourced. The question posed by the novel is where might the will and energy for wider contexts, adult relationships and artistic production come from if one is caught in the net of such a fading utopia?

---

12   Christina Stead, *The People with the Dogs* (1952; London: Virago, 1992), 3. All subsequent references are to this edition and appear in parentheses in the text.

Property

Property is an essential element of Stead's New York trilogy. Where *Letty Fox* opens on a hot night in the Village with a snappy audit of Letty's finances as an index of her sexual fortunes, and *A Little Tea, A Little Chat* opens on the Mid-Upper East Side (never a good sign in Stead) with an enumeration of Peter Hoag's value as a fixer to his set of gangster and buccaneer chums, *The People With the Dogs* opens with a fabulous portrait of Manhattan's housing shortage after the war from the point of view of a female real estate agent. Stead was interested in the political economy of property in New York (and more practically she had rented several properties in Manhattan and Brooklyn), as well as the materiality of specific houses and environments. It is the false utopian promise of property as freedom and power that Stead investigates, rather gently for her, in this last work of the New York trilogy. In 1954, in his curious work, *Understanding the Americans*, Bill Blake made this comment about Americans and property:

> So the American fear is simply the most extreme example of a universal tendency, that property is the basis of cowardice, hence its defence is the incentive to brutality. Property is the most diffused in the shape of creature comforts and creature comforts make men soft.[13]

The Massine properties (city and country) are the reason that the family is insufficiently politicised and tends to be inward-looking, passive and focussed only on their own family networks. Edward is an expression of this privileged provinciality: "when he walked, the district he reached seemed to be an extension of the few streets in which he had been born, lived, and in which, for the present, he intended to die" (1). The longstanding family ownership of a beautiful property called the Whitehouse in the Catskills, first established by Edward's grandfather as an anarchists commune and utopian experiment, was also a source of circumscription and ennui. It is to the Whitehouse, as the principal residence of the insular "Republic of Massine", that the extended family and their dogs always retreat for the middle third of the year, to escape the New York heat. The rural property rests on a long low ridge in the Catskills:

> Whitehouse has been open to anyone since my grandfather's day. He left his house and land to the family undistributed under certain conditions: Peace, liberty, a roof for everyone, all claims equal. If it is all coming down to us two, Oneida and me … still it is a piece of land left for communal living and it is so used. My grandfather said that no one could buy it, no one could own it absolutely and we and our friends, those that we accepted as friends, must have the hospitality of Whitehouse without question. (87–88)

---

13 Blake, *Understanding the Americans*, 96.

The Massine family forebears are Russian migrants and the anarchist experiment overlays elements of European political thinking with the American value for liberty. The intention of the property as it is to be passed down the generations is that it be a haven of enlightened hospitality. No house could be further from the plantation trauma in *The Man Who Loved Children*. Nevertheless, the novel suggests that Edward must leave this family idyll and connect to the world or become buried in a soft and undifferentiated life.

The housing shortage in Manhattan is used to dramatise the nature and effects of the Massine wealth, and to play the urgency of Manhattan housing shortages across the slow pace of the upstate rural idyll. The following exchange produces quite a Grantian moment, when a friend of Edward's equates property with a woman:

> "Property is a woman. You do not leave a woman you want with your neighbour or your best friend or your cousin, for she becomes the woman of your cousin or best friend. If he doesn't try to steal her, no credit to her. She's there to be stolen. The whole thing in a nutshell. Now I don't say woman to mean woman. A woman with property acts like a man ... Like being married, property gives you a special viewpoint. You understand the law and society ..." (345)

The special viewpoint of property was the ownership of the means of production – the great dividing line in class identity and capital relations. "The poor people" who "think you cheated it out of them" are the people without property. The hard luck of this market is the luck of capital that has become so familiar during the American novels. Property gives you a firm base from which to negotiate with society because of the subjectivity one earns in holding it; like marriage, it gives you standing. This energetic and hard-nosed assessment of capital wealth and property argues that a competitive position must be taken around property. Yet, Edward Massine derives little energy from his capital good fortune.

One of the effects of Edward's property inheritance is a kind of beatific inertia. Jenny Gribble argues that this work is "Chekhovian in its atmosphere of dying pastoral", and I would argue that this true even when the Massines are in the city.[14] Edward's privilege leaves him pacified, non-productive, like a teenager or man-child. In Chekhov we would refer to *ennui*. This inertia takes the form of sleeping, endlessly traversing the old paths, the stasis of his romantic relationship and his lack of paid work. Even as an actor and artisan he has no drive and no ideas. When we come across Edward in the novel, after the bustling of the female real estate agent, we find him asleep: "Edward was a good sleeper. He had come to the surface several times during the morning and heard the house sounding with heavy weights, thumps, men's voices and on the same floor, back-stage sounds; he heard

---

14 Jennifer Gribble, *Christina Stead* (Melbourne: Oxford University Press, 1994), 89.

Musty's snuffling and scratching" (14–15). When he is eventually awake, he thinks, "behind him stretched the perfect life of sleep; and now he had various irritating little things to do. He felt disgusted and bored. He was a very kind man, and had a hundred things to do for friends, but no interesting project for himself" (20).

Edward is adrift in post-war New York, where getting back to business signals a new world of abundance, conservatism and entrepreneurship. Edward declines to be involved in this: "'I have enough to eat and women are keeping me,' said Edward, referring to his tenants. He went on to explain that he had his army savings, his separation pay, and he felt sure there would be another bonus with so many fellows coming back and finding nothing to do" (25). The zeal of the other returned servicemen is hard for him to share. Edward sees his economic privilege based in property, but he has the larger task of discovering whether he has any will. In the 1930s and 1940s Stead claimed that she had been reading Stanislavski for his sense that the function of the artist was to let a given character express his or her will. The Chekhov and Stanislavski connection supports my argument that *The People with the Dogs* offers something more than nostalgia. Stead's portrait of Edward investigates the premise of how to write a relatively content character of no appreciable will. What emerges here is a critique of inherited wealth and provincial insularity, because it is Edward's comfort that means his creative drives are banked in an apolitical collective and a pacifying utopia:

> "Some of them have property and they'll be safe. The value of my houses will go up for the time being. I won't be able to raise my rents, but I'm not that kind of roughneck anyhow. As long as I've got a roof over my head, I don't think of my houses that way ... Communism is a great mistake; when one fellow has the property, he's ever so much better off." (25)

With the Republic of Massine, Edward has no need for other politics touching on social relations. Because of inherited property he seems quite determined not to work for a living and rather to stay at home forever, in a formation of arrested development and fixity, despite his physical movement around Manhattan: "Staying at home this way I save a lot of money. Pay is handy but for a man like me with a rents background, I'd be ruined ... Work for me would be a waste of time and money and from the point of view of my character, ruination" (31–32). As Al Burrows responds, with some perspicacity: "Yes, but your object in not marrying, not getting an ordinary job like other men, it's that you're afraid to measure yourself with anything and find out you're just another one of eleven million" (84). Edward's girlfriend of ten years of non-committal relationship, Margot, calls this out another way: "If anyone could have heard you just then! I'm tired of hearing about the good, the kindhearted, the wonderful Edward and knowing what I know about you: that you're selfish to the core, monstrously selfish, that nothing disturbs you" (85–86). Margot links Edward's inertia to his inheritance of city and country properties, and especially the involvement with the Whitehouse experiment. His lack of agency is specifically attached to generational legacies and lingering afterlives of inheritance: "Can you imagine a man who marries what his grandfather's ghost dictates?" (87). She goes on to connect his arrested development with his inability to function outside the Republic of Massine: "The trouble is you cannot love. So old aunts and such come first. And ideas of a roof over everyone's head" (87–88).

Urban Pastoral and the City of Stories

Unlike Letty and Robbie, who range far and wide in their economic and libidinal restlessness and avidity, Edward knows his favourite New York like the back of his hand: "He thought with pride that here he was at home. 'New York is my village. Yes, it is true, it *is* better to die in New York than live elsewhere else'" (282). He has no desire to travel anywhere except in pursuit of company or pleasant affect. Family is not a large enough unit for proper adult political commitment, the novel suggests, because it has made Edward Massine short-sighted, though very much at home:

> He took Musty with him and walked on uptown, crossing the park over to Broadway. He loved New York, especially at this time of night. It was rich and tender with neon. There was a faint shine with big gobs of light in the duck pond at the end of Central Park. Edward loved all the town, even the broken parts of Sixth Avenue. He walked from block to block, store to store, recognising all the names, signs, kinds of wares: he was quite at home. He and Lou walked everywhere. (55–56)

The ironic undertow that surrounds Edward's amateur movement is revealed in the description of neon as "rich and tender", and in the fact that the light shining on the Central Park duck pond appears as "big gobs". The ironised pleasure of practised urban recognition suggests that Edward is not only an amateur, he is an incurable provincial in the most cosmopolitan of cities. Although he loves the country life with his family – a summer sojourn upstate every year – his walking in New York City (as well as his titanic sleeping) seems to be the most rewarding aspect of Edward's life, bar swapping stories.

What Stead clearly treasured is the only real drive of the Massine clan apart from their dogs, and that is their inveterate storytelling. The telling of stories maps the streets around the Lower East Side where the family congregate, all the way uptown to Al Burrow's pharmacy. The houses of the Massine family, the brownstones full of people to whom Edward rents and the theatre spaces in which he desultorily works, are full of thriving, multiplying, exchanged and moderated stories. The "chicken's story" from Annichini is an absolute homage to the power of the New York story (28): "Edward smiled. 'Do you know the latest line of story? What's noo? The sea burned up. Well, a lot of fried fish. What's noo?'" (91). The storytelling of New York is altogether the most energetic and attractive aspect of Edward, who, though selfish, energetically exchanges stories. His story exchange has the drive of human community and tale-telling that Stead declares in her essay for the *Kenyon Review* in 1968 and continued to talk about in interviews throughout the mid to late 1970s.[15] Storytelling is a particular kind of circulation and exchange, an alternative economy to capital, though never apolitical. Its home is the market-place, but it offers a powerful and oceanic alternative to market forces.

In *The People with the Dogs* storytelling is not about survival, swindling or marriage; it is grounded in the comforts of property and belonging. Freed from the survivalist amorality of Letty and predations of Robbie, Edward Massine exists in a non-alienated, potentially deeply attractive totality of an encompassing family, with ideologies of communality at the core of his relationships and common histories. In a post-war New York City, rife with housing shortages, Edward and the wider Massine family have access to inherited property. This is what makes this communality possible and may indeed feed a troublesome Chekhovian inertia, mild dilettantism and suspended development. Some energy can and does come from habitual pleasures of the daily Manhattan round, such as interactions with the extended Massine community, tall-tale telling and the well-known and well-loved features of their Manhattan haunts. Yet, Edward himself has no creative ideas or personal momentum – he is stuck in habits and relationships from ten years previously. His romantic relationship dates from the mid-1930s and it is clear that both parties in the relationship are wasting their lives in a passive-aggressive round of habit and recrimination, with Edward's childlike self-absorption (and family-absorption) as his main characteristic in this context.

The "Cherry Orchard Family"

Stead had a large and beloved family of Russian émigré New Yorkers in mind for a novel since she met them. These were the American Karamazovs she referred to in her letter to Thistle Harris in 1939, though that title indicates a much more philosophical novel, perhaps, than the one she eventually wrote. Asa Zatz was Blake and Stead's landlord in 1940–42 when they moved into one of his brownstones on 16th Street. They knew Zatz very well by the end of their time in New York and though they only lived in one of his houses until mid-1942, they stayed in touch as neighbours. Zatz saw Stead onto the boat bearing her back to Europe just after Christmas in 1946. Hazel Rowley tells us that Zatz was struck later with how Stead had captured the way he talked and the sheer truth of the portrait of the family: "He remembered her asking a lot of questions and marvelled to think that this quiet woman was digesting his family with this verisimilitude".[16] Rowley reports

---

15 Christina Stead, "England", *Kenyon Review* 30, no. 4 (1968) 444–450.
16 Hazel Rowley, *Christina Stead: A Biography* (Port Melbourne: Minerva, 1994), 269.

that Stead loved his communal kitchen in the 16th Street basement and she thought of Zatz and his extended family as the "cherry orchard family".[17] It was through Zatz that Stead came to know her other great New York friends and correspondents, Aida and Max Kotslarsky. They were Asa's favourite aunt and her husband: Max had studied with the pianist and composer Artur Schnabel and they had dogs they treated as surrogate children. The Dolinskis were Zatz's family on his mother's side and they provide a wonderful snapshot of the Russian émigré communities with deep roots in New York and upstate rural New York stretching back to the nineteenth century.

Zatz's grandfather had owned and developed several acres near Hunter in the Catskills, an estate originally built on radical ideals like those of the Oneida community, various cottages built on the estate for his nine children, of which Aida was the youngest. Stead and Blake would visit several times over the years, particularly in the summers of 1944 and 1945. Stead had notes on the nineteenth-century utopian socialists William Morris and Charles Fourier from the 1930s. She neatly records her boredom at the social pointlessness of anarchistic utopia: "Yawn, yawn, the whole summer" (101). It might be true to say that, unlike many a radical thinker (including Marx), Stead had no interest whatsoever in utopias. Utopian communal living, though perhaps hugely attractive in short bursts for a writer, is portrayed as juvenile, inert and the enemy of vitality in the long term. The Massine utopia is associated with the sentimental and more manageable substitution of dogs for children. Dogs provided the mass of bodies that communal living required, without the family having actually to live with anyone outside the magic circle of their own networks.

The possibility of mapping a Moscow-to-Melikhovo kind of retreat from the stifling Moscow summer is in view in this novel. *The Cherry Orchard* (1903), Chekhov's last play, written after a famous short story, *The Lady with the Dog* (1899), dramatises the imminent loss of a beloved, if fading, world. Cherished family land must be sold to avoid financial ruin, and the centrepiece of this loss is the proposed destruction of the beloved cherry orchard, which signals the end of a certain kind of fading world characterised by civility and ennui. Michael Goldman, in *The Actor's Freedom*, has suggested that the combination of a paradoxical tone of comedy and tragic pathos is "part of a deeper pathos; the [comic] stumbles are not pratfalls but an energized, graceful dissolution of purpose".[18] Chekhov's tragicomic engagement with the everyday, with family, economic struggle, disillusionment and a lack of energy or direction in the face of change offers a wonderfully apposite set of formal propositions for the story of Edward Massine.

Bakhtin's description of the idyll chronotope offers an account of the world of Chekhov's late play – a fictional world that is static and hermetic. In this idyll, the

---

17 Christina Stead to William Blake, 7 May 1942, in Rowley, *Christina Stead*, 268.
18 Michael Goldman, *The Actor's Freedom: Toward a Theory of Drama* (New York: Viking, 1975), 72.

hero is wholly engrossed in the "little world" of his own home, his countryside and his country, inevitably becoming conventional.[19] This describes the Chekhovian universe very well:

> The unity of the life of generations (in general, the life of men) in an idyll is in most instances primarily defined by the *unity of place*, by the age-old rooting of the life of generations to a single place, from which this life, in all its events, is inseparable. This unity of place in the life of generations weakens and renders less distinct all the temporal boundaries between individual lives and between various phases of one and the same life. The unity of place brings together and even fuses the cradle and the grave (the same little corner, the same earth), and brings together as well childhood and old age (the same grove, stream, the same lime trees, the same house), the life of the various generations who had also lived in that same place, under the same conditions, and who had seen the same things. This blurring of all temporal boundaries made possible by a unity of place also contributes in an essential way to the creation of the cyclic rhythmicalness of time so characteristic of the idyll.[20]

The People with the Dogs offers a moving homage to this sense of the unity of place and generation. In the famous and much quoted vine pruning sequence (150–51), Stead draws a direct parallel between the Republic of Massine and *The Cherry Orchard*; between the vision of this mighty vine and that the dreadful sound as the woodcutters start to destroy the orchard at the end of Chekhov's play. This vine, so strongly wrapped around the Whitehouse, shows signs of recovery. It is still strong and renewal is indicated rather than a fading world because Edward Massine, the main candidate for "sapling root", will marry and become more independent, though he will never leave Manhattan or fail to visit family at the Whitehouse: "In a few days, the injured roots completed their repairs and sent up a new line of roots and leaves and the work of monopoly went on" (151). The vine seems to me to be a figure for the Massine family and all is generations, connected friends and abundance over the years of the property. The dogs also provide this image of collectivity, plenitude and mass, but the tone is neither of nostalgia nor of resignation. The passage is intent on conveying the scale of the vine, "the body of the great being" in its huge vitality.

---

19 Mikhail M. Bakhtin, "Forms of Time and the Chronotope in the Novel", *The Dialogic Imagination: Four Essays*, ed. Michael Holquist, trans. Caryl Emerson and Michael Holquist (Austin: University of Texas Press, 1981), 232.
20 Bakhtin, "Forms of Time and the Chronotope in the Novel", 225. My emphasis.

Utopia and Its Discontents

The utopia of slow aging and long life beautifully summons up Chekhov's tragi-comic oeuvre, particularly *Uncle Vanya*. Vanya and the The Cherry orchard foreground the lives of characters of great promise who have somehow sacrificed or been robbed of their potential in favour of sheltered lives conducted on the periphery. As the world grapples with modernity outside the magic circle of the estate, or the old family and its friends and retainers enact depleted formalities and tussle for power and meaning in the lazy late days of summer. Lost vitalities and desire are caught as echoes in the anachronistic world of the rural retreat in these late great plays. In Stead's equivalent 'Cherry Orchard family', who have both rural and urban pastoral settings, the dazed lack of action is as much about the rich appreciation of present pleasures as a distinct lack of political action, commitment or idea. Lack of action ultimately means a lack of revolution, though the utopian retreat was founded on hard-won anarchist principles. To make matters worse, it seems that the anachronistic utopia is inimical to both politics and art. The vitality required for both has turned to idleness. As Walt bursts out, in a fond judgement of the utopian Republic of Massine:

> "You only understand the communal life, that's why you don't want to marry, isn't it? ... You need abundant multiple life around you like Whitehouse, like the Massines; the perfect still life, eh? Ha-ha. Fruitfulness with grapes and rabbits dropping over the edges of an oak table on a woven cloth – and many dogs and dishes and many children and many days? ... And all without any theory, Anarchist, Socialist, what-have-you, just the Massine Bill of Rights. You're born in the Golden Age just because old Dad Massine established the Fiftieth State of the Union, the Massine Enclave, with the following sweet words: 'I leave Whitehouse to furnish a roof for you all, rich, poor, working, idle.'" (94–95)

The communitas of the Massine-Solway family is based on a communal ideal that Stead reads as an excuse for exhausted retreat. Art and ideas cannot seriously thrive in these contexts, and neither can radical action. The community of family, the exhausted communal ideal and the dogs that bind these things together with hustle and bustle, do not add up to political commitment or even fundamental drive. Art cannot seriously be made in these contexts and neither can genuine radical action. The community/family is too endogenous, especially in the pacifying rural idyll. The much-travelled Massine circuit between the Catskills and the Lower East Side is one of the most precious aspects of the life of the Massine family, but it is not a regenerating mobility, it is ceremonial and it is stultifying. The timelessness of Shangri-La hangs over the Whitehouse (isolationist centre of the Republic) and this promises melancholy and stasis rather than rejuvenation. Unawareness of age seems to convey arrested development and pathos rather than vitality:

> As they entered the country of upland valleys and high mountains in which Whitehouse lies he had forgotten the dark blood and smoke and sorrow of New York. All this during the war had lain and was then as now, and his family's life had been the same. The years flew past, they did not know they were getting older, neither did he. (246)

In fact, Edward's character is being ruined by inertia, ambivalence and parochialism: "that is the weakness of living all your life in one setting. You get shortsighted" (80–81). Vera, the artist whom Edward sees onto the boat for her voyage to Europe, is the antithesis of this kind of parochial inertia. She is a true artist, with the gifts and burdens that this entails. Vera's concert is an epiphany for Edward, but perhaps one with which he can do nothing since she is leaving, and he is still too immature.

The Massine-Solways are isolationists and Stead foregrounds this self-sufficiency and insularity of her fictional Russian family as both naïvely unproductive and self-centred. Stead seems to imply that this endogamous self-regard means that the younger generation (without vitality or influence from the outside) is really a series of biddable and loving dogs. The generational vitality of these property-owning anarchists is direly threatened by both postwar and mid-century 'arrest' and the more obvious psychological symptoms of arrested development: "Oneida laughed and fondled Musty's ears. 'No one shall ever beat us, no one will ever get the better of us because we don't want anything, do we, we only want each other'" (100–101). Like the Republic of America, they are "the Republic of Massine" and with all the weaknesses of the isolationist and exceptionalist America. Edward, like New York City, is emerging into the world after the war and it is time to go into the world: "I'm happy. I think I am. I know I've been acting strange. I can't help it. I've led such a scattered life and I suppose I've lived for us all. But I'd like to live for myself" (332). Hearing another echo from *The Man Who Loved Children,* there is a sense here of the importance of leaving home, even a *loving* collective home. *The People with the Dogs* records Stead's homage to New York and its well-loved circuits and modes of community. I would suggest that in the form of her criticism of the utopian idyll, the repetitive circulation of story and the dearth of thinking or inspiration, we see her own account of why it was time to leave Manhattan. Politics and art require energies that the well-worn routes and secular rituals could not provide.

The Dogs, Fake Communality and Weak Radicalism

The Massine dogs are curiously ambivalent in Stead's novel. They are a sign of generosity, love, and vitality; they bring the natural world and community into the city but also pose questions around maturity and political engagement. The dogs are a sign of community but also of a kind of misplaced idealism or arrested childhood. The family dogs are a form of instant and almost multitudinous community such as their grandfather may have created in the early days of the Whitehouse commune. Several generations down, the sense of numbers seems to come from the colourful array of the Massine hounds, with all their names and histories and needs. They are a manifestation of ethical care, but the book implies that there is something less textured in this relation, and some unhealthy rehearsal of arrested development. The dogs are not children; they will never grow up and leave of their own volition:

> She said, "Edward, if I went away and left the dogs to Lou, he wouldn't even feed them." He laughed. She added, after a while, "I can live without them, never fear. But, Edward, without them at all in the world, the world would seem empty. You have to have something to take care of and love; and to have something love you unquestioningly." (202)

Oneida can be as abundantly maternal and caregiving in her relationship to the dogs, but there is something a little arrested in her development in this case, too – the dogs will not grow up to question authority or leave. They are like Edward before he meets his future wife:

> Oneida cried out, "Oh Edward, I think a love of dogs makes you understand human beings. You learn how to take care of everybody. You *realise* people have their weaknesses and faults but they have their wants too, isn't that what you feel?" (319–20)

Stead sees that the Massine utopia and utopian thinking (in the city and in the country) offers a kind of refuge in the past, and the anarchist's dreams in the past offer a stranglehold in the present. Utopian thinking was the provenance of activists (and anarchists) who were privileged already. When the utopian conditions disappeared and the going got tough, these radicals disintegrated and *I'm Dying Laughing* is a portrait of this. Again, there appears to be lack of real theory to ground a genteel radicalism, and the fact that the anarchist culture of the family (that originally justified and powered the Whitehouse property) goes generations back and has subsided into the self-protection of one extended family, with the dogs standing in for the collectivity that once informed their sociality.

In the last hundred pages of this novel, there is a sense that it is a series of cumulative episodic events that happen *to* Edward about town that are the catalyst to his coming of age. He is overtaken by some momentum at last, even if it is external. Although he will not leave Manhattan, it seems he may marry Lydia and create a more independent life. An ambiguous but important aspect of this last section of the novel is Edward's interactions with the great singer, Vera, who displays the restiveness and drive that seem synonymous with the artist. Vera's farewell indicates that for the artist, inertia is not an option; only vitality and will – expressed in Vera's need to travel – can support art (280).

In the complementary portraits of the New York *picaro*, Stead has given us a portrait of a market velocity and related instances of reification so intense and so dark that the players recede from humanity into gigantic and prolix figures of Jacobean farce. The fact that hiding squalid adulterous letters from himself is the apex of Robbie Grant's actual capacity for pleasure supports this point. He is an evacuated subject, completely at the mercy of his lack of interiority and the rapacious turnover of the market that will defeat him in the end. The alternative portrait of a genial, albeit selfish, man wandering about in a state of jovial arrested development offers an almost antithetical New York masculinity. *The People with the Dogs* moves between loving recollections of the Lower East Side and the Catskills as the comparative urban and rural pastorals, as part of a muted but persistent critique of the effects of inherited property, the ineffectual nature of faded utopias and the suffocations of an otherwise loving family. The genuine politics of collectivity have been subsumed into memories of things past and the delightful but ambiguous care for the dogs in the present. The question of the forms and works of the female artist dominates the next chapter on *I'm Dying Laughing*. Whereas Stead's domestic and picaresque fictions are intent on exposing hidden contradictions and entanglements of political economy in the lives of their characters, *I'm Dying Laughing* makes contradiction its central preoccupation.

6
Gargantuan Contradictions and the Supercession of Limits in *I'm Dying Laughing: The Humourist*

> Politics is a specific form of strain between men in which both sides play for the realisation of vital impulses; and that these passions, these conflicts are the essence of drama, the stuff of new literature.[1]

> She was a great friend of mine and she was a woman of immense energy. She was a sort of Danton – I always thought she was Danton in skirts, you know – but she wasn't; she didn't have political integrity, she didn't really have any integrity except she was a very great person, she was wonderful.[2]

I'm Dying Laughing is the tragic account of a successful comic writer and passionate radical who falls into disarray and insanity through her transgression of all meaningful limits in an historical period of seemingly impossible choices. Gargantuan forces, both political and aesthetic, that have been held in some relationship of opposition or tension within and around her expansive body, finally dissolve in one last aporetic image: her madly laughing as her unfinished work of historical tragedy flies in the wind at the steps of the Forum Romanorum. It is a last image of dissolution in an ironically unfinished and perhaps unfinishable work, given that the book that captures this moment was also unfinished and perhaps unfinishable. It is hard to imagine another such work from the American mid-century; a conflicted and loquacious female writer towering over the many excesses of this massive novel, including the mass of her own writing, with her genius and her follies on display in equal measure. Emily Wilkes, the eponymous

---

1 Christina Stead, *I'm Dying Laughing: The Humourist* (1986; London: Penguin, 1989), 61. All subsequent references are to this edition and appear in parentheses in the text.
2 Anne Whitehead, "An Interview with Christina Stead", *Australian Literary Studies* 6, no.3 (1974), 246.

humourist, embodies the dynamism of crisis, contradiction, excess and accumulation in action. She represents an exhilarating and self-destructive economy out of kilter and a system geared to fail. In some sense, she represents contradictory impossibilities of all kinds, including true American radicalism or a stable system of capital.[3]

I'm Dying Laughing occupies a complex double position as two moments of culmination. It was Stead's last novel, published posthumously. It was also the last novel she wrote about America and it strives, I would argue, to deliver the force and synthesising ambition of a summative declaration about the country which she had found so important for a decade and then left. It is both an achingly sad and typically remorseless anatomy of the failure of the American Left. It is a portrait that seeks to diagnose, at the same time, the question of Americans as such, not to mention the function of history as a form of tragedy unfolding in the present. The vital gangster realism of *A Little Tea, A Little Chat* is put to work in the service of a quasi-biography of the extraordinary Emily Wilkes as writer-gangster-comedienne. Based on the talented and tragic Ruth McKenney, she is Stead's most powerful example of the positives and negatives of America and Americans. It is also a realist chronicle that most anatomises the deforming effects of capital on the fundamental possibility of radicalism or revolution in America. Though the cohesion of synthesis bored Stead; she favoured the irregularities of life and its immersive and verbose possibilities, this masterpiece is perhaps the closest Stead ever moved toward the unities of epic and away from the encyclopaedic. Certainly, there is no greater evidence that Stead's fundamental modus operandi was critique of a very Frankfurt School kind. She sits almost on top of her object of study; criticism is often levelled at a very confusingly close range, the intimacy of critique suggesting both loving engagement and harrowing and fearless indictment.

The title of Christina Stead's posthumous novel is a phrase used when someone is laughing so hard it becomes unmanageable. In Stead's American novels, comedy and laughter have connoted vitality and life, as well as ambivalence about power or intention under the misleading sign of the democratic. "Dying" indicates the supercession of a certain limit, when the physical delight in response to something comic becomes so extreme that it threatens to become its opposite. This is not a promised moment of Hegelian synthesis, where one term contradicts the other in the pair and they resolve together into a new term. Instead, laughter is the state in which a pair of opposites, physical delight and physical obliteration, are suspended together and there is no dialectical progression. "I'm Dying Laughing" is thus a phrase that indicates a continuous and indefinite present, where suspension

---

3   This chapter owes an important conceptual debt both to Susan Sheridan's work in "Christina Stead's Last Book: The Novel and the Bestseller." *JASAL: Journal for the Study of Australian Literature* 2 (2003), 41–52, and to Nicholas Birns' essay "'Merely Unfriendly or Slightly Critical': Christina Stead, the Left and *I'm Dying Laughing*", *Australian Literary Studies* 31, no. 6 (2016). https://doi.org/10.20314/als.57f2e7a7ce.

is emphasised over resolution. Dying and laughing together generate a kind of impossible orbit of locked forces, one that is both generative and destructive, multiplying pleasure as well as scenes and sites of struggle and limit-testing. It may be a matter of time before the laughing passes, or the contradictory social elements resolve, but the liminal time of suspension, especially if it is extended, carries the potential for degradation and monstrosity, as well as *jouissance*. It is a heightened period of interminable and terminating crisis.

Laughter is a moment or scene that might just flout the dialectic. Often involuntary, laughter opens up an unfettered space in which deep contradiction is expressed. Likewise, comedy can be the place in which the contradictions of political life find expression and negotiation. It is the philosophical forces of tragedy that come in after the laughter has died away to assess meaning and deliver insight. The truncated textual history of *I'm Dying Laughing* means that while the powerful impasse of held contradictions in an ongoing present of crisis is clear, the philosophical work of the tragic historical novel remains unfinished and is perhaps unfinishable. While I think that Stead's ambition for the novel was that it be an American Tragedy, what we have instead is a tragicomic chronicle of the American dilemma as it informs the life and times of a radical couple, and a brilliant woman writer in particular. Gabriel García Márquez's brilliant novel, *Chronicle of a Death Foretold* (1981), comes to mind in this context. Stead's *magnum opus* does communicate the sense of an unbearable foretelling of the decline of American radicalism. The fact that the central role is given to an extraordinary female clown (a female Gargantua) complicates Stead's reputation as a dour Cassandra prophesising doom, which is well in keeping with the contradictions that saturate this novel. As Randall Craig reminds us: "whereas earlier theories of comedy and laughter were often based on incongruity, the humour of the tragicomedians arises from a more emphatic and self-conscious sense of contradiction".[4] The unbearable consciousness, or knowing, so essential for tragedy is deployed in *I'm Dying Laughing* not as a consciousness of end times, but of unmanageable contradiction.

The focus of this chapter on Stead's posthumous masterpiece is the shape and nature of contradiction. Contradiction was an indispensable conceptual piece of the Hegelian Marxist assessment of history and of capital, and much of Stead's work in the American novels was to expose hidden contradictions and reveal the inner engineering of capitalist modernity. Her critique of capital in the American novels achieves just this. In *I'm Dying Laughing,* Stead explores contradiction as such, revealing that, in the form of a dilemma, it is lodged at the very heart of American national identity. The political life and times of the humourist of the title is not a sequence of contradictions to be exposed from the obscure places of everyday lives, but a matter of understanding the massive and unruly contradictions sitting in plain sight at a complex and demanding moment in history for American radicals.

---

4 Randall Craig, *The Tragicomic Novel: Studies in a Fictional Mode from Meredith to Joyce* (Newark: University of Delaware Press, 1989), 38.

The critique powering Stead's American anatomy swings away from the hidden or secret life of the home and city and comes to focus on the answer to an historical question: why and how did certain American radicals betray their cherished beliefs during the Cold War? American radicals come under scrutiny, but so too does American national identity and the ideologies and impossibilities upon which it rests.

The last book in Stead's American anatomy is a tragicomic chronicle of the rise and decline of radical commitment in the period from the Popular Front to the early Cold War. The central subject of this chronicle is a midwestern writer called Emily Wilkes, a very successful American comic writer and, for a period from the 1930s to the 1950s, a committed communist. She is a figure of tremendous scope and scale because of the complex and contradictory categories of identity and affiliation that she negotiates. The terms American and communist, humourist and radical, clown and woman, comedian and serious political writer are all pairs that exist in some kind of incongruous or unlikely relation and they are increasingly difficult to reconcile as the world changes around formerly committed Leftists. Emily's prolific writing, substantial body and tremendous appetites all convey her vital expansiveness in response to the challenge of maintaining her balance among multiple positions and ironic oppositions. This expansion endures for an extraordinary length of time, to which the novel bears witness, until it disintegrates, without resolving into a new form, at the end of the novel.

The balance of this chapter will devote itself to the moments, scenes, figures and sequences where various fields of opposed forces previously held together as viable contradictions either inflate, collapse or become inverted. This investigation of the supercession of limits at the scene of contradiction commences with a starting point in the portrait of a contradictory marriage, progresses to the irony at the heart of American humour and then works into Stead's manifestations of textual inflation and gigantic scale. Political trouble with limit emerges and, finally, the dreaded figure of the renegade arises as the litmus test of transgression that is inimical to stable identity. The greatest supercessions of limit and category-breaking are finally expressed as abject collapse.

The first general arena of struggle and opposition we find in *I'm Dying Laughing*, though it is not strictly a contradiction, is the marriage between a rich scion of an industrial family turned radical, Stephen Howard, and a brilliant but poor journalist from the Midwest, Emily Wilkes. Their marriage forms a materialist *Grand Guignol* of class, gender and regional difference that plays out as a Punch and Judy show of domestic and professional conflict. Stead's real life models for her Punch and Judy Show were Ruth McKenney and Richard Bransten, hard-working American communists who Stead met at the *New Masses* offices in about 1937 and for whom *I'm Dying Laughing* could almost operate as an unofficial biography, or even a *roman-à-clef*. There is a great deal of energy and affection in this unlikely partnership at the beginning of the novel, though much of their relationship is conducted in environments of frenzy and uproar that one might expect in a radical partnership that thematises Marx's views about historical class struggle. Although I will treat Emily as the unambiguously central figure of this work, the dyad of Emily and Stephen is essential for the rhetoric of struggle and opposition in this work.

Contradiction 1: Miss America is an American Humourist and Radical Writer

If Sam Pollit is Mr America and Letty Fox is Miss New York City, then Emily Wilkes is Miss America. As Stead said to Jonah Raskin in an interview: "The novel is about a great character who goes astray: it's a tragedy. It's about Miss America too, about the American girl. I saw that at the end, not the beginning".[5] Like Sam Pollit, Emily displays American vitality and energy, expressed in folkloric storytelling and wisecracking humour, as well as fountains of Vesuvius speech and childlike appetites and demands. Unlike Sam, Emily is a persuasive and energetic radical, though she possesses an astonishing materialism and greed that powers terrible corruption at the very same time. She is also enormously vulnerable to an entrenched American ideology of individualism, and the beating pressure on the individual to succeed.

Emily Wilkes is the first and only substantial female writer of Stead's *oeuvre*. *I'm Dying Laughing* paints an extremely valuable portrait of a woman writer whose talent has had no opportunity to flower, and who becomes mired in her own contradictions and related corruption of capacity. Emily's American-ness, her appetitive nature, her marriage into the ruling class and the times in which she finds herself has prevented the full expression of her literary talent. The tragic novel about the American radical movement that she should and could write is stymied by national ideologies of success and money, and her talent is prostituted for the sake of the fast buck and the wild bestseller. She should write the great American tragedy she yearns to write, but instead becomes the raw material for just such a narrative. The interleaved categories of gender, national identity, comedy and political commitment are quite dizzying, and the echo chamber of identifications between the author and central subject are vertiginous.

The female comic is also a relatively rare figure in narrative, especially when she is in charge of the successful jokes. It is significant that Emily Wilkes is associated with the comic, and successfully so, since comedy is a space or practice where opposition and incongruity can manage to have a reasonable shelf life. Emily Wilkes is certainly the trickster woman, boundary-violator and limit tester of this piece. She is deeply ambivalent; full of vitality, courage and talent incarnate as well as greed, cowardice and hypocrisy. She flouts norms of femininity and decorous textuality; she jumps boundaries, mixes genres and becomes a figure of pure limit

---

5   Christina Stead quoted by Jonah Raskin, "Christina Stead in Washington Square", *London Magazine* 9, no. 11 (1970), 74.

as she ends up outside productive affiliation or legible coordinates of identity. It is unusual in the genealogies of American humour for there to be a female humourist, though not unheard of, given the success of Dorothy Parker and Anita Loos in New York and Hollywood in the 1920s and 1930s. Emily gives us a clear humourist canon with which she wishes to be associated, and it basically includes only James Thurber:

> in James Thurber – in – this and that – she saw faint shades of herself. American humour based on the American dilemma, based on, what you want most, you'll never have, but the plastic makeshift – ha-ha-ha! ... Small-town girl – she had left her impression on the language, on the nation, on the USA, a great nation of humorists. (57)

In this tradition, the humourist is a teller of witty and ironic tales about the quandaries and incongruities of everyday life. Emily is amazingly good at this stuff, producing reams and reams of commercially popular material, seemingly without thought:

> She earned a living with what she called her Toonerville tales, short amusing anecdotes, in simple language, recollections, stories about uncles, parents, cousins, grocers, mailmen, townspeople of the small towns; a doctor on the wrong side of the tracks who was always drunk but a loved, reliable bone-setter; a woman with one tooth who won the corn-on-the-cob eating contests every year, drilling her way furiously along the rows; an uncle who stewed cheese-rind with anchovies, the first eater of yogurt in Toonerville. (43)

This is easily cooked up, middlebrow humour about embarrassing provincial relations, but it earned both Ruth McKenney and Emily Wilkes a fortune as writers. Emily's humourist material, involving the stories of her family and small-town American life, earns her big money with "nothing but family hokum, a belly-laugh or two and a shovelful of sentiment" (137). Emily often takes her own impropriety (of body, size, region and gender) and generates comic gold: "a typical Middle-Western Mamma, with a beer-barrel waist, overstuffed dewlaps, panting about looking for an ice-cream soda" (310). However, as a writer of talent and insight and a background in serious political journalism, Emily wants to move from popular culture ("hix in the stix") to high culture, and write novels dealing with political topics, including revolution, wartime concentration camps and the French Resistance. Unfortunately, her earning capacity and the attention and success it has garnered her have introduced an addiction to luxury, which entices her to continue with her humourist pieces.

Emily Wilkes' position on American humour is fascinating. Her wit and genius are more evident in her description of the anatomy of American comedy than almost anything else she writes, because it combines her perspicacity and her vernacular flair in the pursuit of analysis:

> "Well, that's the bitter truth, the savagery of life which staggers you, keeps you rooted to the spot and your outcries stop your breath; and yet it is wildly out of line with all our ideals, humanity, peace, brotherly love, do unto others, until you laugh, shout, you understand your own simplicity and wickedness and denseness and greed – that's American humour ... You listen to any Hollywood dialogue in a modern film and you'll hear such a mash of good sense, brashness, earthy wit, impudence – that's American wisdom, that's our humour ... it bites to the bone ... American humour is another way of seeing the truth; and what a vision! ... it is homespun, godlike truth stalking in from the plains and the tall timber, coonskin and deerhide, with a gun to disturb our little home comforts". (20–21)

American humour is founded in the double perspective of irony; in the capacity to see the opposed and the incongruous. Stephen claims that humourists actually "have both worlds ... They see the sinister truth and they can laugh." Emily agrees, but puts this another way, stressing the knowing duplicity of insight and the division it entails: "I'm a wise guy. I've got the angles. I know the score ... I'm like a doll with two faces glued together" (212). What arises from this identification of the engine of American humour is that American national identity is, by extension, also a matter of troubling doubles. Like American humour, or because American humour is the original American characteristic, American-ness is seen by Emily and Stephen as constituted by both great idealism and immense materialism. Proliferating pairs stem from this insight: Americans want to be both good and successful; they want to help others, but they want to succeed at all costs; they want to act together, but the fundamental ideology of individualism is overmastering, and so on.

On the boat to Paris, Emily delivers another of her wonderful monologues to a range of international listeners about this double and divided nature of American identity. Her hometown display of idiomatic language is knowing and waggish, but the analysis and deprecation, the political mind, is obvious:

> "We have two shovels in our hands, right for digging gold, left for digging graves. And it has always been so. We're miserable people, leanfaced, dismal Uncle Sams. Isn't our history all struggle, all terror, all bloodshed; and at the same time, all hooraying, all success? America the Golden ... Other countries have history; we have nothing but contradictions. We haven't even got a system; or if we have, no one knows what it is. American get-ahead, that's the only system we know ... " (21)

Emily points out the unmanageable contradictions at the heart of the American identity and American history, listed by her as a stand-off between success and bloodshed, terror and celebration, Lincoln and General Motors. The twin gods of capital/success and freedom/integrity show the bipolar spectrum of American ideology that political critique reveals, with American idealism (goodness) at one end and American obsession with success (capital) at the other. The desire for success, or even notoriety, and fear of the obscurity or failure are described as the "American dilemma".

Contradiction 2: The American Dilemma and the Radical Dilemma

In 1973, during an interview in England with Joan Lidoff, Stead summarised her unfinished work with inspiring precision:

> It was all about the passion – I use passion in almost the religious sense – of two people, two Americans, New Yorkers, in the thirties. They were politically minded. They went to Hollywood. They came to Europe to avoid the McCarthy trouble. Of course, they were deeply involved. And then, they lived around Europe, oh, in a wild and exciting extravagant style. But there was nothing to support it. At the same time, they wanted to be on the side of angels, good Communists, good people, and also to be very rich. Well, of course … they came to a bad end.[6]

As Stead suggests so succinctly, radical identity and radical politics are all very well when there is no great pressure, but it just may be true (based on what Stead herself witnessed) that in general, Americans cannot manage to be both wealthy and comfortable *and* good revolutionaries in tough times. Market forces, money, success and individuality were finally too firmly planted at the heart of national identity for radical politics to thrive when historical forces were stacked against many American radicals. Failure, discomfort, poverty, collective action, idealism and Marxist notions of social change were difficult to manage in the pressure cooker of the McCarthy era. The American dilemma thus becomes the radical dilemma and, as Stead predicts, "they came to a bad end." The American dilemma – that failure was an anathema and success was an essential good – comes to inflect American radicalism and the impossible negotiations with which it was challenged during the transition from a buoyant and financially viable 1930s into a world of ever-increasing political and commercial difficulty.

---

6 Joan Lidoff, "Interview with Christina Stead", June 1973, in Joan Lidoff, *Christina Stead* (New York: Frederick Ungar, 1982), 181. Stead refers here to *I'm Dying Laughing* as "the big novel".

For Emily, the measure of success was, on one hand, the wealth generated by her middlebrow writing and her commercial success in Hollywood as a screenwriter. It was also a sign of failure, because she knew as she was doing it that there was much more important politically committed work to achieve. There was art to create. However, the commercial failure that was sure to follow her move into genuine work could not be hazarded by Wilkes or all the people who depended on her capacity to earn. Creative writing became the battleground of success and failure, ersatz and real, commercial and artistic. The double jeopardy of genres and modes was organised by Stead into the genre that writes the conflicted and contradictory woman – the tragicomic novel. As Randall Craig has suggested: "consistently dualistic, tragicomic fiction both originates in and evokes a contradictory aesthetic emotion. A trenchant perception of human limitation and suffering, combined with an empathic and amused acceptance of them, is the form of humour characteristic of tragicomedy".[7]

Contradiction 3: The Tragicomic Chronicle

When you have a comic genius and radical protagonist that falls into an historical abyss created, in part, by their own huge and hugely ambivalent qualities, the obvious thing might be to write a tragedy of their rise, their struggle and their fall. This was the book Stead was trying to write, but the very history with which she was engaged continued to unfold around her across the book's long period of gestation, making the purchase required by tragedy a little difficult without resorting to an example in the historical past, like Arthur Miller's *The Crucible* (1953). *I'm Dying Laughing* is a fictionalised account of the life and times of two American radicals Stead knew, who struggled with themselves and their fundamental coordinates of national, regional and personal identity in the historical forces they found ultimately impossible to negotiate. In response to blacklisting on the one hand and political exile on the other, these former political idealists betray everything they know. As it is neither a transnational epic, nor a *roman-à-clef*, the term chronicle best describes the complex and compendious genre of *I'm Dying Laughing* that holds life, history and art together in a strange and magnificent hub. The chronicle is associated with a long-form account of events in chronological order, like *The Anglo-Saxon Chronicle*, but it was often focused on the scope of one life or a period of time in a life, and often circumscribed by a region or ruler. It is a form that earned its contemporary political and experimental stripes in Latin and South America, as an intensely malleable genre that mixed a capacity for literary representation with a long-standing and almost journalistic obligation to inform. In the context of *I'm Dying Laughing*, it is also interesting that it is a genre that famously mixes high and low cultural material in its twentieth-century renditions. In Latin America,

---

7   Craig, *The Tragicomic Novel*, 13.

specifically in Brazil, the chronicle has been used increasingly by writers, travel writers and public intellectuals to record political and social events, and in this process, it has shared affinities with the function of testimonial narrative.[8] As a thinly fictionalised record of an actual person and an actual marriage that are installed as allegorical staging posts for the failure of the American Left, *I'm Dying Laughing* deploys the capacious and mixed elements of the chronicle genre to tell the history of a very difficult and very personal present.

Like the allegorical novel of domesticity, the chronicle is a compendious genre fit to house the matter of the nation. For a nation like America on the eve of the Cold War, which Stead sees as characterised by plenty and poverty, sorrow and laughter, the decline and fall elements of tragedy would be met and complicated by the vitality and democratic vision of comedy. For her last great elaboration of the matter of America, especially with a degree of political turmoil and loss that was so close to her, Stead focuses her vision of America on a single (if massive) figure whom she frames through a poetics of contradiction and crisis. First and foremost, this work is a tragic account of a comedian. Thus, it is to the unstable and capacious mode of tragicomedy that she turns. *Tragicomedia* was a term originally coined by the Roman playwright Plautus (d.184 BCE), and is associated with dramatic tragedies that have comic scenes or characters, with examples from Euripides to Shaw, Chekhov and Beckett and, most famously, Shakespeare's late romances. David Hirst suggests that modern tragicomedy is:

> The only mode capable today of coping with the ethical and aesthetic burdens formerly divided between tragedy and comedy in times when thoughtful men were largely agreed about the metaphysical and theological structure of the universe (a structure composed of absolutes) and could depend upon that structure to provide universal ethical and aesthetic norms. As a result, playwrights and play-goers were agreed that there are two different, but not finally antagonistic ways of assessing human existence, one tragic and one comic, and that individual dramatists could have their say in any of the dramatic modes expressive of these two ways. No such situation prevails today …[9]

The contradictions so resoundingly thematised in *I'm Dying Laughing* could only be held and formed in some protean way by the glossing of the chronicle genre as tragicomic in mode. This double narrative form was intended to broker a kind of balance between opposing tendencies and proliferating ironies without collapsing. Stead's *The People with the Dogs*, with its obvious debt to Chekhov, had already experimented with the uneven tonal range of the comic crossed with notes from

---

8   Viviane Mahleux, "The Chronicle", *Oxford Bibliographies*, https://doi.org/10.1093/OBO/9780199766581-0092.
9   David B. Hirst, *Tragicomedy* (London and New York: Methuen, 1984), 1.

the tragic and folded into a twilight sense of a fading world both celebrated and criticised. Ibsen was another tragicomic playwright whose work Stead knew well, but neither Chekov nor Ibsen quite catches the tonal range required for the American political tragedy of the female humourist dramatised in *I'm Dying Laughing*. The twentieth-century novel, seeking to represent heterogeneous order and a lack of balance or harmony without the assistance of Fate or Fortune, embraced the complexity of tone and composition tragicomedy implied. The tragicomedy in the modern period was associated with a problematic and protean protagonist – a modern day version of the Elizabethan and Jacobean fool. These modern tragicomedies more often than not had a sad clown at their heart, and Stead's late masterpiece elects a female clown and woman writer to be at the centre of hers.

This complex fool who must negotiate contradiction of every stripe and seemingly at every turn, is both a political woman writer and a humourist, which expands yet further the astonishing originality of Stead's tragicomic novel in the context of mid-century writing, as well as the reflexive hall of mirrors between author and protagonist. Randall Craig suggests that the author of the tragicomic novel (and he includes in his study George Meredith, Henry James and James Joyce) is necessarily fascinated with contradiction because the tragicomic novel can be identified by "its dualistic vision and emphasis on unresolved tensions, its double sense of self-consciousness, its affective contradictions, and its realism".[10] Craig thus nominates tragicomedy as a genre centred on the "double occasion" that produces a "double vision".[11] Of course, once a double has been identified, sweeping proliferation is often a consequence. The representation of proliferation is dealt with here as a matter of inflation and expansion, which is inexorably gendered in *I'm Dying Laughing*. No other prolix and hypocritical clown in Stead's American anatomy was also thematised through bodily dimensions. It is an ambivalent critique on this point, because although Emily is physically vast, so is her output, her creative prodigiousness and her earning power. Whatever else Stead thought about lowbrow comedy as a way for a female genius to make a living, she acknowledges Emily's sheer power to turn inventiveness into viable economic returns.

Contradiction 4: Scale Inflation

In Stead's anatomy, Emily Wilkes is the figure we might identify most with the notion of scale, which is certainly saying something given Sam and Henny Pollit, Letty Fox and Robbie Grant. Her expansiveness inheres in her capacity to talk *ad infinitum,* to write in a variety of genres, raise money and make money, generate

---

10   Craig, *The Tragicomic Novel*, 13.
11   Craig, *The Tragicomic Novel*, 38.

ideas and just as easily cast them away. The generosity of her dimensions is built on the sense that she (like her country) is a volcano of contradictions, and only the large scale can possibly offer a stage large enough to house her. Stead wrote to her friend Edith Anderson about the potential "dimensions" of the book about "Mme Gargantua", the "big, noisy, ravenous and alive" Ruth McKenney.[12] These dimensions referred to the site of the "terrific struggle" of a "death of conscience" narrative and the contradictory pulls of political affiliation, idealism and personal greed. Stead commented that: "It is a fascinating subject. Here is a gargantua who marries $1,000,000 – and decides to go in for Despair, and it *is* a tragedy, it's not just talk ... What dimensions. I hope I am able to do it, that's all".[13]

Susan Stewart's work on the gigantic in *On Longing: Narratives of the Miniature, the Gigantic, the Souvenir, the Collection* is of great interest for the characterisation of Emily. I pick up Stephen's rhetoric of Emily as an overwhelming "natural force" as well as the "great roaring of big lungs and a strong heart". Earlier in the text Stephen says affectionately: "'You are a public danger, a monster, a terror, but never a bore, if a bore, well, the sort that has never been seen before; and so a phenomenon'" (354). Stewart relates that the giant was a stalwart of hyperbole in grotesque realism and was associated with the market fair and attendant feasts. The giant was a symbol of surplus and licentiousness, of overabundance and unlimited consumption, of supercession of limit. The giant (Gargantua again) also possesses the tremendous capacity to be both destructive and productive.[14] Emily similarly possesses a vast creativity that bears within it the capacity for self-destruction. The giant symbolises an exaggerated physical force and lawlessness, and an overabundance of the natural that is an affront to cultural demarcations. This affront threatens abjection, too. We can see this gendered threat of abjection, or loss of proper boundary, in the categorical challenges generated by the improperly prolific generation of text in multiple genres, the mobile identifications of unfixed political partisanship and the amoral approach to maternity, not to mention the boundary-crossing threat that emerges from too much body, food and fecundity.

Emily Wilkes – Stead's literary fat lady – must be read within the historical context of twentieth-century fictional critiques of capitalism, which use and re-use a series of fat-inflated figures to trope capitalist decadence and corruption. Where Patricia Parker's investigation of the textual figure of the "literary fat lady" works mainly in the early modern period, it nonetheless sheds substantial light on the rhetorical and ideological operations of *I'm Dying Laughing*. Parker's position on the intersection of rhetoric, gender and generativity resonates with Stead's satirical project in *I'm Dying Laughing*. Parker's aim is to demonstrate "the link between

---

12 Christina Stead to Edith Anderson, 20 January 1950. Quoted in Hazel Rowley, *Christina Stead: A Biography*, (Port Melbourne: Minerva, 1994), 361.
13 Stead to Anderson, Rowley, *Christina Stead*, 363.
14 Susan Stewart, *On Longing: Narratives of the Miniature, the Gigantic, the Souvenir, the Collection* (Durham, NC: Duke University Press, 1992).

the amplification of discourse and the expansive textual figure of the 'fat lady' both within the Renaissance and beyond".[15] In her account of the links between "female *copia*, of body and of word, and the copiousness of texts" Parker argues that the collocation between copious textual/feminine body depends not so much on authorship as "the existence and adoption of a form which involves a combination and double movement of textual expansion with closure or 'point'".[16] The gender of authorship is of some consequence in this consideration of the development and continuation of misogynist topoi such as women's endless talkativeness and, by extension, their boundary-less bodies. *I'm Dying Laughing* uses the rhetorical modes of dilation and *copia* that are inflected by long traditions of misogynist figures, but there is also a sense that Emily is a force to be reckoned with and not just a trick of narrative *copia*. She is a typhoon system that attracts the admiration of reader, husband, publishers and political comrades.

I'm Dying Laughing continues to offer the idea that Emily is more than capable of a serious work of political commitment, of truth, but her husband-manager-editor dissuades her from work that might not earn the dividends they require for the high life. For the Wilkes-Howards, politics is compatible with writing and earning insofar as it provides material for novels and prevents or encourages market success. Emily can balance her double world when the comic writing supports a viable sense of her political belonging and political work. When the Left straighten her out and then expel her from the party, she is bereft of her political anchor. The comic writing continues but her national and political coordinates of identity become less and less stable. She turns to tragedy as a genre or mode that might establish again for her a sense of what really counts, but the contradictions of her life multiply and overwhelm her. She thinks she can keep instability at bay, but she is too far 'beyond the pale'.

Contradiction 5: Bohemian Political Exile

The Howards begin on the Left of the party; Emily is at least faithful to international socialism over American exceptionalism; both partners were for the workers, and hard working for the cause. Yet their faithfulness erodes as McCarthyism begins to be felt in American political life. Eventually fear, opportunism and corruption make them traitors to their early ideals. First, though, they are tripped up by one aspect of the American dilemma as it related to collective politics – the value of individualism. In the post-Browder era of purges and recriminations in the Communist Party of the United States of America, formerly treasured people on the correct side were suddenly seen as the opposite – as obstructive individualists.

---

15 Patricia Parker, *Literary Fat Ladies: Rhetoric, Gender, Property* (London and New York, Methuen, 1987), 2.
16 Parker, *Literary Fat Ladies,* 34.

This is not an anticipated transgression of the party line or negotiation of limit, but it is the first such challenge Emily, in particular, faces, and its rhetorical mode very much concerns limit and control of her body, talent, texts and political position.

The "Straightening Out" in chapter six presents a long scene in which Emily and Stephen are disciplined by the Hollywood branch of the party for their dissident, because progressive, positions. Stead unflinchingly anatomises the regulatory mechanisms of the Left, which work, in this scene, to contain the "individualist" and "bohemian" Emily. Vera Holinshed, the wife of Jim Holinshed, a moving force in the Hollywood Communist Party, says to Emily:

> Don't you think you ought to accept more discipline? Do you think your own individual opinion is so important? I don't believe you're just a Bohemian; and for that matter, we've talked it over and put it down to your coming from New York. Everyone knows that New Yorkers are more Bohemian, more individualist than we are, especially the writers. Here, we've got a mass of working writers who are unionised, work for big bosses, just like factory workers. The writer working in a cellar on his own ideas, is almost unknown: it belongs to the handloom epoch. (89)

The use of bohemian here does not carry the explicit charge of amoral decadence. Rather, it implies theoretical irregularity. To be bohemian in this context is to be dissident (too radical), having affiliations with the New York literary and political scene and an attachment to romantic notions of individualism and textual production. The accusation of "escapists and bohemian adventurers" (232) also carries the charge of lightweight zealots acting outside party direction. Vera Holinshed's statement ("woman-to-woman") employs an East Coast–West Coast distinction within the American Left, a distinction also revealed in a letter Stead wrote to Stanley Burnshaw while working in Hollywood in 1942: "it looks, after all, as if the Lion's Roar (M.G.M) is going to take me in – but when, I don't know: I have to wait, though a director, an M.G.M intellectual, now please be good – has given a firm promise and there's talk of a 30 week contract and all that".[17]

In this letter Stead alludes to an east–west distinction between real intellectual work (east) and mass-produced writing (west). *I'm Dying Laughing* scrutinises Hollywood's strangely elitist Communist Party branch, with its hierarchy of powerful and well-paid filmmakers and writers. Emily asks, "Do the intellectuals in Hollywood join a separate branch? The writers' branch of fighting progressives in Hollywood is by long miles separate isn't it, from the vulgar Mexican worker downtown?" (90). The east coast party members are represented thus:

---

17 Christina Stead to Leda and Stanley Burnshaw, 29 October 1942. Stanley Burnshaw Papers, Harry Ransom Humanities Research Center, University of Texas, Austin. Quoted with permission from Stanley Burnshaw.

> There were impudent people, devoted followers with no minds of their own, a noisy but ever loyal Connecticut editor, who was rude to all intellectuals and particularly rude to communist intellectuals, because he was one himself, and people from New York ... Almost everyone was drunk and the usual brutal personal attacks, parlour analyses were going on, along with all brands of economic and political discussion ... The words "wreckers, saboteurs, Trotskyists, bastards, petty bourgeois poseurs, rich crackpots" had already been shouted at Emily and Stephen by certain partisans led by the suspect district organiser. (159–60)

Emily positions herself in the context of the Party's actions as a writer whose creativity has been stifled by orthodoxy. As a writer, she claims that she must have access to a wider view; she must "see both sides": "'Oh, dear, if I am a sort of candidate for the tumbrils in the end, still it is worth it. I can see why they did it ... I see behind the scenes. Why shouldn't I see both sides?'" (171).

Although Emily Wilkes is branded a bohemian individualist and a renegade by the party, she sees herself as a political exile, compelled to move from the American west coast, then to the east coast, and finally to Paris during the early McCarthy period. It is an interesting instance of renegadism. Political exile is a mode of outlawry, where the movement across national and political borders is grounded in ideological principle. The Howards' political exile is twofold: from their own party and from the increasingly conservative national political topoi of the House Un-American Activities Committee hearings. In addition to the rhetoric of the witch-hunts, Emily reiterates an ongoing formulation of crossing the line(s) as road and train nightmares. Trotsky's fate is always in view here. Both Emily and Stephen refer to the "renegade's train" (387), a version of the revolutionary icon associated with Lenin. They return a number of times to this nightmare of movement on the road or tracks at night, unable to make out "the sign", the moment of transgression from which there is no return. They rehearse between them the stages in the evolution of the renegade: individualist, then renegade and finally traitor. Emily begins watching for the signs in the night.

Contradiction 6: The Political Renegade and the Absolute Limit

I'm Dying Laughing indicates Stead's passionate engagement with concepts of betrayal and political exile. Hazel Rowley reports this of Stead's reception of *Jericho*, a film about the Resistance:

> Stead, who by then had begun to write *I'm Dying Laughing* in earnest – "wept like a fool. I'd never known until then how far this 'traitor' theme I am treating had got under my skin ... I felt how dreadful dreadful dreadful it is for Ruth McK (the only friend I have in that category) to betray. I never thought her

anything but Gargantua, a crazy out-of-size drawing … (Of course I'm writing about the whole thing, so I'm not normal about it)".[18]

Betrayal and exile were everyday realities in the political environment of the late 1940s and early 1950s in which the gestation and first drafts of *I'm Dying Laughing* took place. Stead's use of the terms "traitor" and "betrayal" indicates a horror at the breaking of affiliation through treacherous disclosure of beliefs that locate and orient. The betrayal of intellectual and political affiliation was seen by Stead as the most serious instance of dislocation, disorientation and dis-identification. Stead talked of "the torturing conscience of the traitor" and saw the Emily-Ruth apostasy as a "death of the conscience" narrative.[19] The transgression of national boundary, of language and of genre were secondary to the moral and political transgression produced through a loss of faith. Political discourse was a crucial mode of international identification and affiliation. Socialism was an important form of location in the itinerant life: an ideological "mobile home". Socialism offered a rubric for relationships that allowed for a wide scope of affiliation. The use of the term "fellow traveller" to indicate a like-minded leftist suggests the possibilities of continuous mobility and constant affiliation. Socialist political belief provided Stead and Blake with the ability to be simultaneously mobile and stable.[20]

Renegade derives from *negare*, to deny. To reneg(u)e is to "deny, renounce, abandon" and a renegade is one who deserts a "person, party or principle in favour of another; a turncoat." The turncoat "turns" from a previously held system of beliefs and this "turning" or crossing marks him or her as deserter and traitor. The renegade is even less trustworthy than the enemy because this transgression from inside to outside is more usually seen in the light of self-interest rather than principle.[21] The renegade is tremendously threatening to the maintenance of law as he or she is in breach of regulation and still "at large": a suitable figuration for the "gargantuan" Emily Wilkes. As the enemy from within, the traitorous renegade exits one set of laws, usually for another, with the consequence that the defining boundaries between lawful and lawless are seen to be infinitely mobile and therefore potentially meaningless.

---

18   Christina Stead to Edith Anderson, 13 July 1955. Quoted in Rowley, *Christina Stead*, 361–2.
19   Christina Stead's diary, "The Traveller's Bed and Breakfast", 7 November, 1950, and letter to Edith Anderson, 11 October, 1950 (Christina Stead Papers, National Library of Australia, Notebook and letter by Christina Stead to Edith Anderson, circa 1949-1951, MS 10058).
20   Hazel Rowley, "Christina Stead: Literature and Politics in the Radical Years, 1935–1942", *Meridian* 8, no. 2 (1989), 149. Judith Kegan Gardiner claims that *I'm Dying Laughing* is "Stead's only book to consider seriously and at length her most important aesthetic preoccupation, the connection between writing and politics". Judith Kegan Gardiner, *Rhys, Stead and the Politics of Empathy* (Bloomington: Indiana University Press, 1989), 75.
21   N.I. Matar, "The Renegade in English Seventeenth Century Imagination", *Studies in English Literature 1500–1900* 33, no. 3 (1993), 502.

> "No," said Stephen; for he had been going to say, she's a renegade, she's deserted all she truly believed in; but he could not say it. He felt his gorge rise. He foresaw their slow separation from the Party, the beliefs of the Roosevelt era. He had a suspicion that Emily, who had jibbed at all marking time or trimming, would throw herself bodily over the Rubicon, would jump, laughing and hurrahing, the narrow deep river while he might forever hesitate on the banks. He thought to himself, Emily's bad, she doesn't hesitate; and I would be a villain to say the words, to encourage her to make that jump. (275)

Stead's commitment to the theme of the "traitor" or renegade can be seen in her choice of the epigraph to Part II of *I'm Dying Laughing*, which is from Goethe's *Faust*. Faust's turning to Satan is a famous occasion of apostasy in literature. Faust chooses freely to renounce his faith and is punished by death and eternal damnation. Goethe's fiction of betrayal and renunciation is based in religious apostasy, and renegade is a word used traditionally in the context of religious apostasy, usually the renunciation of Christian faith for Islam, rather than the renunciation of faith *per se*.[22] Making the link between religious and political apostasy, Stephen Howard declares that he can never give up his belief in the party and the Soviet Union because: "If I didn't believe in that, what would I believe in? It would be as if I suddenly did not believe in the ideas of Galileo; or after being an atheist all my life, woke up one morning believing there was an old bearded tribal God" (164).

After he has "sung" to the American Embassy and before his suicide, Stephen comments with bitter irony: "The renegade husband and wife, the perfect American couple, loyal to each other and to the country" (437). Stephen has betrayed the party and is now also a "Man Without a Country" and has even considered leaving his beloved wife. He muses on the meaninglessness generated by the total lack of affiliation:

> To be thought of as a quitter, as leaving the United States – and the cause, too – that would be the end. Nothing – my wife and children, success, family, money – nothing of that would mean anything to me. That's my honour. That's my soul. It is. There would be no future. It would be the black day: *dies irae*. (183)

Stephen's declaration of "blind" party affiliation engages an evangelical rhetoric of personal insufficiency and the need for salvation:

> "I can only follow blindly; but I intend to follow. I went into Marxism for personal salvation. I know, a despicable reason; but I have to stick to it, or where am I? Just a failure; not even a playboy."

---

22 Matar, "The Renegade in English Seventeenth Century Imagination", 490.

"I'm not going to follow anyone into a quagmire; and I don't want to be saved."

"You're an individualist; individualists become renegades."

She sprang up from her chair. "Don't call me a renegade! I'll scratch your nose. I won't stand that." (53)

Where Stephen identifies a certain adherence as better than failure and dislocation ("I have to stick to it, or where am I"), Emily sees a quagmire instead. Emily firmly states her independence from any blind loyalty to party lines but reacts strenuously to the charge of being an individualist, which leads to renegade. She focuses at this point, and repeatedly throughout the novel, on the horror of the position of renegade or traitor: "No turning back is always dread ... Oh, what dread to turn from a world we know well to one we don't know" (252). Emily's cry echoes Stephen's dread of not being anywhere, cast adrift by the Left and Right in a rather terrible set of historical circumstances:

> "... I know we're going to be blackballed. I know we've got our feet on a road from which there is no turning back. I don't know where this road is going," she said sadly, "but I know in the night, one night, we passed a signpost, I dreamed about it and when I woke up, I shuddered. I shivered all day long, for we had passed the sign in the night, in our sleep and there was no going back." (164)

In this land where the sign has passed in the night, there are no coordinates and there is no return, there is not even the volition of being awake. This is the limit space of illegibility, trauma and repetition.

Contradiction 7: Abjection at the Limits

As Julia Kristeva suggests in *Powers of Horror: An Essay on Abjection*:

> It is not lack of cleanliness or health that causes abjection but what disturbs identity, system, order. What does not respect borders, positions, rules ... The traitor, the liar, the criminal with a good conscience ... any crime, because it draws attention to the fragility of the law, is abject, but premeditated crime, cunning murder, hypocritical revenge are even more so because they heighten the display of such fragility.[23]

Abjection is that which challenges functioning identity and draws one toward a place where meaning collapses. The idea that abjection must be policed at the

---

23 Julia Kristeva, *Powers of Horror: An Essay on Abjection*, trans. Leon S. Roudiez (Columbia: New York University Press, 1980), 242.

boundary, so that identity, system and order are preserved is critically interesting for a work of mixed genre, which seems to be able to sit with the mixed and open-ended nature of human experience without foreclosing too quickly on meaning. Abjection brings us back to Louisa Pollit in a full circle from the American mid-1930s to the mid-1950s. Whereas Louisa's abjection was revolutionary and resistant in tenor, Emily's derives from her position as committed political writer who transforms into the premeditated traitor. The renegade position is a double position for Emily, and she has driven towards both limits with all the effort of her individualist and passionate soul. She exists on a double outside (from Left and Right) and her map for functioning identity is not available in the land she has come to inhabit, post-war and post-collaboration France. In the return to the scene of triumphal radicalism as a traitor and outlaw, Emily tries to obviate the effect of abjection by calling up the autonomy of the artist: "They lost me. I am free. I can think and write without being compelled by narrow petty mumbo-jumbo orthodox views and strait-jacket childish loyalties. Like the child who has to hit every railing with a stick, I had to hit every tenet of my faith with my pen when I wrote" (382).

Emily wants to be able to see both sides, she is interested in the whole vision and in the world at large but she does not finally want to be on the wrong side or uncomfortable or cold, and here is the American dilemma again:

> "I don't like to be a martyr, I won't be a martyr. I don't want to be on the wrong side. I wasn't born for that. How short life is! And what about the children? Oh, my, my! For them, one can't be on the wrong side: and yet we have to choose. What's the right side? I mean morally, and in terms of our natural lives? Oh, Lord! We can be torn to pieces. I won't give up the kids; and your mother and Florence will drag Olivia and Christy from us like lightning; and Giles and Lennie will be homeless. They'd have every right to grab them if we became outcasts, outlaws with the community riding us on a rail and throwing stones through our windows … " (73)

The contradiction of the desire to survive in comfort, feeding various middle-class addictions and compulsions, and the desire to be good and faithful revolutionaries, must, as Stead tells us, make for a bad end. The end in sight is not the loss of political faith one might think, but the opposite move; the reacquisition of national and class belonging by selling out their beliefs to the McCarthyists in order to placate and assuage Stephen's mother in return for financial support: "April 1950: You see, they told me that you had already done it, so I thought I'd make the record perfect. The renegade husband and wife: the perfect American couple, loyal to each other and to their country" (437).

Stead's American Tragedy

Understanding the Americans (1954) was written by Blake for Frederick Muller in London at the about the same time as the Branstens were imploding politically and personally, along with much of the American radical Left. Blake wrote about American literary history: "as with history, so with tragedy. It has been said that Americans have no sense of tragedy. But tragedy arises largely out of national defeats, or, at the least thwarted national histories"[24]. The dust jacket of Blake's *Understanding the Americans* contained this description of him: "The author, an American, ex-editor of the *Magazine of Wall Street*, believes that the depths of his people are best revealed through the medium of comedy. But even fun cannot wholly obscure the tragic-inflections of the multi-coloured play." Blake's own novels had been works of historical fiction and bore the trace of Lukács' influence, in particular *The Historical Novel* (1937).

The question of the history of this period, and its meaning for Stead and Blake's generation, made the novel deeply important to Stead, but she, like Emily, had trouble with history and with tragedy. Dreiser was the model Emily and Stead both turn to for an example of the work they most wanted to write in order to capture the epicentre of radical crisis and contradiction:

> This is what I should be doing, she thought. Dreiser is stupid, dull, his language is Teutonic, but Dreiser is powerful, dramatic, overwhelming; it's because he's honest. He's overcome by humble human tragedy and he doesn't care who knows he is. He's awestruck by riches, that's true – not me; but he's awestruck by human nature, too; and so am I; *but he's cold, penetrating and suffering, humane, an adult*. All I can do is to try to squeeze out belly-laughs and horse-laughs … "Oh, Stephen, to choose such a doomed soul! Listen, Stephen! Like us, perhaps! He makes you feel it is like us … to show this severe terrible compassion – such compassion, oh, is terror, terror." She shuddered, "Oh, I feel so cold, such terror – suppose we were all to be shown up like that; and yet," she said, straightening and looking at him with red face and brimming eyes, "*that is art*, never would I ask for another sort of sentence from the most compassionate judge! Never for the dreamstuff. He says, 'Here is the remorseless, logical, inescapable doom, he brought on himself and the twentieth century brought on him and America brought on all'. He is not, I am not, sorry for myself, or Dreiser or Clyde or us – yes, I am. Behold his unspeakable suffering, so puny, so unworthy, his, the tragedy of the century, the century of the common man, so common, so wretched … Suppose we are all to be shown up like that – *the severe terrible compassion* – *the remorseless, inescapable, logical doom*" (350–51, my emphasis).

---

24 William J. Blake, *Understanding the Americans* (London: Frederick Muller, 1954), 150.

Emily Wilkes declares this admiration for Dreiser in a conversation with Stephen late in the second half of *I'm Dying Laughing*, when Emily becomes preoccupied with undertaking "real" work. This means trying with all her might to give up writing the lucrative comic sketches that maintain the family in style and move instead into serious historical fiction. Her specific idea is to write a novel based on the late days of Marie Antoinette, who she feels is swept up and trapped in historical forces of successful revolution, much as she and Stephen are caught on the wrong side (the ironically inverse position of the now failed worker's revolution in America). Emily's insight about Dreiser's cold empathy is heartbreakingly powerful, indicating the dimension of her mind and talent as well as the impossibilities she faces in writing the kind of book that Stead writes about her.

Stead works for the first time with the question of the tragic forces of history. Stead's work was generally tied to the present of the real life models she used as characters or the present of the settings that inspired her. Her step away from contemporary events and settings and into the dialectical progress of a period and a generation was powerful, but it gave her trouble. Had she published the work when she had a first draft – in 1951 or 1952 – *I'm Dying Laughing* would have been available at roughly the same time as the early productions of Arthur Miller's *The Crucible* (1953), probably under the title of *The Renegade*. However, the real life of her models also kept running away with the novel in tragic ways. It was in 1955 that Richard Bransten, the model for Stephen Howard, committed suicide, and Ruth McKenney, the model for Emily, experienced a long-term breakdown. Stead carried the manuscript of "The Renegade" around with her, and worked on it solidly into the late 1960s, but the burden of history, the strained and strange temporalities of composition and her difficulty in finding the right detachment or distance meant that she never properly finished and fully integrated the narrative.

In *I'm Dying Laughing*, the humourist has lost all the key markers of identity and faith that stabilised her impressive dimensions. Everything has become all at once opposed to itself. Once the ironic and wise commentator on cosmic folly, the fool has instead become the centrepiece of tragic narrative in the mid twentieth-century in which nothing can be made to make sense. In light of this, Emily's end is equivocal. She seems to be disintegrating/dissolving, but this is not a resolution; it reads more as the present continuous tense of a national and personal crisis: "she began to laugh and could not stop. She lay on and rolled about the steps, endless laughter" (447). The physicality and the semiosis of Emily in this moment is overpowering as she literally stages a rehearsal of the laughing/dying predicted by the title and the epigraphs that reference appetite and denunciation. The contradiction of dying and laughing are not sublated here into a third term; they inflate instead. Emily's personal and textual inflations index the ambivalent conflict of a romantic individualism and a commitment to collective identity. Other modes of exaggeration in a rhetoric of ambivalence include the childish, the feminine and the mad, all of which Emily engages at one time or another, and here perhaps all at once.

I'm Dying Laughing is not only one of Stead's master works, it is one of the rare Anglophone literary accounts of the complex abandonment of the Left by previously committed Left supporters in the early Cold War. To this complex work, Stead brings her fearlessness about form, her commitment to the matter of life. Emily's powerful excesses, her transgressions of order, of size and speech, her disrespect for the law, her overproduction, her rebelliousness and her disruption are as much desired as they are censured by Stead's text. Her end is a cautionary tale about limit and the breaking of filiation, but also about creativity and individuality. It is very much a tale, told by an experienced fellow traveller, about the necessity of an inside of identification to secure and sustain the outside. For Stead this was political commitment and both she and Blake saw this through to the end of both their lives. They had a system – Marxism – that continued to give them a set of ideological coordinates to steer by well into the Cold War years. It was the enduring problem of no system and no theory that ensured Letty Fox, Edward Massine and Emily Wilkes could not manage to gain any purchase in their day to day struggles with American modernity. *I'm Dying Laughing* chronicles the logic of this inability to frame the capitalist totality and draws it out as an account of multiplying illegibilities and losses.

Conclusion

During Christina Stead's American years and slightly after, she produced a sequence of enormous and experimental realist novels that worked with distinct genres to deliver portraits of American life. These included domestic life in the later years of the New Deal, a revolving and evolving series of portraits of New York from the mid 1930s to the immediate post-war period, and a final portrait of national and transnational scale that addressed the McCarthyist period. This sequence delivers a certain kind of anatomy of America from an experimental realist and a woman writer situated both inside and outside the nation to which she addressed herself.

Stead's American sequence represents a powerful and unusual meditation on the matter of a nation in which the writer is a sojourner. This point of view was grounded for Stead, until the later days of drafting *I'm Dying Laughing*, in a productive and stable affiliation as a fellow traveller. This sympathy with socialist politics and aesthetics is also articulated in her work as an experimental critical realist, with an originality and scope that align her, in the twentieth century, with Thomas Mann: a fascinating comparison. Her critique of America takes up the idea that this nation in particular operates as a synonym for capital and she approaches this as an experimental realist with an interest in the clamouring and trials of her bourgeois characters.

One of my key claims in this book concerns Stead and realism. She arrived in America with a newly re-focused commitment to realism, and the American material shaped this realism as she proceeded with her sequence. I constructed an account of Stead's evolving politics and aesthetics, from her origin in Sydney through her time in Europe to the mid 1930s, and then to America (and its aftermath), demonstrating that Stead was a writer of totalities from a very early age (this explains the emphasis on Lukács in this period and in this monograph). From her provincial background she drew a sense of scale and vital materiality. In addition to growing socialist convictions, this inclined her to experiment with Surrealism and other avant-garde influences in Paris in the early 1930s and although Popular Front urgencies saw a move away from modernist experiments, the marks and traces of surrealist intensity never leave her work. Speech becomes the site for these intensities, and it comes, in time, to power Stead's novelistic totalities, as well as support the oceanic qualities that accompanied her earliest insights and inspirations as a writer. In the American novels, this intensity can and did express itself through Stead's determination to capture the American voice, both for ethnographic and political purposes. Speech and the gendering of genre are the points of focus in this book that lead the reader back again and again to the question of the literary in Stead's work.

I claim that *The Man Who Loved Children* is Stead's first American novel, following Louise Yelin's convincing move in this direction in the 1990s and Michael Ackland's more recent work on the novel in light of the New Deal years. *The Man Who Loved Children* is positioned here as a domestic novel that uses allegory to convey the scope of Stead's vision of the downwardly mobile days of the Great Depression in America. In the Washington/Annapolis house that stands in for the nation, a portrait of petty domination is foregrounded and this patriarchal domination is met by a gendered resistance, which culminates in the performance of the necessary autonomy of the revolutionary artist and the inevitability of her exit from the house of the nation.

The New York trilogy, comprising *Letty Fox: Her Luck, A Little Tea, A Little Chat* and *The People with the Dogs*, showcases a virtuosic set of modulations of the picaresque. This is the genre of wide-ranging episodic and contingent structures of incident and therefore the genre most able to display the scale and complexity of the city of New York. It is also the genre that puts its rogue protagonist to work as the only centre of action. Each of the three novels deploys a *picara* or *picaro* suited to the portrait of relations under capital that interest Stead. For Letty Fox, the "love market" and its contingencies dominate action. For Robbie Grant, financier-libertine and corrupt racketeer, the obsessive and mobile speculation in the market of women and commodities culminates in a darkly comic end. For Edward Massine, the Chekhovian dilettante and mobile family storyteller, ennui and inertia is partially surrendered for an acknowledgement that the miasma of utopia and the privilege of property ownership is not productive. He does not surrender his beloved family collective (and their collective of dogs), but he does acknowledge the changing post-war world and its requirements for him to individuate, to find energy and purpose.

I'm Dying Laughing is the American novel with the greatest scope of all, and the greatest challenges. Again, Stead focuses her response on the question of America through genre and character, and in this tragicomic masterpiece, the aperture onto America is Emily Wilkes, the female humourist. It is a novel which, as it works through questions of art, political affiliation, historical development and the fate of the radical generation of the 1930s, moves inexorably to become an American Tragedy, like the great work by Dreiser that Stead's book so often cites. In this sense, the culminating work in Stead's American sequence is a tragedy about a female

Conclusion

clown, and some of the difficulty of the work relates to this breathtakingly original move with genre and form.

Stead's capacity to focus with such intention and attention on the matter of a nation that was not her own was the product of transnational movement. Theories of the world literary space and of transnational writing have been crucial to thinking through this work, particularly the material shaped by a focus on gender. What has become even more apparent in the writing of this book is Stead's unswerving interest in the secret history and true story of women in modernity. Although Stead's work is often thought of as deploying the masculine prerogatives of epic scale and satirical criticism, nevertheless, her account of femininity and mid-century American modernity is sustained with important focus.

In her work on the great matter of America and capital, Stead's critique was choreographed through gender, genre and language, particularly speech. This fiction was powered by her sense that her proper work, apart from vitality, presence and truth, was to reveal what was hidden in social, political and economic relations. In this sense, Stead's work speaks to the contemporary work of Lauren Berlant in her national sentimentality project because of Berlant's cognate interest in uncovering the sentimental and gendered fantasies that drive the political project of nation. Her sense that a realist account of the space of national fantasy produces new genres full of the incoherent, awkward, non-ideal and messy is a tremendous rubric for reading Stead's American novels. Her discussion about her most recent project is similarly thought-provoking for work on Stead:

> My Guggenheim project, *Matter of Flatness*, approaches these questions of attachment from a different perspective. Scholars of political emotion and publics need better tools to think about multiple registers of the social/political, rather than presuming that dramatic intensities and orchestrated events are of greater significance than diffused, unaccounted-for, loosely organised, comic, or episodic forms of life.[1]

Although Berlant's great work is on affect and affectivity in the nation space, I would like to highlight her view that "loosely organised, comic or episodic forms of everyday life" are "unaccounted for" and that better tools to think about "multiple registers of the social/political". I would reiterate that Stead's secret histories of America have been achieving just this set of effects and texts since 1940. Another provocative coordinate for the scope and nature of Stead's "hidden life" project emerges in Jacques Rancière's notion of political *dissensus*:

> Political action consists in showing as political what was viewed as "social", "economic" or "*domestic*" … It is what happens whenever "domestic" agents

---

1 Lauren Berlant, quoted by Earl McCabe, "Depressive Realism: An Interview with Lauren Berlant", *Hypocrite Reader* 5 June 2011. hypocritereader.com/5/depressive-realism

– workers or women, for instance – reconfigure their quarrel as a quarrel concerning the common, that is concerning what place belongs and does not belong to it and who is able or unable to make enunciations and demonstrations about the common. It should be clear therefore that there is politics when there is a disagreement about what is politics, when the boundary separating the political from the social or the public from the domestic is put into question. Politics is a way of re-partitioning the political from the non-political. This is why it generally occurs "out of place" in a place which was not supposed to be political.[2]

Rancière's meditation on the issue of space and the terms of distribution of the boundaries of what is included or excluded, central or peripheral, visible or invisible, forms the heart of what he terms "the distribution of the sensible".[3] It seems clear that Stead's American novels worked to redistribute what can be known and counted as political, and her writing is energised and focussed by this very task of redistribution.

My claim that Stead is one of the great political women writers of the twentieth century rests at least partially on this work to redistribute what can be known and counted as political as such. She brought the transnational scope of her aesthetics and the international breadth and complexity of her political understanding to the task of engaging and representing the material specifics and symbolic resonances of the matter of America. In thinking about what has been occluded or obscured, it is exciting to note all kinds of avenues of new work arising from this attention to Stead's American novels. I suspect a productive rivalry with Faulkner in *The Man Who Loved Children*, and a less visible but no less important and fascinating set of underground dialogues between Stead and American radical women writers such as Josephine Herbst, Meridel Le Sueur and Tillie Olsen (to name a few), who were working alongside her in America during the Popular Front years. There are also inductive claims to be made about political women's writing in the transnational space from the mid-century forward, and I will argue in ongoing work that Rebecca West, Doris Lessing, Nadine Gordimer, Jamaica Kincaid and Toni Morrison are the company of writers, thinking so powerfully about the intersection of politics and aesthetics, in which Stead needs to be read.

This book emerged in tandem with new and exciting literary critical developments in the study of realism. The work of Jed Esty and Colleen Lye, Joe Cleary, Lauren Goodlad and Frederic Jameson's *The Antinomies of Realism*, has heralded the emergence of realism and realist aesthetics as newly renovated after

---

2   Jacques Rancière, "The Thinking of Dissensus: Politics and Aesthetics", in *Reading Rancière*, eds. Paul Bowman and Richard Stamp (London: Continuum, 2011), 4.
3   Jacques Rancière, *The Politics of Aesthetics: The Distribution of the Sensible,* (London: Continuum, 2004), 1.

a period of poststructuralist submergence.[4] As Lauren Goodlad has so helpfully elaborated:

> In the last decade or so a new generation of artists, historians, and literary scholars has seemed to anticipate Thomas Piketty in affirming the realist novel as an indispensable feature in the ongoing story he tells in *Capitalism in the Twenty-First Century* (2014). The sociology Giovanni Arrighi has provided a compelling frame for studying the recurrence of realisms in and across *longues durees* … Cognizant of realism's centuries-long plurality and vitality, scholars in various fields now hold that realist fiction, which responds to capitalist permutations across space and time, is a transnational medium shot through with aesthetic possibility.[5]

The terms of much of this discussion have been given over to negotiating the solidity of the Cold War binary of realism–modernism and key modernist critics have contributed work in this area. In addition to this, the study of peripheral realisms is emerging from work on transnational and world literatures. Even though there is a problem with mapping literary and political periods, and historical flattening out to be avoided, much of this analysis is provocative for thinking about Stead's work. The serious re-imagining of literary realism away from the European imperial centres is exciting for work on Stead, to which the analysis of this book contributes. With similar methodological problems with a simple diffusionist model of centre and periphery, but with no less excitement, Alison Shonkwiler and Leigh Claire La Berges' work on capitalist realism is extremely promising for Stead studies:

> Capitalist realism is both an old and a new concept for literary studies. Realism, after all has long been considered the aesthetic mode most intimate to capitalism . It is this intimacy that in the view of its admirers generates realism's depth and incisiveness of critique.[6]

---

[4] Jed Esty and Colleen Lye, "Peripheral Realisms Now", *Modern Language Quarterly* 73, no. 3 (2012), 269–88; Joe Cleary, ed, *The Cambridge Companion to Irish Modernism* (Cambridge: Cambridge University Press, 2014) and "Realism after Modernism and the Literary World-System", *Modern Language Quarterly* 73, no. 3 (2012), 255–68. See also Fredric Jameson, "Antinomies of the Realism-Modernism Debate", *Modern Language Quarterly* 73, no. 3 (2012), 475–86; *Representing Capital: A Reading of Volume One* (London: Verso, 2011); *The Political Unconscious: Narrative as a Socially Symbolic Act* (London: Routledge, 2007).

[5] Lauren Goodlad, *The Victorian Geopolitical Aesthetic: Realism, Sovereignty and Transnational Experience* (Oxford: Oxford University Press, 2015), 183.

[6] Alison Shonkwiler and Leigh Claire La Berge, eds, *Reading Capitalist Realism* (Iowa City: University of Iowa Press, 2014), 1.

Christina Stead's American sequence showcases "realism's depth and incisiveness of critique", its vitality and its set of aesthetic possibilities. Stead's American sequence started its life in some of the political and aesthetic forms of *Seven Poor Men of Sydney* at the global periphery, and perhaps even earlier in her juvenilia. Her American sequence was elaborated at the semi-periphery of America just as it was transforming into a global centre, though this was also at the moment in which Stead's political centre was being destabilised. Given that Stead was then reviewed and circulated at the centre of traditional world literary markets from the 1960s on, we must see her American sequence as a unique moment in long-form transnational twentieth-century realism. In these literary contexts, Stead's position as the greatest political woman writer of the twentieth century, who developed her American realism through the aesthetic richness and potential transgressions of the folk, the vernacular, the comic and the tragicomic is properly revealed. Further work on the secret histories of the Left experimental realists of the 1930s, effectively buried during the Cold War, will only assist this timely recognition.

Works Cited

Aaron, Daniel. *Writers on the Left: Episodes in American Literary Communism*. New York: Columbia University Press, 1992.
Ackland, Michael. "Breeding 'Reptiles of the Mind': Blake's Dialectics of Vision and Stead's Critique of Pollitry in *The Man Who Loved Children*." *Studies in the Novel* 38, no. 2 (2006): 234–49.
——. "Christina Stead and the Politics of Covert Statement." *Mosaic* 41, no. 1 (2010): 127–42.
——. *Christina Stead and the Socialist Heritage*. New York: Cambria Press, 2016.
——. "'Socialists of a New Socialism'? Christina Stead's Critique of 1930s America in *The Man Who Loved Children*." *ELH* 78, no. 2 (2011): 387–408.
Ades, Dawn and Matthew Gale. "Surrealism." *Grove Art Online*. Oxford University Press, 2003. http://bit.ly/2Ypa2gC.
Adorno, Theodor. *Notes to Literature II*. Edited by Rolf Tiedemann. Translated by Shierry Weber Nicholson. New York: Columbia University Press, 1991.
Agamben, Giorgio. *Infancy and History: The Destruction of Experience*. (1993) London: Verso, 2007.
——. *The Signature of All Things: On Method*. Translated by Luca di Santo. New York: Zone Books, 2010.
——. *Sovereign Power and Bare Life*. Translated by Daniel Heller-Roazen. Stanford: Stanford University Press, 1998.
——. *State of Exception*. Translated by Kevin Attell. Chicago: University of Chicago Press, 2005.
Agar, Jolyon. *Rethinking Marxism: From Kant and Hegel to Marx and Engels*. London: Routledge, 2006.
Ahmad, Dohra. *Rotten English: A Literary Anthology*. New York: W.W. Norton & Co, 2007.
Amariglio, Jack, Joseph W. Childers and Stephen E. Cullenberg, eds. *Sublime Economy: On the Intersection of Art and Economics*. London: Routledge, 2009.
Anderson, Edith. *Love in Exile: An American Writer's Memoir of Life in Berlin*. South Royalton, VT: Steerforth Press, 1999.
Anderson, George P. *American Modernism, 1914–1945* (Research Guide to American Literature, vol. 5). New York: Facts on File, 2010.

Appadurai, Arjun. *Modernity at Large: Cultural Dimensions of Globalization*. (1996) Minneapolis: University of Minnesota Press, 2008.
Aragon, Louis. *Paris Peasant*. (1926) Boston: Exact Change, 1994.
Aravamudan, Srinivas. "Subjects/Sovereigns/Rogues." *Eighteenth-Century Studies* 40, no. 3 (2007): 457–65.
Arendt, Hannah. *On Revolution*. (1963) London: Penguin, 1990.
Armstrong, Nancy. *Desire and Domestic Fiction: A Political History of the Novel*. Oxford: Oxford University Press, 1990.
Armstrong, Tim. *The Logic of Slavery: Debt, Technology, and Pain in American Literature*. Cambridge: Cambridge University Press, 2012.
Aronowitz, Stanley. *The Death and Rebirth of American Radicalism*. New York: Routledge, 1996.
Arthur, Jason. *Violet America: Regional Cosmopolitanism in US Fiction Since the Great Depression*. Iowa City: University of Iowa Press, 2013.
Ashcroft, Bill. *Caliban's Voice: The Transformation of English in Post-Colonial Literatures*. London: Routledge, 2009.
Atwood, Margaret. *Payback: Debt and the Shadow Side of Wealth*. Toronto: Anansi, 2008.
Auerbach, Erich. *Mimesis: The Representation of Reality in Western Literature*. Princeton, NJ: Princeton University Press, 2013.
Baker, Rebecca. "Christina Stead: The Nietzsche Connection." *Meridian: The La Trobe University English Review* 2, no. 2 (1983): 116–120.
Bahr, Ehrhard. *Weimar on the Pacific: German Exile Culture in Los Angeles and the Crisis of Modernism*. Berkeley: University of California Press, 2007.
Baker, Jennifer J. *Securing the Commonwealth: Debt, Literature, and Community in Eighteenth-Century America*. Baltimore, MD: Johns Hopkins University Press, 2005.
Bakhtin, Mikhail. "Forms of Time and of the Chronotope in the Novel." In *The Dialogic Imagination: Four Essays*, edited by Michael Holquist, translated by Caryl Emerson and Michael Holquist. Austin: University of Texas Press, 1981.
——. *Speech Genres and Other Late Essays*. Translated by Vern W. McGee. Austin: University of Texas Press, 1986.
Ballaster, Rosalind. "Manl(e)y Forms: Sex and the Female Satirist." In *Women, Texts and Histories 1575–1760*, edited by Clare Brant and Diane Purkiss. London: Routledge, 1992. 217–41.
Balshaw, Maria. *Looking for Harlem: Urban Aesthetics in African-American Literature*. London: Pluto Press, 2001.
Balzac, Honoré. *Cousin Bette*. Translated by Sylvia Raphael. (1846) Oxford: Oxford University Press, 2008.
——. *The Human Comedy: Selected Stories*. Translated by Linda Asher, Carol Cosman and Jordan Stump. New York: New York Review of Books, 2014.
——. *Père Goriot*. Translated by A.J. Krailsheimer. (1835) Oxford: Oxford University Press, 2009.
——. *The Wild Ass's Skin*. Translated by Helen Constantine. (1831) Oxford: Oxford University Press, 2012.
Barnard, Rita. *The Great Depression and the Culture of Abundance: Kenneth Fearing, Nathanael West, and Mass Culture in the 1930s*. Cambridge: Cambridge University Press, 1995.

Works Cited

Barnard Eldershaw, M. *Essays in Australian Fiction*. Melbourne: Melbourne University Press, 1938.

Barnes, Elizabeth. *States of Sympathy: Seduction and Democracy in the American Novel*. New York: Columbia University Press, 1997.

Barrish, Phillip. *The Cambridge Introduction to American Literary Realism*. Cambridge: Cambridge University Press, 2011.

Bartolovich, Crystal and Neil Lazarus, eds. *Marxism, Modernity, and Postcolonial Studies*. Cambridge, UK: Cambridge University Press, 2002.

Batchelor, David, Briony Fer, and Paul Wood. *Realism, Rationalism, Surrealism: Art between the Wars*. New Haven, CT: Yale University Press, 1994.

Bauman, Zygmunt. *Liquid Modernity*. Cambridge: Polity Press, 2000.

——. *Wasted Lives: Modernity and Its Outcasts*. (2004) Cambridge: Polity Press, 2011.

Baym, Nina. "Uncle Tom's Cabin and American Culture." *The Journal of American History* 72, no. 3 (1985): 691–92.

——. *Women's Fiction: A Guide to Novels by and about Women in America, 1820–1870*. Urbana: University of Illinois Press, 1992.

Baym, Nina and Robert S. Levine, eds. *The Norton Anthology of American Literature, Vol. 2: 1865 to the Present* (The Shorter Eighth Edition). New York: WW Norton, 2012.

Beaumont, Matthew, Andrew Hemingway, Esther Leslie and John Roberts, eds. *As Radical As Reality Itself: Essays on Marxism and Art for the 21st Century*. Bern: Peter Lang, 2007.

Beaumont, Matthew, ed. *A Concise Companion to Realism*. Malden, MA: Wiley-Blackwell, 2010.

Begam, Richard and Michael Valdez Moses, eds. *Modernism and Colonialism: British and Irish Literature, 1899–1939*. Durham, NC: Duke University Press, 2007.

Beilharz, Peter. *Zygmunt Bauman: Dialectic of Modernity*. London: Sage, 2000.

Bell, Michael, ed. *The Cambridge Companion to European Novelists*. Cambridge: Cambridge University Press, 2012.

Bender, Thomas. *The Unfinished City: New York and the Metropolitan Idea*. New York: The New Press, 2002.

Benhabib, Seyla. *The Reluctant Modernism of Hannah Arendt*. Rev. ed. Lanham, MD: Rowman & Littlefield Publishers, 2003.

Benjamin, Walter. *Charles Baudelaire: Lyric Poet in the Era of High Capitalism*. (1973) London: Verso, 1997.

——. "Surrealism: The Last Snapshot of the European Intelligentsia." In *Reflections: Essays, Aphorisms, Autobiographical Writings*, edited by Peter Demetz. (1978) New York: Schocken, 1986.

Bennett, David. *The Currency of Desire: Libidinal Economy, Psychoanalysis and the Sexual Revolution*. London: Lawrence & Wishart, 2016.

Bennett, Jane. *The Enchantment of Modern Life: Attachments, Crossings, and Ethics*. Princeton, NJ: Princeton University Press, 2001.

——. *Vibrant Matter: A Political Ecology of Things*. Durham, NC: Duke University Press, 2010.

Benstock, Shari. *Women of the Left Bank: Paris, 1900–1940*. London: Virago, 1994.

Berlant, Lauren. *The Anatomy of National Fantasy: Hawthorne, Utopia and Everyday Life*. Chicago: University of Chicago Press, 1991.

Berlant, Lauren and Sianne Ngai. "Comedy Has Issues." *Critical Inquiry* 43 (2017): 233–49.
Berman, Jessica. *Modernist Commitments: Ethics, Politics, and Transnational Modernism*. New York: Columbia University Press, 2011.
Bertens, Hans, and Theo D'Haen. *American Literature: A History*. London: Routledge, 2014.
Beston, John. "An Interview with Christina Stead." *World Literature Written in English* 15, no. 1 (1976): 87–95.
Birns, Nicholas. *Contemporary Australian Literature: A World Not Yet Dead*. Sydney: Sydney University Press, 2015.
——. "'Merely Unfriendly or Slightly Critical': Christina Stead, The Left and I'm Dying Laughing." *Australian Literary Studies* 31, no. 6 (2016).
Bjornson, Richard. *The Picaresque Hero in European Fiction*. Madison: University of Wisconsin Press, 1977.
Blackburn, Alexander. *The Myth of the Picaro: Continuity and Transformation of the Picaresque Novel, 1554–1954*. Chapel Hill: University of North Carolina Press, 1979.
Blake, Angela. *How New York Became American, 1890–1924*. Baltimore, MD: Johns Hopkins University Press, 2009.
Blake, Ann. *Christina Stead's Politics of Place*. Nedlands: University of Western Australia Press, 1999.
Blake, William J. *An American Looks at Karl Marx*. New York: Cordon Company, 1939.
——. *The Copperheads*. New York: Dial Press, 1941.
——. *Elements of Marxist Economic Theory and its Criticisms*. New York: Cordon and Co., 1940.
——. *The Painter and the Lady*. London: Cassell & Co, 1939.
——. *Understanding the Americans*. London: Frederick Muller, 1954.
Bloch, Ernst, Theodor Adorno, Walter Benjamin, Bertolt Brecht and Georg Lukács. *Aesthetics and Politics*. Afterword by Frederic Jameson. London: Verso, 1977.
Blower, Brooke Lindy. *Becoming Americans in Paris: Transatlantic Politics and Culture between the World Wars*. Oxford: Oxford University Press, 2011.
Boehn, Max and Josephine Calina. *Dolls and Puppets*. London: G.G. Harrap, 1932.
Bogardus, Ralph F, and Fred C. Hobson, eds. *Literature at the Barricades: The American Writer in the 1930s*. Tuscaloosa: University of Alabama Press, 1982.
Bohn, Willard. *The Rise of Surrealism: Cubism, Dada, and the Pursuit of the Marvelous*. Albany, NY: State University of New York Press, 2002.
Boland, Brooke. "Matter that Matters: Towards an Embodied World Literature." PhD diss. University of New South Wales, 2017.
Boone, Joseph Allen. "Of Fathers, Daughters and Theorists of Narrative Desire: At the Crossroads of Myth and Psychoanalysis in *The Man Who Loved Children*." *Contemporary Literature* 31, no. 4 (1990): 512–41.
——. *Libidinal Currents: Sexuality and the Shaping of Modernism*. Chicago: University of Chicago Press, 1998.
Boose, Lynda E. and Betty S. Flowers. *Daughters and Fathers*. Baltimore, MD: John Hopkins University Press, 1989.
Bouvet, Vincent and Gérard Durozoi. *Paris between the Wars, 1919–1939: Art, Life and Culture*. New York: Vendome Press, 2010.
Bradley, Fiona. *Surrealism*. Cambridge: Cambridge University Press, 1997.

Brandon, Ruth. *Surreal Lives: The Surrealists, 1917–1945*. New York: Grove Press, 1999.
Breckenridge, Carol A., et al. *Cosmopolitanism*. Durham, NC: Duke University Press, 2002.
Breton, André. *Manifestoes of Surrealism*. Translated by Richard Seaver and Helen R. Lane. (1962) Ann Arbor: University of Michigan Press, 2008.
——. *Nadja*. (1928) New York: Grove Press, 1999.
Brigham, Ann. *American Road Narratives: Reimagining Mobility in Literature and Film*. Charlottesville: University of Virginia Press, 2015.
Brister, Rose. "Placing Women's Bodies in Eran Riklis's *The Syrian Bride*." *Signs* 39, no. 4 (2014): 927–48.
Brody, David. *The American Labor Movement*. New York: Harper and Row, 1971.
Bronner, Stephen E. *Modernism at the Barricades: Aesthetics, Politics, Utopia*. New York: Columbia University Press, 2012.
——. "Modernism, Surrealism, and the Political Imaginary." *Logos: A Journal of Modern Society and Culture* 11, no. 1 (2012).
Brooks, Peter. "Introduction." *The Human Comedy: Selected Stories by Honore de Balzac*. New York: New York Review of Books, 2014. vii–xxi.
——. *The Melodramatic Imagination: Balzac, Henry James, Melodrama and the Mode of Excess*. New Haven, CT: Yale University Press, 1976.
Brooker, Peter. *New York Fictions: Modernity, Postmodernism, the New Modern*. London: Longman, 1996.
Brown, Heather A. *Marx on Gender and the Family: A Critical Study*. Chicago: Haymarket Books, 2013.
Brydon, Diana. *Christina Stead*. London: Macmillan, 1987.
Budd, Louis J. "The American Background." In *The Cambridge Companion to American Realism and Naturalism: Howells to London,* edited by Donald Pizer. Cambridge: Cambridge University Press, 1995. 21–46.
Bürger, Peter. *Theory of the Avant-Garde*. (1973) Minneapolis: University of Minnesota Press, 2002.
Burke, Kenneth. *The Philosophy of Literary Form: Studies in Symbolic Action*. Berkeley: University of California Press, 2000.
Burns, Graham. "The Moral Design of *The Man Who Loved Children*." *Critical Review* 14 (1971): 38–61.
Burns, Lorna. "Uncovering the Marvellous: Surrealism and the Writings of Wilson Harris." *Journal of Postcolonial Writing* 47, no. 1 (2011): 52–64.
Byron, Glennis. *Dramatic Monologue*. London: Routledge, 2003.
Cahan, Abraham. *The Rise of David Levinsky*. Mineola, NY: Dover Publications, 2002.
Calderbank, Michael. "Surreal Dreamscapes: Walter Benjamin and the Arcades." *Papers of Surrealism* 1 (2003): 1–13.
Calisher, Hortense. "Stead." *Yale Review* 76 (1987): 169–77.
Campbell, Donna. "American Literary Naturalism: Critical Perspectives." *Literature Compass* 8, no. 8 (2011): 499–513.
Carter, Angela. *Expletives Deleted: Selected Writings*. London: Vintage, 1993.
Carter, David. *Always Almost Modern: Australian Print Cultures and Modernity*. Melbourne: Australian Scholarly Publishing, 2013.
Carter, David, and Roger Osborne. *Australian Books and Authors in the American Marketplace 1840s–1940s*. Sydney: Sydney University Press, 2018.

Casanova, Pascale. *The World Republic of Letters*. Translated by Malcolm DeBevoise. (1999) Cambridge, MA: Harvard University Press, 2007.
Casey, Janet Galligani, ed. *The Novel and the American Left: Critical Essays on Depression-Era Fiction*. Iowa City: University of Iowa Press, 2004.
Cassuto, Leonard and Clare Virginia Eby, eds. *The Cambridge Companion to Theodore Dreiser*. Cambridge: Cambridge University Press, 2004.
Cather, Willa. *The Song of the Lark*. (1915) New York: Penguin Books, 1999.
Caute, David. *The Fellow-Travellers: Intellectual Friends of Communism*. New Haven, CT: Yale University Press, 1988.
Cavarero, Adriana. *For More Than One Voice: Toward a Philosophy of Vocal Expression*. Trans. Paul A. Kottman. Stanford: Stanford University Press, 2005.
Ceplair, Larry and Steven Englund. *The Inquisition in Hollywood: Politics in the Film Community, 1930–60*. Urbana: University of Illinois Press, 2003.
Childs, Peter. *Modernism and the Post-Colonial: Literature and Empire 1885–1930*. London: Continuum, 2007.
Clark, John R. *The Modern Satiric Grotesque and Its Traditions*. Lexington: The University Press of Kentucky, 1991.
Clark, Katerina. "M.M. Bakhtin and 'World Literature.'" *Journal of Narrative Theory* 32, no. 3 (2002). 266–92.
——. *Moscow, the Fourth Rome: Stalinism, Cosmopolitanism, and the Evolution of Soviet Culture, 1931–1941*. Cambridge, MA: Harvard University Press, 2011.
Cleary, Joe, ed. *The Cambridge Companion to Irish Modernism*. Cambridge: Cambridge University Press, 2014.
——. "Realism after Modernism and the Literary World-System." *Modern Language Quarterly* 73, no. 3 (2012): 255–268.
Clifford, James. "On Ethnographic Surrealism." *Comparative Studies in Society and History* 23, no. 4 (1981): 539–564.
——. *Routes: Travel and Translation in the Late Twentieth Century*. Cambridge, MA: Harvard University Press, 1997.
Clingman, Stephen. *The Grammar of Identity: Transnational Fiction and the Nature of the Boundary*. Oxford: Oxford University Press, 2009.
Cohen, Margaret. *The Novel and the Sea*. Princeton, NJ: Princeton University Press, 2012.
——. *Profane Illumination: Walter Benjamin and the Paris of Surrealist Revolution*. Berkeley: University of California Press, 1995.
Cohen, Margaret and Christopher Prendergast, eds. *Spectacles of Realism: Body, Gender, Genre*. Minneapolis: University of Minnesota Press, 1995.
Conn, Peter J. *The American 1930s: A Literary History*. Cambridge: Cambridge University Press, 2009.
Connor, Steven. *Dumbstruck: A Cultural History of Ventriloquism*. Oxford: Oxford University Press, 2000.
Coole, Diana H, and Samantha Frost, ed. *New Materialisms: Ontology, Agency, and Politics*. Durham, NC: Duke University Press, 2010.
Cooney, Terry A. *The Rise of the New York Intellectuals: Partisan Review and Its Circle*. Madison: University of Wisconsin Press, 1986.
Cooppan, Vilashini. *Worlds Within: National Narratives and Global Connections in Postcolonial Writing*. Stanford: Stanford University Press, 2009.

Costello, Bonnie. "The Tragicomic Mode in Modern American Poetry: 'Awful but Cheerful.'" In *A Companion to Poetic Genre*, edited by Erik Matiny. Hoboken, NJ: Wiley-Blackwell, 2012.

Cottington, David. *The Avant-Garde: A Very Short Introduction*. Oxford: Oxford University Press, 2013.

Cowden, Stephen. "Christina Stead and the 'Marxist Imaginary.'" *Southerly* 63, no. 3 (2003–4): 63–75.

Craig, Randall. *The Tragicomic Novel: Studies in a Fictional Mode from Meredith to Joyce*. Newark: University of Delaware Press, 1989.

Crane, Stephen. *Maggie, a Girl of the Streets and Selected Stories*. (1893) New York: Signet Classics, 2006.

Cruz, Anne J. *Discourses of Poverty: Social Reform and the Picaresque Novel in Early Modern Spain*. Toronto: University of Toronto Press, 1999.

Cunningham, David. "The Contingency of Cheese: On Fredric Jameson's *The Antinomies of Realism*." *Radical Philosophy: Philosophical Journal of the Independent Left* 187 (2014).

Cunningham, Valentine. "Twentieth-Century Fictional Satire." In *A Companion to Satire*, edited by Ruben Quintero. Malden, UK: Blackwell Publishing, 2007. 400–33.

Damrosch, David. *How to Read World Literature*. Chichester: Wiley-Blackwell, 2009.

David-Fox, Michael. "The Fellow Travellers Revisited: The 'Cultured West' through Soviet Eyes." *The Journal of Modern History* 75, no. 2 (2003): 300–35.

Davidson, Cathy N. *Revolution and the Word: The Rise of the Novel in America*. New York: Oxford University Press, 1986.

Davis, D.D. *Breaking Up (at) Totality: A Rhetoric of Laughter*. Carbondale: Southern Illinois University Press, 2000.

Dawes, Greg. "Realism, Surrealism, Socialist Realism and Neruda's 'Guided Spontaneity.'" *Cultural Logic* 6 (2003).

Day, Gary. *Class*. London: Routledge, 2001.

De Kretser, Michelle. "*The Man Who Loved Children* by Christina Stead." *The Monthly*, November 2010. http://bit.ly/2M2HXdN.

Debouzek, Jeanette. "The 'Ethnographic Surrealism' of Jean Rouch." *Visual Anthropology* 2 (1989): 301–15.

Deleuze, Gilles. *Bergsonism*. Translated by Hugh Tomlinson and Barbara Habberjam. (1988) New York: Zone Books, 2006.

Den Tandt, Christophe. *The Urban Sublime in American Literary Naturalism*. Urbana: University of Illinois Press, 1998.

Denning, Michael. *The Cultural Front: The Laboring of American Culture in the Twentieth Century*. London: Verso, 1998.

——. *Culture in the Age of Three Worlds*. London: Verso, 2004.

Dentith, Simon. *Bakhtinian Thought: An Introductory Reader*. London: Routledge, 1996.

Derrida, Jacques. *Rogues: Two Essays on Reason*. Stanford: Stanford University Press, 2005.

——. *Specters of Marx: The State of the Debt, the Work of Mourning and the New International*. Translated by Peggy Kamuf. New York: Routledge, 2006.

Derwin, Susan. *The Ambivalence of Form: Lukács, Freud and the Novel*. Baltimore, MD: Johns Hopkins University Press, 1992.

Dietrich, Julia. *The Old Left in History and Literature*. New York: Twayne Publishers, 1996.

Dimock, Wai Chee. "Literature for the Planet." *PMLA* 116, no. 1 (2001): 173-188.
———. *Through Other Continents: American Literature Across Deep Time*. Princeton, NJ: Princeton University Press, 2006.
Dionne, Craig, and Steve Mentz, eds. *Rogues and Early Modern English Culture*. Ann Arbor: University of Michigan Press, 2006.
Dixon, Robert. "Australian Literature, Scale, and the Problem of the World". In *Text, Translation, Transnationalism: World Literature in 21st Century Australia*, edited by Peter Morgan. Melbourne: Australian Scholarly Publishing, 2016. 173-95.
———. "National Literatures, Scale and the Problem of the World". *JASAL: Journal of the Association for the Study of World Literature* 15, no. 3 (2015): 1-10.
Dixon, Robert and Nicholas Birns, eds. *Reading Across the Pacific: Australia–United States Intellectual Histories*. Sydney: Sydney University Press, 2010.
Dixon, Robert and Veronica Kelly, eds. *Impact of the Modern: Vernacular Modernities in Australia 1870s–1960s*. Sydney: Sydney University Press, 2008.
Dizard, Robin. "Changing the Subject: The Early Novels of Christina Stead". PhD diss., University of Massachusetts, 1984. ProQuest (AAI8500069).
Dorman, Joseph. *Arguing the World: The New York Intellectuals in Their Own Words*. Chicago: University of Chicago Press, 2001.
Dos Passos, John. *Manhattan Transfer*. (1925) Boston: Houghton Mifflin, 2000.
Douglas, Ann. *Terrible Honesty: Mongrel Manhattan in the 1920s*. New York: Farrar, Straus & Giroux, 1996.
Doyle, Jennifer. "The Rhetoric of Prostitution". In *Sublime Economy: On the Intersection of Art and Economics,* edited by Jack Amariglio, Joseph W. Childers and Stephen E. Cullenberg. London: Routledge, 2009. 275-90.
Doyle, Laura and Laura A. Winkiel, eds. *Geomodernisms: Race, Modernism, Modernity*. Bloomington: Indiana University Press, 2005.
Dreiser, Theodore. *An American Tragedy*. (1925) New York: Signet Classics, 2010.
———. *The Financier*. (1914) New York: Penguin Books, 2008.
Duffy, Julia. "The Grain of the Voice in Christina Stead's *The Man Who Loved Children*". *Antipodes* 4, no. 1 (1990): 48-51.
Dunbar, David S., and Kenneth T. Jackson, eds. *Empire City: New York through the Centuries*. New York: Columbia University Press, 2005.
DuPlessis, Rachel Blau. "Quodlibet: Or, The Pleasures of Engagement". *Contemporary Women's Writing* 1, no. 1/2 (2007): 4-13.
During, Simon. "World Literature, Stalinism and the nation: Christina Stead as Lost Object", *Exit Capitalism: Literary Culture, Theory and Post-Secular Modernity*. London: Routledge, 2009.
Duschinsky, Robbie and Emma Wilson. "Flat Affect, Joyful Politics and Enthralled Attachments: Engaging with the Work of Lauren Berlant". *International Journal of Politics, Culture and Society* 28, no. 3 (2015): 179-90.
Duval, Edwin M. "Rabelais and French Renaissance Satire". In *A Companion to Satire*, edited by Ruben Quintero. Malden: Blackwell Publishing, 2007. 70-85.
Eagleton, Terry. "Pork Chops and Pineapples". Review of *Mimesis: The Representation of Reality in Western Literature* by Erich Auerbach, with an introduction by Edward Said. *London Review of Books*, 23 October 2003: 17-19.

Edmunds, Susan. *Grotesque Relations: Modernist Domestic Fiction and the US Welfare State*. Oxford: Oxford University Press, 2008.
Eldridge, David. *American Culture in the 1930s*. Edinburgh: Edinburgh University Press, 2010.
Ellis, Edward R., and Jeanyee Wong. *The Epic of New York City*. New York: Carroll & Graf, 2005.
Emery, Mary Lou. "The Poetics of Labour in Jean Rhys's Carribbean Modernism". *Women: A Cultural Review* 23, no. 4 (2012).
Engels, Friedrich. *The Origin of the Family: Private Property and the State*, rev. trans. Alec West. (1884) New York: International, 1972.
Entin, Joseph B. *Sensational Modernism: Experimental Fiction and Photography in Thirties America*. Chapel Hill: University of North Carolina Press, 2007.
Esty, Jed and Colleen Lye. "Peripheral Realisms Now." *Modern Language Quarterly* 73, no. 3 (2012): 269–88.
Faulkner, William. *Absalom, Absalom!* (1936) New York: Vintage, 2005.
——. *As I Lay Dying: The Corrected Text*. (1930) New York: Vintage Books, 1990.
——. *Light in August*. (1932) New York: Vintage Books, 2005.
——. *The Reivers: A Reminiscence*. (1962) New York: Vintage books, 1999.
——. *The Sound and the Fury*. (1929) New York: Vintage Books, 2005.
Feenberg, Andrew. *The Philosophy of Praxis: Marx, Lukács, and the Frankfurt School*. London: Verso, 2014.
Felman, Shoshana. *The Scandal of the Speaking Body: Don Juan with J.L. Austin, or Seduction in Two Languages*. Stanford: Stanford University Press, 2003.
Ferraro, Thomas J. *Ethnic Passages: Literary Immigrants in Twentieth-Century America*. Chicago: University of Chicago Press, 1993.
Ferris, David S. *The Cambridge Introduction to Walter Benjamin*. Cambridge: Cambridge University Press, 2008.
Fetterley, Judith and Marjorie Pryse. *Writing Out of Place: Regionalism, Women, and American Literary Culture*. Urbana: University of Illinois Press, 2003.
Fielding, Henry. *The History of Tom Jones: A Foundling*. (1749) London: Collins, 1955.
Filewood, Alan. "Authorship, Left Modernism, and Communist Power in *Eight Men Speak*: A Reflection". *Canadian Literature: A Quarterly of Criticism and Review* 209 (2011): 11–30.
Fitch, Noel Riley. *Sylvia Beach and the Lost Generation: A History of Literary Paris in the Twenties and Thirties*. New York: Norton, 1985.
Flaubert, Gustave. *Sentimental Education: The Story of a Young Man*. Translated by Helen Constantine and Patrick Coleman. (1869) Oxford: Oxford University Press, 2016.
Fluck, Winfried. "American Culture and Modernity: A Tale Twice Told". In *Theories of American Culture, Theories of American Studies*, edited by Winfried Fluck and Thomas Claviez. Tubingen: Gunter Narr Verlag, 2003: 65–80.
Friedman, Ellen G. "Where Are the Missing Contents? (Post)Modernism, Gender, and the Canon". *PMLA* 108, no. 2 (1993): 240–52.
Foley, Barbara. *Radical Representations: Politics and Form in US Proletarian Fiction, 1929-1941*. Durham, NC: Duke University Press, 1993.
Folsom, Franklin. *Days of Anger, Days of Hope: A Memoir of the League of American Writers*. Colorado: University of Colorado Press, 1994.

Foucault, Michel. "What Is Critique?" In *The Politics of Truth: Michel Foucault*, edited by Sylvère Lotringer and Lysa Hochroch. New York: Semiotext(e), 1997. 23–82.

Fowler, Alistair. *Kinds of Literature: An Introduction to the Theory of Genre and Modes.* Cambridge, MA: Harvard University Press, 1982.

Fox, Ralph. *The Novel and the People.* London: Lawrence & Wishart, 1937.

Fraiman, Susan. *Extreme Domesticity: A View from the Margins.* New York: Columbia University Press, 2017.

——. *Unbecoming Women: British Women Writers and the Novel of Development.* New York: Columbia University Press, 1993.

Francus, Marilyn. *Monstrous Motherhood: Eighteenth-Century Culture and the Ideology of Domesticity.* Baltimore, MD: Johns Hopkins University Press, 2012.

Friedman, Edward H. *The Antiheroine's Voice: Narrative Discourse and Transformations of the Picaresque.* Columbia: University of Missouri Press, 1987.

Freeman, Joseph et al., eds. *Proletarian Literature in the United States: An Anthology.* New York: International Publishers, 1935.

Frow, John. *Character and Person.* Oxford: Oxford University Press, 2014.

——. *Genre.* London and New York: Routledge, 2006.

Frye, Northrop. *Anatomy of Criticism: Four Essays.* (1957) Princeton, NJ: Princeton University Press, 2000.

Fuchs Abrams, Sabrina, ed. *Literature of New York.* Newcastle upon Tyne: Cambridge Scholars Publishing, 2009.

Gallagher, Catherine. *The Body Economic: Life, Death and Sensation in Political Economy and the Victorian Novel.* Princeton, NJ: Princeton University Press, 2008.

Gallagher, Dorothy. *Lillian Hellman: An Imperious Life.* New Haven, CT: Yale University Press, 2014.

Gardiner, Judith Kegan. "Male Narcissism, Capitalism and the Daughter of The Man Who Loved Children". *The Magic Phrase: Critical Essays on Christina Stead*, edited by Margaret Harris. St Lucia: University of Queensland Press, 2000. 145–62.

——. *Rhys, Stead, Lessing and the Politics of Empathy.* Bloomington: Indiana University Press, 1989.

Gatti, Alberta. "Satire of the Spanish Golden Age". In Ruben Quintero, *A Companion to Satire*. Malden, MD: Blackwell Publishing, 2007. 86–100.

Geering, R.G. Preface to *I'm Dying Laughing: The Humourist* by Christina Stead. (1986) London: Penguin, 1989.

——. "I'm Dying Laughing: Behind the Scenes". *Southerly* 4, no. 3 (1987): 309–17.

——. *Christina Stead.* New York: Twayne, 1969.

Genter, Robert. *Late Modernism: Art, Culture, and Politics in Cold War America.* Philadelphia: University of Pennsylvania Press, 2010.

Gilbert, James. *Writers and Partisans: A History of Literary Radicalism in America.* New York: Columbia University Press, 1992.

Giles, Paul. *Antipodean America: Australasia and the Constitution of US Literature.* Oxford: Oxford University Press, 2014.

Gillen, Paul and Devleena Ghosh. *Colonialism and Modernity.* Sydney: UNSW Press, 2007.

Godden, Richard. *Fictions of Capital: The American Novel from James to Mailer.* Cambridge: Cambridge University Press, 1990.

Goffman, Ethan and Daniel Morris, eds. *The New York Public Intellectuals and Beyond: Exploring Liberal Humanism, Jewish Identity, and the American Protest Tradition*. West Lafayette, IN: Purdue University Press, 2009.

Gold, Michael. *Jews without Money*. New York: Public Affairs, 2009.

Goldman, Michael. *The Actor's Freedom: Toward a Theory of Drama*. New York: Viking Press, 1975.

Goodlad, Lauren. Introduction: Worlding Realisms Now. *Novel* 1 August 2016 49, no. 2: 183–201.

———. *The Victorian Geopolitical Aesthetic: Realism, Sovreignty and Transnational Experience*. Oxford: Oxford University Press, 2015.

Gorky, Maxim, "Soviet Literature". In *Soviet Writer's Congress 1934: The Debate on Socialist Realism and Modernism in the Soviet Union*. By Maxim Gorky, Karl Radek, Nikolai Bukharin, Andrey Zhdanov. et al. London: Lawrence & Wishart, 1977.

Gorky, Maxim, Karl Radek, Nikolai Bukharin, Andrey Zhdanov et al. *Soviet Writer's Congress 1934: The Debate on Socialist Realism and Modernism in the Soviet Union*. London: Lawrence & Wishart, 1977.

Graeber, David. *Debt: The First 5000 Years*. New York: Melville House, 2014.

Gray, Richard T. *Money Matters: Economics and the German Cultural Imagination, 1770–1850*. Seattle: University of Washington Press, 2008.

Green, Dorothy. "*The Man Who Loved Children*: Storm in a Tea-Cup". In *The Australian Experience: Critical Essays on Australian Novels*, ed. W.S. Ramson. Canberra: Australian National University Press, 1974. 174–208.

Grewal, Inderpal and Caren Kaplan, eds. *Scattered Hegemonies: Postmodernity and Transnational Feminist Practices*. Minneapolis: University of Minnesota Press, 1994.

Gribble, Jennifer. *Christina Stead*. Melbourne: Oxford University Press, 1994.

Griffin, Dustin H. *Satire: A Critical Reintroduction*. Lexington: University Press of Kentucky, 1994.

Grosz, Elizabeth A. *Becoming Undone: Darwinian Reflections on Life, Politics, and Art*. Durham, NC: Duke University Press, 2011.

———. *The Nick of Time: Politics, Evolution, and the Untimely*. Durham, NC: Duke University Press, 2004.

Guilhamet, Leon. *Satire and the Transformation of Genre*. Philadelphia: University of Pennsylvania Press, 1987.

Guillen, Claudio. *The Anatomies of Roguery: A Comparative Study in the Origins and the Nature of Picaresque Literature*. New York: Garland Publishers, 1987.

Guillory, John. *Cultural Capital: The Problem of Literary Canon Formation*. Chicago: University of Chicago Press, 1995.

Gurock, Jeffrey S. *Jews in Gotham: New York Jews in a Changing City, 1920–2010*. New York: New York University Press, 2012.

Halttunen, Karen. *Confidence Men and Painted Women: A Study of Middle-Class Culture in America, 1830–1870*. New Haven, CT: Yale University Press, 1982.

Hardwick, Elizabeth. *A View of My Own: Essays on Literature and Society*. New York: Ecco Press, 1982.

———. *American Fictions*. New York: The Modern Library, 1999.

Harris, Margaret. "Christina Stead's Earliest Publications". *Australian Literary Studies* 31, no. 6 (2016).

——. "Christina Stead's Human Comedy: The American Sequence". *World Literature Written in English* 32, no. 1 (1992): 42–51.

——, ed. *Dearest Munx: The Love Letters of Christina Stead and William Blake*. Carlton, Vic.: Melbourne University Press, 2005.

——. Introduction to *The Salzburg Tales* by Christina Stead. Carlton, Vic.: Melbourne University Press, 2016. vii–xv.

——, ed. *The Magic Phrase: Critical Essays on Christina Stead*. St Lucia: University of Queensland Press, 2000.

Harker, Jamie. *America the Middlebrow: Women's Novels, Progressivism, and Middlebrow Authorship between the Wars*. Amherst: University of Massachusetts Press, 2007.

Hart, Matthew. *Nations of Nothing but Poetry: Modernism, Transnationalism, and Synthetic Vernacular Writing*. New York: Oxford University Press, 2010.

Hartley, Daniel. "The Concept of Totality in Lukács and Jameson". Draft working paper for the Historical Materialism Conference, London, 2010.

Hatten, Charles. *The End of Domesticity: Alienation from the Family in Dickens, Eliot, and James*. Newark: University of Delaware Press, 2010.

Hedges, Inez. Review of *Morning Star: Surrealism, Marxism, Anarchism, Situation-ism, Utopia* by Michael Lowy. *Socialism and Democracy* 24, no. 2 (2010). http://bit.ly/2WhIDQu.

Hefner, Brooks E. "'You've Got to Be Modernistic': American Vernacular Modernism: 1910-1937." Dissertation, City University of New York, 2009.

Hemingway, Andrew. *Artists on the Left: American Artists and the Communist Movement, 1926-1956*. New Haven, CT: Yale University Press, 2002.

Herbst, Josephine. *Pity Is Not Enough*. Urbana: University of Illinois Press, 1998.

Hill, Barry. "Christina Stead at 80 Says Love is her Religion", *Age*, 17 July 1982, 2.

Hirst, David B. *Tragicomedy*. London: Methuen, 1984.

Hodgart, Matthew. *Satire: Origins and Principles*. (1970) New Brunswick, NJ: Transaction Publishers, 2010.

Hollier, Denis. "Surrealism and Its Discontents". *Papers of Surrealism* 7 (2007): 1–16.

Holquist, Michael. *Dialogism: Bakhtin and His World*. (1990) London: Routledge, 2002.

Hooton, Joy. "Mermaid and Minotaur in *The Man Who Loved Children*". *Meridian: The La Trobe University English Review* 8, no. 2 (1989): 127–39.

Hopkins, David. *Dada and Surrealism: A Very Short Introduction*. Oxford: Oxford University Press, 2004.

Horkheimer, Max and Theodor W. Adorno. *Dialectic of Enlightenment*. Edited by Gunzelin Schmid Noerr. Translated by Edmund Jephcott. Stanford: Stanford University Press, 1992.

Hussey, Andrew. "Paris: Symbolism, Impressionism, Cubism, Surrealism". In *The Oxford Handbook of Modernisms*, edited by Peter Brooker, Andrzej Gasiorek, Deborah Longworth and Andrew Thacke. Oxford: Oxford University Press, 2010. 655–68.

Hyde, Lewis. *Trickster Makes this World: Mischief, Myth and Art*. New York: Farrar, Straus & Giroux, 1998.

Hyman, Louis. *Debtor Nation: The History of America in Red Ink*. Princeton, NJ: Princeton University Press, 2011.

Indyk, Ivor. "Provincialism and Encyclopaedism". *Island* 127 (2011): 78–92.

Irr, Caren. *The Suburb of Dissent: Cultural Politics in the United States and Canada during the 1930s*. Durham, NC: Duke University Press, 1998.

Jackson, Robert. *Seeking the Region in American Literature and Culture: Modernity, Dissidence, Innovation*. Baton Rouge: Louisiana State University Press, 2005.

Jacobson, Kristin J. *Neodomestic American Fiction*. Columbus: Ohio State University Press, 2010.

James, David. "Realism, Late Modernist Abstraction, and Sylvia Townsend Warner's Fictions of Impersonality". *Modernism/Modernity* 12, no. 1 (2005): 111–31.

Jameson, Fredric. *The Antimonies of Realism*. London: Verso, 2013.

——. "Antinomies of the Realism-Modernism Debate." *Modern Language Quarterly* 73, no. 3 (2012). 475–86.

——. *The Political Unconscious: Narrative as a Socially Symbolic Act*. (1981) London: Routledge, 2007.

——. "Realism and Utopia in *The Wire*." *Criticism* 52, no. 3 (2010): 359-372.

——. *Representing Capital: A Reading of Volume One*. London: Verso, 2011.

——. "Third-World Literature in the Era of Multinational Capitalism" *Social Text*, no. 15, (1986), 65–88. https://doi.org/10.2307/466493.

Jarrell, Randall. "An Unread Book". Introduction to *The Man Who Loved Children* by Christina Stead. Harmondsworth: Penguin Books, 1970.

Jay, Martin. *Marxism and Totality: The Adventures of a Concept from Lukács to Habermas*. Berkeley: University of California Press, 1984.

Joannou, Maroula. *Women Writers of the 1930s: Gender, Politics and History*. Edinburgh: Edinburgh University Press, 1999.

Jolas, Eugene. "Proclamation". *Transition* 16/17 (June 1929).

Jones, Donna. *The Racial Discourses of Life Philosophy: Négritude, Vitalism and Modernity*. New York: Columbia University Press, 2010

Jones, Gavin R. *Failure and the American Writer: A Literary History*. Cambridge: Cambridge University Press, 2014.

——. *Strange Talk: The Politics of Dialect Literature in Gilded Age America*. Berkeley: University of California Press, 1999.

Joseph, Philip. *American Literary Regionalism in a Global Age*. Baton Rouge: Louisiana State University Press, 2007.

Jumonville, Neil. *Critical Crossings: The New York Intellectuals in Postwar America*. Berkeley: University of California Press, 1991.

——. *The New York Intellectuals Reader*. New York: Routledge, 2007.

Kadarkay, Arpad. *The Lukács Reader*. Oxford: Blackwell, 1995.

Kairoff, Claudia Thomas. "Gendering Satire: Behn to Burney", In *A Companion to Satire*, edited by Ruben Quintero. Malden, MD: Blackwell Publishing, 2007. 276–92.

Kalaidjian, Walter B. *American Culture between the Wars: Revisionary Modernism and Postmodern Critique*. New York: Columbia University Press, 1993.

——. *The Cambridge Companion to American Modernism*. Cambridge: Cambridge University Press, 2008.

Kaplan, Amy. *The Anarchy of Empire in the Making of US Culture*. Cambridge, MA: Harvard University Press, 2005.

——. *The Social Construction of American Realism*. Chicago: University of Chicago Press, 1992.

Kazin, Alfred. *On Native Grounds: An Interpretation of Modern American Prose Literature*. San Diego: Harcourt Brace, 1995.

Kazin, Alfred. Review of *House of All Nations* by Christina Stead, *New York Herald Tribune*, 12 June, 1938, 1.

Keavney, Kay. "Ranked with the Immortals: Christina Stead", *The Australian Women's Weekly*, 17 November 1976, 71–72.

Kelly, Julia. "The Ethnographic Turn". In *A Companion to Dada and Surrealism*, edited by David Hopkins. New York: John Wiley, 2016. 319–33.

Kennedy, J Gerald. *Imagining Paris: Exile, Writing, and American Identity*. New Haven, CT: Yale University Press, 1993.

Kerman, Sarah. "Speaking for American: Modernist Voices and Political Representation 1910–1940". Dissertation. University of Pennsylvania, 2010.

Kessner, Thomas. "Fiorello H. LaGuardia and the Challenge of Democratic Planning". In *Landscape of Modernity: Essays on New York City 1900–1940*, edited by David Ward and Olivier Zunz. New York: Russell Sage Foundation, 1992.

Kinross-Smith, Graeme. "Christina Stead: A Profile". *Westerly* 1 (1976): 67–76.

Kiralyfalvi, Bela. *The Aesthetics of György Lukács*. Princeton, NJ: Princeton University Press, 2015.

Kohlmann, Benjamin. *Committed Styles: Modernism, Politics, and Left-Wing Literature in the 1930s*. Oxford: Oxford University Press, 2014.

Kreilkamp, Ivan. *Voice and the Victorian Storyteller*. Cambridge: Cambridge University Press, 2005.

Kristeva, Julia. *Powers of Horror: An Essay on Abjection*. Translated by Leon S. Roudiez. Columbia: New York University Press, 1980.

Kuhn, Rick. *Henryk Grossman and the Recovery of Marxism*. Urbana: University of Illinois, 2007.

Kunkel, Benjamin. "Forgive Us Our Debts: The History of Debt". *London Review of Books* 34, no. 9 (10 May 2012), 23–29.

Kutulas, Judy. *The Long War: The Intellectual People's Front and Anti-Stalinism, 1930–1940*. Durham, NC: Duke University Press, 1995.

Lambert, Joshua N. *American Jewish Fiction: A JPS Guide*. Philadelphia, PA: The Jewish Publication Society, 2009.

Landay, Lori. *Madcaps, Screwballs and Con Women: The Female Trickster in American Culture*. Philadelphia: University of Pennsylvania Press, 1998.

Lang, Jessica. "Scratching the Surface: Reading Character in Female Quixotism". *Texas Studies in Literature and Language* 51, no. 2 (2009): 119–41.

Lardner, Ring, Jr. *The Ecstasy of Owen Muir*. (1954) Amherst, NY: Prometheus Books, 1997.

Larsen, Neil. "Preselective Affinities: Surrealism and Marxism in Latin America". *Socialism and Democracy* 14, no. 1 (2000): 21–34. .

Laskin, David. *Partisans: Marriage, Politics, and Betrayal Among the New York Intellectuals*. Chicago: The University of Chicago Press, 2001.

Lawall, Sarah, ed. and Introduction. *Reading World Literature: Theory, History, Practice*. Austin: University of Texas Press, 1994.

Lawson, Elizabeth. "Louie's Mother: The Feminist Inscape of *The Man Who Loved Children*". *Meridian: The La Trobe University English Review* 8, no. 2 (1989): 114–26.

Lazzarato, Maurizio. *The Making of the Indebted Man: An Essay on the Neoliberal Condition*. Los Angeles, CA: Semiotext(e), 2012.

Lazzarato, Maurizio and Joshua Jordan. *Governing by Debt*. South Pasadena, CA: Semiotext(e), 2015.

Le Sueur, Meridel. *The Girl*. (1978) Albuquerque, NM: West End Press, 2006.

Lears, Jackson. *Something for Nothing: Luck in America*. Penguin: New York, 2003.

Lee, Benjamin and Edward LiPuma, "Culture of Circulation: The Imaginations of Modernity", *Public Culture* 14, no. 1 (2002): 191–213.

Lee, Judith Yaross. "The International Twain and American Nationalist Humor: Vernacular Humor as a Post-Colonial Rhetoric". *The Mark Twain Annual* 6 (2008).

Lehan, Richard. "The European Background". In *The Cambridge Companion to American Realism and Naturalism: Howells to London*, edited by Donald Pizer. Cambridge: Cambridge University Press, 1995. 47–73.

Leichner, Amber Harris. "'To Bend Without Breaking': American Women's Authorship and the New Woman, 1900–1935." Dissertation. University of Nebraska, 2012.

Leitch, Vincent B. *American Literary Criticism Since the 1930s*. 2nd ed. London: Routledge, 2010.

Levenson, Michael. *The Cambridge Companion to Modernism*. Cambridge University Press, 2011.

———. *Modernism*. New Haven, CT: Yale University Press, 2011.

Lever, Susan. "Christina Stead's Workshop in the Novel: How to Write a 'Novel of Strife.'" *JASAL: Journal of the Society for the Study of the Australian Literature* 2 (2003): 81–91.

———. Lever, Susan. *Real Relations: The Feminist Politics of Form in Australian Fiction*. Rushcutters Bay, NSW: Halstead Press, 2000.

Lever, Susan and Anne Pender. "*The Man Who Loved Children* by Christina Stead." In *The Encyclopedia of the Novel*, edited by Paul Schellinger. London: Routledge, 1998. 1272–1274.

Lewis, Sinclair. *Babbitt*. (1922) New York: Signet Classics, 2015.

Lidoff, Joan. *Christina Stead*. New York: Frederick Ungar Publishing Co., 1982.

———. "Domestic Gothic: The Imagery of Anger, Christina Stead's *The Man Who Loved Children*". *Studies in the Novel* 11, no. 2 (1979): 201–15.

Lindner, Christoph. *Imagining New York City: Literature, Urbanism and the Visual Arts 1890–1940*. Oxford: Oxford University Press, 2015.

Lionnet, Françoise, and Shu-mei Shih, eds. *Minor Transnationalism*. Durham, NC: Duke University Press, 2005.

Loos, Anita. *Gentlemen Prefer Blondes: The Illuminating Diary of a Professional Lady; and, But Gentlemen Marry Brunettes*. (1925) New York: Penguin Books, 1998.

Lottman, Herbert R. *The Left Bank: Writers, Artists, and Politics from the Popular Front to the Cold War*. Chicago: University of Chicago Press, 1998.

Love, Nancy S. *Marx, Nietzsche, and Modernity*. New York: Columbia University Press, 1986.

Lowy, Michael. "The Current of Critical Irrealism: 'A Moonlit Enchanted Night.'" In *A Concise Companion to Realism*, edited by Matthew Beaumont. Malden, MA: Wiley-Blackwell, 2010.

———. *Morning Star: Surrealism, Marxism, Anarchism, Situationism, Utopia*. Austin: University of Texas Press, 2009.

——. *The Theory of Revolution in the Young Marx*. Chicago: Haymarket Books, 2005.
Lukács, Georg. *Essays on Thomas Mann*. Translated by S. Mitchell. (1964) London: Merlin, 1979.
——. *History and Class Consciousness: Studies in Marxist Dialectics*. Translated by R. Livingstone. (1923) London: Merlin, 1971.
——. *The Historical Novel*. (1955) Lincoln: University of Nebraska Press, 1983.
——. *The Meaning of Contemporary Realism*. (1963) London: Merlin, 2006.
——. "Realism in the Balance". In *Aesthetics and Politics*, by Bloch, Ernst, Theodor Adorno, Walter Benjamin, Bertolt Brecht and Georg Lukacs, 28–59. London: Verso, 1977.
——. *The Sociology of Modern Drama*. Oshkosh, WI: Green Mountain Editions, 1965.
——. *Soul and Form*. Translated by Anna Bostock. (1908) London: Merlin, 1974.
——. *Studies in European Realism*. (1950) New York: Howard Fertig, 2002.
——. *The Theory of the Novel*. (1962) Cambridge, MA: MIT Press, 1974.
Lutz, Tom. *Cosmopolitan Vistas: American Regionalism and Literary Value*. Ithaca, NY: Cornell University Press, 2004.
Lyotard, Jean-Francois. *Libidinal Economy*. Translated by Iain Hamilton Grant. (1974) London: Bloomsbury 2004.
MacClancy, Jeremy. "Surrealism and Anthropology" *Oxford Bibliographies*. DOI 10.1093/obo/9780199766567-0140.
Mahleux, Viviane. "The Chronicle". *Oxford Bibliographies*, DOI: 10.1093/OBO/9780199766581-0092.
Maiorino, Giancarlo. *At the Margins of the Renaissance: Lazarillo De Tormes and the Picaresque Art of Survival*. University Park: Pennsylvania State University Press, 2003.
——. *The Picaresque: Tradition and Displacement*. Minneapolis: University of Minnesota Press, 1996.
Malouf, David. "David Malouf Examines Christina Stead's *A Little Tea, A Little Chat*", *Australian*, 1 October 2016, http://bit.ly/2PPyeWp.
——. "Stead Is Best at Egotistical Monsters". *Sydney Morning Herald*, 17 July 1982: 36.
Mandrell, James. "Questions of Genre and Gender: Contemporary Versions of the Feminine Picaresque", *NOVEL: A Forum on Fiction* 20, no. 2 (1987): 149–70.
Manganaro, Marc. *Culture, 1922 and After: Conversations in Anthropology and Literary Study*. Princeton, NJ: Princeton University Press, 2002.
——. *Modernist Anthropology*. Princeton, NJ: Princeton University Press, 2014.
——. *Myth, Rhetoric, and the Voice of Authority: A Critique of Frazer, Eliot, Frye, and Campbell*. New Haven, CT: Yale University Press, 1992.
Mann, Thomas. *Confessions of Felix Krull, Confidence Man: The Early Years*. (1954) New York: Vintage, 1992.
——. *The Magic Mountain*. Translated by H.T. Lowe-Porter and Adam Foulds. (1924) London: Vintage, 2011.
Marcus, Greil and Werner Sollors, eds. *A New Literary History of America*. Cambridge, MA: Harvard University Press, 2009.
Martin, Susan K. "'The Other Seven Little Australians': *The Man Who Loved Children* Reads Ethel Turner". *Australian Literary Studies* 25, no. 3 (2010): 35–48.
Marx, Karl. *Grundrisse: Foundations of the Critique of Political Economy*. Translated by Martin Nicolaus. (1939) London: Penguin Books, 1993.

Marx, Leo. "The Vernacular Tradition in American Literature". *Die Neuren Sprachen* 3 (1958). 46–57.
Matar, N.I. "The Renegade in English Seventeenth Century Imagination". *Studies in English Literature 1500–1900* 33, no. 3 (1993): 490.
Matthews, John T., ed. *A Companion to the Modern American Novel 1900–1950*. Chichester: Wiley-Blackwell, 2013.
Matz, Aaron. *Satire in an Age of Realism*. Cambridge: Cambridge University Press, 2010.
McCabe, Earl. "Depressive Realism: An Interview with Lauren Berlant". *Hypocrite Reader* 5 (2011). http://hypocritereader.com/5/depressive-realism.
McCarthy, Mary. *Intellectual Memoirs: New York, 1936–1938*. San Diego: Harcourt Brace, 1993.
McDonald, Gail. *American Literature and Culture: 1900–1960*. Malden, MD: Blackwell, 2008.
McDonell, Jennifer. "House Arrest: Domestic Space in Christina Stead's Fiction". *Crossing Lines: Formations of Australian Culture – Proceedings of ASAL Adelaide 1995* (1996): 136–43.
——. "Christina Stead's *The Man Who Loved Children*". *Southerly* 44, no. 4 (1984): 394–413.
McGurl, Mark. "Gigantic Realism: The Rise of the Novel and the Comedy of Scale". *Critical Inquiry* 43, no. 2 (2017): 403–30.
McKeon, Michael. *The Secret History of Domesticity: Public, Private and the Division of Knowledge*. Baltimore, MD: Johns Hopkins Press, 2005.
Meade, Marion. *Lonelyhearts: The Screwball World of Nathanel West and Eileen McKenney*. New York: First Mariner Books, 2010.
Melville, Herman. *The Confidence-Man: His Masquerade*. (1857) London: Penguin, 1991.
——. *Moby-Dick*. (1851) New York: Norton, 2002.
Mencken, Henry Louis. *The American Language: An Inquiry into the Development of English in the United States*. West Valley City, UT: Waking Lion Press/The Editorium, LLC, 2011.
Mendelson, Edward. "Encyclopedic Narrative, from Dante to Pynchon". *MLN* 91, no. 6 (1976): 1267–75.
Mendola, Tara and Jacques Lezra. "Introduction: Allegory and Political Representation", *The Yearbook of Comparative Literature* 61 (2015): 3
Michels, Tony. *A Fire in Their Hearts: Yiddish Socialists in New York*. Cambridge, MA: Harvard University Press, 2005.
——. *Jewish Radicals: A Documentary History*. New York: New York University Press, 2012.
Miller, Marc. *Representing the Immigrant Experience: Morris Rosenfeld and the Emergence of Yiddish Literature in America*. Syracuse, NY: Syracuse University Press, 2007.
Miller, Stuart. *The Picaresque Novel*. Cleveland, OH: The Press of Case Western Reserve University, 1967.
Miller, Tyrus. *Late Modernism: Politics, Fiction, and the Arts between the World Wars*. Berkeley: University of California Press, 1999.
Montefiore, Janet. *Men and Women Writers of the 1930s: The Dangerous Flood of History*. London: Routledge, 1996.
Moody, Theo. "'I really am a Puritan,' Christina Stead says". *Daily Telegraph*, 25 October 1946. 23–24.

Moore, Nicole. "The Totally Incredible Obscenity of Letty Fox". *JASAL: Journal of the Society for the Study of the Australian Literature* 2 (2003): 67–79.

Moretti, Franco. "Conjectures on World Literature." *New Left Review* 1 (Jan–Feb 2000): 54–68.

Morley, Catherine. *Modern American Literature*. Edinburgh: Edinburgh University Press, 2012.

Morris, Pam. *Realism*. London: Routledge, 2004.

Morrison, Fiona. "The American Introduction: Perfect Readers, Unread Books and Christina Stead's *The Man Who Loved Children*". In *Republics of Letters: Literary Communities in Australia*, edited by Robert Dixon and Peter Kirkpatrick. Sydney: Sydney University Press, 2012. 127–36.

——. "Modernist/Provincial/Pacific: Christina Stead, Katherine Mansfield and the Expatriate Home Ground." *JASAL: Journal of the Association for the Study of Australian Literature* 13, no. 2 (2013): 1–12.

——. "'A Vermeer in the Hayloft': Christina Stead, Unjust Neglect and Transnational Improprieties of Place and Kind'". *Australian Literary Studies* 31, no. 6 (2016).

Mullen, Bill and Sherry Linkon, eds. *Radical Revisions: Rereading 1930s Culture*. Urbana: University of Illinois Press, 1996.

Murphy, Geraldine. "Romancing the Center: Cold War Politics and Classic American Literature". *Poetics Today* 9, no. 4 (1988): 737–47.

Murphy, Richard J. *Theorizing the Avant-Garde: Modernism, Expressionism, and the Problem of Postmodernity*. Cambridge: Cambridge University Press, 1999.

Murray, Alex. *Giorgio Agamben*. London: Routledge, 2010.

Nealon, Christopher S. *The Matter of Capital: Poetry and Crisis in the American Century*. Cambridge, MA: Harvard University Press, 2011.

Nekola, Charlotte and Paula Rabinowitz, eds. *Writing Red: An Anthology of American Women Writers, 1930–1940*. New York: Feminist Press at the City University of New York, 1987.

Nelson, Brian. *The Cambridge Introduction to French Literature*. Cambridge: Cambridge University Press, 2015.

Nelson, Deborah. *Tough Enough: Arbus, Arendt, Didion, McCarthy, Sontag, Weil*. Chicago: University of Chicago Press, 2017.

Nestor, Pauline. "An Impulse to Self-Expression: *The Man Who Loved Children*." *Critical Review* 18 (1976): 61–78.

Newlin, Keith. *The Oxford Handbook of American Literary Naturalism*. New York: Oxford University Press, 2011.

Newsinger, John. *Fighting Back: The American Working Class in the 1930s*. London: Bookmarks, 2012.

Nicholls, Peter. *Modernisms: A Literary Guide*. New York: Palgrave Macmillan, 2009.

Nicholson, Colin. *Writing and the Rise of Finance: Capital Satires of the Early Eighteenth Century*. Cambridge: Cambridge University Press, 1994.

Nietzsche, Friedrich W. *Thus Spoke Zarathustra: A Book for Everyone and No One*. Translated by R J Hollingdale. (1885) Baltimore, MD: Penguin Books, 1966.

Nokes, David. *Reading 1922: A Return to the Scene of the Modern*. Oxford: Oxford University Press, 2002.

North, Michael. *Dialect of Modernism: Race, Language and Twentieth-Century Literature*. Oxford: Oxford University Press, 1998.
Olsen, Tillie. *Yonnondio: From the Thirties*. (1974) Lincoln: University of Nebraska Press, 2004.
Ong, Walter J. *The Presence of the Word: Some Prolegomena for Cultural and Religious History*. Binghamton, NY: Global Publications, 2000.
Paenhuyson, An. "Surrealism in the Provinces: Flemish and Walloon Identity in the Interwar Period". *Image & Narrative* 13 (2005). http://bit.ly/2VXj0F9.
Paine, Thomas. *The Living Thoughts of Tom Paine*, edited by John Dos Passos. (1940) London: Cassell & Co, 1946.
Palmeri, Frank. "Narrative Satire in the Nineteenth Century". In *A Companion to Satire*, edited by Ruben Quintero. Malden: Blackwell Publishing, 2007. 361–76.
Papanikolas, Theresa. "Towards a New Construction: Breton's Break with Dada and the Formation of Surrealism". In *Surrealism, Politics and Culture*, edited by Raymond Spiteri and Donald LaCoss. Aldershot: Ashgate, 2003. 37–51.
Parker, Patricia. *Literary Fat Ladies: Rhetoric, Gender, Property*. London: Methuen, 1987.
Pellon, Gustavo and Julio Rodríguez-Luis, eds. *Upstarts, Wanderers or Swindlers: Anatomy of the Picaro: A Critical Anthology*. Amsterdam: Rodopi, 1986.
Pells, Richard H. *Radical Visions and American Dreams: Culture and Social Thought in the Depression Years*. New York: Harper & Row, 1973.
Pender, Anne. *Christina Stead: Satirist*. Altona, Vic.: Common Ground Publishing, 2002.
Perkins, Elizabeth. "Energy and Originality in Some Characters of Christina Stead". *Journal of Commonwealth Literature* 15, no. 1 (1980): 107–13.
——. "Learning to Recognise Wicked People: Christina Stead's *A Little Tea, A Little Chat*". *World Literature Written in English* 32, no. 1 (1992): 13–25.
Petersen, Teresa. *The Enigmatic Christina Stead: A Provocative Re-Reading*. Carlton: Melbourne University Press, 2001.
Petry, Ann. *The Street*. (1946) Boston: Houghton Mifflin, 1991.
Pippin, Robert B. *Introduction to Nietzsche*. Cambridge: Cambridge University Press, 2012.
Pizer, Donald. *American Expatriate Writing and the Paris Moment: Modernism and Place*. Baton Rouge: Louisiana State University Press, 1996.
——. "Introduction: The Problem of Definition". In *The Cambridge Companion to American Realism and Naturalism: Howells to London*, edited by Donald Pizer. Cambridge: Cambridge University Press, 1995. 1–18.
Platt, Susan N. *Art and Politics in the 1930s: Modernism, Marxism, and Americanism: A History of Cultural Activism During the Depression Years*. New York: Midmarch Arts Press, 1999.
Poovey, Mary. *Genres of the Credit Economy: Mediating Value in Eighteenth and Nineteenth-Century Britain*. Chicago: University of Chicago Press, 2008.
Prendergast, Christopher. *Balzac: Fiction and Melodrama*. London: Hodder & Stoughton, 1978.
Puchner, Martin. *Poetry of the Revolution: Marx, Manifiestos, and the Avant-Gardes*. Princeton, NJ: Princeton University Press, 2006.
Quigley, Mark. *Empires Wake: Postcolonial Irish Writing and the Politics of Modern Literary Form*. New York: Fordham University Press, 2013.

Rabb, Melinda Alliker. "The Secret Life of Satire". In *A Companion to Satire*, edited by Ruben Quintero. Malden, MD: Blackwell Publishing, 2007. 568–84.

Rabinowitz, Paula. *American Pulp: How Paperbacks Brought Modernism to Main Street*. Princeton, NJ: Princeton University Press, 2014.

——. *Labor and Desire: Women's Revolutionary Fiction in Depression America*. Chapel Hill, NC: University of North Carolina Press, 1991.

Rahv, Philip. *Literature in America: An Anthology of Literary Criticism*. New York: Meridian Books, 1967.

Rancière, Jacques. *The Politics of Aesthetics: The Distribution of the Sensible*. London: Continuum, 2004.

Raskin, Jonah. "Christina Stead in Washington Square". *London Magazine* 9, no. 11 (1970): 70–77.

Reading, Amy. "Gambling and Grace, Profit and Providence". *Reviews in American History* 32, no. 4 (2004): 532–38.

Rico, Francisco. *The Spanish Picaresque Novel and the Point of View*, translated by Charles Davis with Harry Sieber. Cambridge: Cambridge University Press, 1969.

Rifkind, Candida. *Comrades and Critics: Women, Literature and the Left in 1930s Canada*. Toronto: University of Toronto Press, 2009.

Ritivoi, Andreea D. *Intimate Strangers: Arendt, Marcuse, Solzhenitsyn, and Said in American Political Discourse*. New York: Columbia University Press, 2014.

Robb, David, ed. *Clowns, Fools and Picaros*. Amsterdam: Rodopi, 1994.

Rodriguez-Luis, Julio. "Picaras: The Modal Approach to the Picaresque". *Comparative Literature* 31, no. 1 (1979): 32–46.

Rooney, Brigid. "Christina Stead's 'The Kelly File': Politics, Possession and the Writing of *Cotters' England*". *Australian Literary Studies* 31, no. 6 (2016).

——. "Crossing the Rubicon: Abjection and Revolution in Christina Stead's *I'm Dying Laughing*". *JASAL: Journal of the Association for the Study of English Literature* 2 (2003): 29–39.

——. "Loving the Revolutionary: Re-reading Christina Stead's Encounter with Men, Marxism and the Popular Front in 1930s Paris." *Southerly* 58, no. 4 (1998–99): 84–102.

——. "'Those Boys Told Me Everything': The Politics of the Secretary of Christina Stead's 1930s Fiction." *Antipodes* 17, no. 1 (2003): 29–35.

——. "Writers Behaving Badly: Stead, Bourdieu and Australian Literary Culture". *Australian Literary Studies* 20, no. 1 (2001): 76–87.

Rosenberg, Fernando J. *The Avant-Garde and Geopolitics in Latin America*. Pittsburgh, PA: University of Pittsburgh Press, 2006.

Rosenberg, Harold. "The American Writer's Congress". *Poetry* 46, no. 4 (1935): 222–27.

Ross, Stephen M. *Fiction's Inexhaustible Voice: Speech and Writing in Faulkner*. Athens: University of Georgia Press, 1989.

Roth, Henry. *Call It Sleep*. (1934) New York: Picador, 2005.

Rourke, Constance. *American Humor: A Study of the National Character*. New York: Doubleday, 1931.

Rowe, Kathleen. *The Unruly Woman: Gender and the Genres of Laughter*. Austin: The University of Texas Press, 1985.

Rowley, Hazel. *Christina Stead: A Biography*. Port Melbourne: Minerva, 1994.

——. "Christina Stead: Literature and Politics in the Radical Years, 1935–1942". *Meridian: The La Trobe University English Review* 8, no. 2 (1989): 149–59.
——. "How Real Is Sam Pollit? 'Dramatic Truth' and 'Procès-Verbal' in *The Man Who Loved Children*". *Contemporary Literature* 31, no. 4 (1990): 499–511.
——. *Richard Wright: The Life and Times*. Chicago: University of Chicago Press, 2008.
Ruan, Felipe E. *Pícaro and Cortesano: Identity and the Forms of Capital in Early Modern Spanish Picaresque Narrative and Courtesy Literature*. Lewisburg, PA: Bucknell University Press, 2011.
Rubin, Louis D., Jr. *The Comic Imagination in American Literature*. (1956) Washington, DC: Voice of America, 1983.
Russo, Elena. "Sociability, Cartesianism and Nostalgia in Libertine Discourse". *Eighteenth-Century Studies* 30, no. 4 (1997): 383–400.
Sante, Luc. *Low Life: Lures and Snares of Old New York*. (1991) New York: Farrar, Straus & Giroux, 2003.
Schehr, Lawrence R. *Rendering French Realism*. Stanford: Stanford University Press, 1997.
Schlichter, Annette. "Do Voices Matter? Vocality, Materiality, Gender Performativity". *Body & Society* 17, no. 1 (2011): 31–52.
Schwartz, Lawrence H. *Marxism and Culture: The CPUSA and Aesthetics in the 1930s*. San Jose: Authors Choice Press, 2000.
Scott, William B. and Peter M. Rutkoff. *New York Modern: The Arts and The City*. Baltimore, MD: Johns Hopkins Press, 1999.
Segerberg, Anita. "Christina Stead: The American Years". Dissertation. University of Auckland, 1991.
——. "Christina Stead in New York". *Antipodes* (Spring 1989): 15–19.
——. "A Fiction of Sisters: Christina Stead's *Letty Fox* and *For Love Alone*". *Australian Literary Studies* 14, no. 1 (1989): 15–25.
Seidel, Michael. *Satiric Inheritance: Rabelais to Sterne*. Princeton, NJ: Princeton University Press, 1979.
Seliniadou, Eleni. *Angela Carter and Christina Stead: The Quicksilver Abyss: Romantic Anachronism in Their Fiction*. Charleston, SC: BookSurge Publishing, 2008.
Selzer, Jack. *Kenneth Burke in Greenwich Village: Conversing with the Moderns, 1915–1931*. Madison: University of Wisconsin Press, 1997.
Shell, Marc. *Islandology: Geography, Rhetoric, Politics*. Stanford: Stanford University Press, 2014.
——. *Money, Language, and Thought: Literary and Philosophical Economies from the Medieval to the Modern Era*. Baltimore, MD: Johns Hopkins University Press, 1993.
Sheridan, Susan. *Christina Stead*. London: Harvester Wheatsheaf, 1988.
——. "Christina Stead's Last Book: The Novel and the Bestseller". *JASAL: Journal of the Association for the Study of Australian Literature* 2 (2003): 41–52.
——. Introduction to *Letty Fox: Her Luck* by Christina Stead. North Ryde, NSW: Angus & Robertson, 1991. v–xi.
——. "*The Man Who Loved Children* and the Patriarchal Family Drama". In *Gender and Fiction: Twentieth Century Australian Women's Novels*, edited by Carole Ferrier. St Lucia: University of Queensland Press, 1985. 136–49.
——."Politics and Passion in Stead's Late Novels". *Australian Literary Studies* 31, no. 6 (2016). http://bit.ly/2YK6PZn.

——. "When Was Modernism? The Cold War Silence of Christina Stead". *Hecate* 35, no. 1/2 (2009): 204–18.

——. "The Woman Who Loved Men: Christina Stead as Satirist in *A Little Tea, A Little Chat* and *The People with the Dogs*". *World Literature Written in English* 32, no. 1 (1992): 2–12.

Sherrill, Rowland A. *Road-Book America: Contemporary Culture and the New Picaresque*. Urbana: University of Illinois Press, 2000.

Shivers, Frank R. *Maryland Wits & Baltimore Bards: A Literary History with Notes on Washington Writers*. Baltimore, MD: Johns Hopkins University Press, 1998.

Shonkwiler, Alison. *The Financial Imaginary: Economic Mystification and the Limits of Realist Fiction*. Minneapolis: University of Minnesota Press, 2017.

Shonkwiler, Alison and Leigh Claire La Berge, eds. *Reading Capitalist Realism*. Iowa City: University of Iowa Press, 2014.

Short, Robert. "The Politics of Surrealism, 1920–36." In *Surrealism, Politics and Culture*, edited by Raymond Spiteri and Donald LaCoss. Aldershot: Ashgate, 2003. 18–36.

Showalter, Elaine. *A Jury of Her Peers: American Women Writers from Anne Bradstreet to Annie Proulx*. London: Virago, 2010.

Shulman, Robert. *The Power of Political Art: The 1930s Literary Left Reconsidered*. Chapel Hill: University of North Carolina Press, 2000.

Sieber, Harry. *The Picaresque*. London: Methuen, 1977.

Sinclair, Upton. *The Jungle: An Authoritative Text, Contexts and Backgrounds, Criticism*, edited by Clare Virginia Eby. (1906) New York: Norton, 2003.

Smedley, Agnes. *Daughter of Earth*. (1935) New York: Dover Publications, 2011.

Smith, Betty. *A Tree Grows in Brooklyn*. (1943) New York: Harper Perennial, 2006.

Smith, Jeanne R. *Writing Tricksters: Mythic Gambols in American Ethnic Literature*. Berkeley: University of California Press, 1997.

Snaith, Anna. *Modernist Voyages: Colonial Women Writers in London, 1890–1945*. Cambridge: Cambridge University Press, 2014.

Snyder, John. "Contemporary Genre Theory". In *Prospects of Power: Tragedy, Satire, the Essay, and the Theory of Genre*. Lexington: University Press of Kentucky, 1991. 1–23.

Spiteri, Raymond. "Surrealism and the Political Physiognomy of the Marvellous". In *Surrealism, Politics and Culture*, edited by Raymond Spiteri and Donald LaCoss. Aldershot: Ashgate, 2003. 52–72.

Sprinker, Michael. *Ghostly Demarcations: A Symposium on Jacques Derrida's Specters of Marx*. London: Verso, 2008.

Stansell, Christine. *American Moderns: Bohemian New York and the Creation of a New Century*. Princeton, NJ: Princeton University Press, 2009.

Stead, Christina. *The Beauties and Furies*. (1936) London: Virago, 1982.

——. "Christina Stead's Earliest Publications". *Australian Literary Studies* 31, no. 6 (2016). https://dx.doi.org/10.20314/als.8b73130f4b

——. *Christina Stead: Selected Fiction and Non-Fiction*. Edited by R.G. Geering and Anita Segerberg. St Lucia: University of Queensland Press, 1994.

——. *Cotters' England*. (1966) North Ryde, NSW: Angus & Robertson, 1989.

——. "England", *Kenyon Review* 30, no. 4 (1968) 444–450.

——. *For Love Alone*. (1945) Sydney: Angus & Robertson, 1966.

——. *House of All Nations*. (1938) North Ryde, NSW: Angus & Robertson, 1988.

——. *I'm Dying Laughing: The Humourist*. (1986) Harmondsworth: Penguin, 1989.
——. "An Interview with Joan Lidoff". In *Christina Stead*, edited by Joan Lidoff, 180–220. New York: Frederick Ungar, 1982.
——. "It Is All a Scramble for Boodle: Christina Stead Sums Up America". *Australian Book Review* 141, no. 6 (1992): 22–24.
——. *Letty Fox: Her Luck*. (1946) Sydney: Angus & Robertson, 1974.
——. *The Little Hotel: A Novel*. (1973) New York: H. Holt & Co, 1992.
——. *A Little Tea, A Little Chat*. (1948) London: Virago, 1981.
——. *The Man Who Loved Children*. (1940) Harmondsworth: Penguin Books, 1970.
——. *Miss Herbert (The Suburban Wife)*. (1976) London: Virago, 1992.
——. *Ocean of Story: The Uncollected Stories of Christina Stead*. Ringwood, Vic.: Penguin, 1986.
——. *The People with the Dogs*. (1952) London: Virago Press, 1992.
——. *The Puzzleheaded Girl: Four Novellas*. (1965) London: Virago, 1984.
——. *The Salzburg Tales*. (1934) North Ryde, NSW: Angus & Robertson, 1989.
——. *Seven Poor Men of Sydney*. (1934) North Ryde, NSW: Angus & Robertson, 1990.
——. *Talking into the Typewriter: Selected Letters, 1973–1983*. Edited by R.G. Geering. Pymble, NSW: Angus & Robertson, 1992.
——. "The View of the Homestead." *The Paris Review* 57 (1974): 124–130.
——. *A Web of Friendship: Selected Letters, 1928–1973*. Edited by R.G. Geering. Pymble, NSW: Angus & Robertson, 1992.
——. "The Writers Take Side." *Left Review* 1, no. 2 (1935): 454.
Stead, Christina, ed. *Great Stories of the South Sea Islands*. London: Frederick Muller, 1955.
Stead, Christina and William Blake. *Modern Women in Love: Sixty Twentieth-Century Masterpieces of Fiction*. New York: Dryden Press, 1945.
Stead, Christina and Jean B. Read. *A Christina Stead Reader*. London: Angus & Robertson, 1981.
Stead, Christina and Rodney Wetherell. "Interview with Christina Stead." *Australian Literary Studies*, 9, no. 4, (1980), 431–448. https://doi.org/10.20314/als.f6039f695d.
Stern, Kate Macomber. *Christina Stead's Heroine: The Changing Sense of Decorum*. New York: Peter Lang, 1989.
Sternlicht, Sanford V. *The Tenement Saga: The Lower East Side and Early Jewish American Writers*. Madison: University of Wisconsin Press / Terrace Books, 2004.
Stewart, Ken. "Heaven and Hell in *The Man Who Loved Children*". *Meridian: The La Trobe University English Review* 2, no. 2 (1983): 121–27.
Stewart, Susan. *On Longing: Narratives of the Miniature, the Gigantic, the Souvenir, the Collection*. Durham, NC: Duke University Press, 1992.
Storrs, Landon R.Y. *The Second Red Scare and the Unmaking of the New Deal Left*. Princeton, NJ: Princeton University Press, 2013.
Strausbaugh, John. *The Village: 400 Years of Beats and Bohemians, Radicals and Rogues: A History of Greenwich Village*. New York: Ecco, 2014.
Stewart, Jules. *Gotham Rising: New York in the 1930s*. London: I.B. Tauris, 2016.
Strehle, Susan. "Chosen People: American Exceptionalism in Kingsolver's *The Poisonwood Bible*". *Studies in Contemporary Fiction* 49, no. 4 (2008): 413–29.

Sturm, Terry. "Christina Stead's New Realism: *The Man Who Loved Children* and *Cotter's England*". In *The Magic Phrase: Critical Essays on Christina Stead*, edited by Margaret Harris. St Lucia: University of Queensland Press, 2000.

Suh, Judy. *Fascism and Anti-Fascism in Twentieth-Century British Fiction*. New York: Palgrave Macmillan, 2009.

Suleiman, Susan R. *Subversive Intent: Gender, Politics, and the Avant-Garde*. Cambridge, MA: Harvard University Press, 1990.

Sussman, Warren. *Culture as History: The Transformation of American Society in the Twentieth Century*. (1973) Washington, DC: Smithsonian Institution Press, 2003.

Szalay, Michael. *New Deal Modernism: American Literature and the Invention of the Welfare State*. Durham, NC: Duke University Press, 2000.

Tallack, Douglas. *New York Sights: Visualizing Old and New New York*. London: Bloomsbury, 2010.

Tally, Robert T., Jr. *Spatiality*. London: Routledge, 2013.

Thiel, Elizabeth. *The Fantasy of Family: Nineteenth-century Children's Literature and the Myth of the Domestic Ideal*. London: Routledge, 2011.

Thompson, James. *Models of Value: Eighteenth-century Political Economy and the Novel*. Durham, NC: Duke University Press, 1996.

Thompson, Michael. *Georg Lukács Reconsidered: Critical Essays in Politics, Philosophy, and Aesthetics*. London: Continuum, 2011.

Tokarczyk, Michelle M., ed. *Critical Approaches to American Working-Class Literature*. London: Routledge, 2014.

Tompkins, Jane P. *Sensational Designs: The Cultural Work of American Fiction: 1790–1860*. Oxford: Oxford University Press, 2013.

Tratner, Michael. *Deficits and Desires: Economics and Sexuality in Twentieth-Century Literature*. Stanford: Stanford University Press, 2001.

Trilling, Lionel. *The Liberal Imagination: Essays on Literature and Society*. New York: New York Review of Books, 2008.

Tyler, Imogen. *Revolting Subjects: Social Abjection and Resistance in Neoliberal Britain*. London: Zed Books, 2013.

Umbach, Maiken and Bernd Hüppauf, eds. *Vernacular Modernism: Heimat, Globalization, and the Built Environment*. Stanford: Stanford University Press, 2005.

Veitch, Jonathan. *American Superrealism: Nathanael West and the Politics of Representation in the 1930s*. Madison: University of Wisconsin Press, 1997.

Vials, Chris. *Realism for the Masses: Aesthetics, Popular Front Pluralism and US Culture, 1935–1947*. Jackson: University of Mississippi Press, 2009.

Vogl, Joseph. *The Specter of Capital*. Translated by Joachim Redner and Robert Savage. Stanford: Stanford University Press, 2015.

Vogel, Lise. *Marxism and the Oppression of Women: Towards a Unitary Theory*. (1983) Chicago: Haymarket Books, 2013.

Wald, Alan M. *American Night: The Literary Left in the Era of the Cold War*. Chapel Hill: University of North Carolina Press, 2012.

——. *Exiles from the Future Time: The Forging of the Mid-Twentieth Century Literary Left*. Chapel Hill: University of North Carolina Press, 2002.

——. *The New York Intellectuals: The Rise and Decline of the Anti-Stalinist Left from the 1930s to the 1980s*. Chapel Hill: University of North Carolina Press, 1987.

——. *Trinity of Passion: The Literary Left and the Antifascist Crusade*. Chapel Hill: University of North Carolina Press, 2007.
Ward, Artemus (Charles Farrar Browne). "Atlantic Cable Celebrations at Baldinsville", *The Complete Works of Artemus Ward* (1871) (Project Gutenberg, November 2004), ebook, n.pag.
Ward, David and Olivier Zunz, eds. *The Landscape of Modernity: New City 1900–1940*. New York: Russell Sage Foundation, 1992.
Walker, Nancy A. *A Very Serious Thing: Women's Humour and American Culture*. Minneapolis: University of Minnesota Press, 1988.
Walker, Shirley. "Language, Art and Ideas in *The Man Who Loved Children*". *Meridian: The La Trobe University English Review* 2, no. 1 (1983): 11–20.
Weil, François. *A History of New York*. Translated by Jody Gladding. New York: Columbia University Press, 2004.
Welter, Barbara. "The Cult of True Womanhood: 1820–1860". *American Quarterly* 18, no. 2 (1966): 151–74.
West, Nathanael. *Miss Lonelyhearts & The Day of the Locust*. (1933) New York: New Directions Book, 2009.
Whitehead, Anne. "An Interview with Christina Stead". *Australian Literary Studies* 6, no. 3 (1974): 230–48.
Whiting, Sarah. "1935: The Skyscraper". In *A New Literary History of America*, edited by Greil Marcus and Werner Sollers. Cambridge, MA: Harvard University Press, 2009. 689–94.
Wicks, Ulrich. *Picaresque Narrative, Picaresque Fiction: A Theory and Research Guide*. New York: Greenwood Press, 1989.
Wilde, Lawrence. "Logic". In *The Cambridge Companion to Marx*, edited by Terrell Carver. Cambridge: Cambridge University Press, 1991. 275–95.
Williams, Chris. *Christina Stead: A Life of Letters*. London: Virago, 1989.
Williams, John Frank. *The Quarantined Culture: Australian Reactions to Modernism 1913–1939*. Cambridge: Cambridge University Press, 1995.
Wilson, Sarah. "New York and the Novel of Manners". In *The Cambridge Companion to the Literature of New York*, edited by Cyrus Patell and Bryan Waterman. Cambridge: Cambridge University Press, 2010. 121–33.
Wirth-Nesher, Hana. *Call It English: The Languages of Jewish American Literature*. Princeton, NJ: Princeton University Press, 2009.
Wolfram, Walt and Natalie Schilling-Estes. *American English: Dialects and Variation*. 2nd ed. Malden, MD: Blackwell, 2008.
Woodward, Wendy. "Calling a Spade a Muck Dig: Discourse and Gender in Some Novels by Christina Stead." In *Crisis and Creativity in the New Literatures in English*, edited by Geoffrey V. Davis and Hena Maes-Jelinek. Amsterdam: Rodopi, 1990. 249–64.
Wright, Richard. *Native Son*. (1940) London: Vintage, 2000.
Yelin, Louise. "Christina Stead in 1991". *World Literature Written in English* 32, no. 1 (1992): 52–54.
——. "Fifty Years of Reading: A Reception Study of *The Man Who Loved Children*". *Contemporary Literature* 31, no. 4 (1990): 472–98.
——. *From the Margins of Empire: Christina Stead, Doris Lessing, Nadine Gordimer*. Ithaca, NY: Cornell University Press, 1998.

——. "Representing the 1930s: Capitalism, Phallocracy, and the Politics of the Popular Front in House of All Nations". In *The Magic Phrase: Critical Essays on Christina Stead*, edited by Margaret Harris. St Lucia: University of Queensland Press, 2000. 71–88.
——. "Sexual Politics and Female Heroism in the Novels of Christina Stead". In *Faith of a Woman Writer*, edited by Alice Kessler-Harris and William Brien. New York: Geenwood Press, 1988. 191–98.
——. "Unsettling Australia: *The Man Who Loved Children* as National Family Romance." In *From the Margins of Empire: Christina Stead, Doris Lessing, Nadine Gordimer*. Ithaca, NY: Cornell University Press, 1998. 17–38.
Zhdanov, Andrey, "Soviet Literature: The Richest in Ideas, The Most Advanced Literature". In *Soviet Writer's Congress 1934: The Debate on Socialist Realism and Modernism in the Soviet Union*. By Maxim Gorky, Karl Radek, Nikolai Bukharin, Andrey Zhdanov. et al. London: Lawrence & Wishart, 1977.

Index

abjection 64, 72, 79–81, 140, 146–147
Adler, Alfred 22
Adorno, Theodor 31
alienation 16, 39, 40, 41, 64, 76, 86, 99–100, 105, 112–115
allegory 9, 39, 47, 50–51
  characters as 71, 73, 97
  of America 47, 50, 60, 62, 63, 82, 138
  of imperialism 59
  postcolonial 50, 51
American Academy of Arts and Sciences 1, 2, 8
American Realism *see* realism: American
anatomy 9–10, 17, 31, 38, 40, 45, 47, 54, 90, 97, 99, 116, 132, 139, 151
Anderson, Edith 140, 144
Armstrong, Tim 70, 74
Australian Book Review 15, 85

Bakhtin, Mikhail 35–36, 57, 122
Balzac, Honoré de 9, 12, 14, 30–31, 37, 40, 108
Barnard Eldershaw, M. 33
Baym, Nina 77
Benjamin, Walter 33–35, 115
Bergson, Henri-Louis 22, 30
Berlant, Lauren 11, 17, 48, 153
Birns, Nicholas ix, 130
Blake, Bill 1, 3, 30–33, 41, 42, 88, 112, 117, 148, 150
Blech, Ruth 87, 91
Blech, William *see* Blake, Bill
"Blondine, the" 107, 108, 109–114
Blount, Kol 30
Boone, Joseph 57
Breton, André 34

Brooks, Peter 31
Burnshaw, Stanley 10, 24, 142

Calisher, Hortense 1–2, 4
capitalism 16, 19, 32, 38, 40, 67, 85–87, 97–101, 105, 108, 109, 114, 140, 155
  and America 93, 99, 118, 131
  and gangster capitalists 90, 93, 95, 100, 116
Chaucer, Geoffrey
  Canterbury Tales, The 27, 43
Chekhov, Anton 104, 115, 118, 122–124, 138
  The Cherry Orchard 72, 122
Clark, Katerina 35–36
class 6, 16, 18, 41, 63, 64, 70, 73, 76, 93, 95, 118, 133, 147
Clifford, James 36
Cohen, Margaret 24
Cold War 17–19, 132, 150, 155
colonial provinces 2
colonialism 16, 22–24, 41, 47, 55, 61, 86
comic writing *see* humour
Communist parties 52, 141, 142
communists 37, 119, 132, 136, 143
confinement and accumulation 66–69
Connor, Steven 54, 58
Cooppan, Vilashini 10
Craig, Randall 131, 137, 139

de Balzac, Honoré *see* Balzac, Honoré de
de Maupassant, Guy *see* Maupassant, Guy de
De Tocqueville, Alexis 86
debt and foreclosure 63, 72–77
Depression, The 8, 51, 65, 152
Derrida, Jacques 14

domestic fiction 3, 10, 11, 45, 47–48, 50–55, 59–62, 66, 71, 73, 77–78, 82, 152
  alienation in 64
  home economy in 81
  incarceration in 17, 48; *see also* oppression
domestic violence 75
Dostoyevsky, Fyodor 4, 36, 57, 86, 108
During, Simon 4
Duschinsky, Robbie 11

Edmunds, Susan 52
enargia 14
"Error of Feminine Riot, The" 98–101

fairy tales 13, 22, 27, 30, 66
fascism 32, 35, 63, 78
"fellow traveller" 8, 35, 144, 150, 151
femininity 25, 93, 133, 153
feminist literature 5
  critics of 9, 18, 63
Foley, Barbara 18, 44
folk tales *see* fairy tales
folk talk *see* vernacular speech
Fox, Ralph 37–42, 45, 47, 53, 103
Frye, Northrop 9
Fuchs Abrams, Sabrina 88

Gardiner, Judith Kegan 4, 58, 144
Geering, Ron 4, 10, 13, 26
gender 3–6, 12, 17, 59, 63, 65, 70, 76, 86, 93, 94, 101, 110, 133, 139–141
genre 3, 9–12, 36, 40, 45, 52, 86, 89, 90, 104, 133, 137–141, 147, 152–153
gold-digger 44, 86, 90, 93–100; *see also* marriage market
Goodlad, Lauren 19, 154
Gothic, the 13, 22, 30, 48, 54, 63, 66, 71
Great Depression *see* Depression, The
Guillen, Claudio 89

Harris, Margaret 3, 9, 30
Harris, Thistle 86
Hartley, Daniel 39
Hirst, David 138
Holinshed, Vera 142
Holt, Rinehart and Winston 1, 4
humour 30, 41–44, 56, 130–137, 139
Hurst, Alf 107, 112
Hyman, Louis 73

imperialism *see* colonialism

Indyk, Ivor 29–30
'Intensity of Speech' 31–35

Jacobson, Kristin 51
James, Henry 89, 139
Jameson, Fredric 7, 19, 51, 154
Jarrell, Randall 1, 4
Jones, Donna 28
Jones, Gail ix
Joyce, James 32, 37, 139

Kaplan, Amy 59
Kinross-Smith, Graeme 25, 26
Krause, Tom 2
Kristeva, Julia 146

League of American Writers 42
Lears, Jackson 86, 98
Lee, Judith Yaross 60
Lenin 6, 53, 143
Lezra, Jacques 50
Lidoff, Joan 4, 6, 10, 136
Lindsays, Norman and Lionel 30
  Vision 30
Lionnet, Francoise 5
"luck" 16, 69, 86, 91, 95, 97–98, 100, 113
Lukács, Georg (György) 11–15, 23, 37–39, 51, 100, 108, 148, 151
Lyotard, Jean-François 89

MacClancy, Jeremy 33–34
Malouf, David 3, 8–9, 106
'man alive' aesthetic 14
man-child 53, 59, 118
Mann, Thomas 14, 38–39, 151
Márquez, Gabriel García 131
marriage market 90, 92, 94, 100, 101, 107, 108; *see also* gold-digger
Martin, Susan 78
Marx, Karl 6, 63, 76
Marxist theory 20, 32, 41, 90, 99, 131, 136
masculinity 58, 104, 115, 127, 153
matter of mothers, The 64–65
Maupassant, Guy de 37, 88
McCarthyism 1, 3, 136, 141, 143, 147, 151
McDonell, Jennifer 55, 63, 82
Melville, Herman 50, 108
Mendola, Tara 50
Mitchell, Margaret 52
mobility 6, 8, 21, 32, 40, 87, 91, 92, 104, 108, 144
modernism 3, 6–7, 17–19, 37, 42, 44, 155

Index

modernity 3, 12, 20, 25, 39, 64, 85, 87, 131, 153
Monroe, Marilyn 112
Muller, Frederick 88, 148
Murphy, Geraldine 42

national identity 4, 8, 20, 22, 24, 131, 133, 135, 136
New Deal economics 47, 51–52, 62, 64, 82, 151
Nietzsche, Friedrich 22

O. Henry 88
ocean *see* sea, connection to the
oceanic totality and the "sea of story" 22–30
oppression 3, 26, 40, 51, 57, 58, 76

Partisan Review 17, 18, 42
patriarchy 53, 55, 58, 59, 152
Pender, Anne 10
picara 44, 86, 87, 89–91, 97, 100, 101, 110, 152
picaro 36, 86, 87, 89, 100, 104, 108, 110, 152
picaresque narrative 10, 45, 83, 85–87, 89–91, 93, 108, 127, 152
political economy 3, 8, 20, 32, 45, 63, 65, 70, 78, 86, 97, 106, 117
Popular Front 3, 19, 35–38, 44, 152
Porter, William Sidney *see* O. Henry
Prendergast, Christopher 5
property ownership 17, 72, 86, 90, 94, 95, 106, 115–119, 121, 127, 152
prostitution 63, 64, 72, 90, 95, 107, 110–111
provinciality 12, 15, 29–31, 40, 117, 134, 151

Rabinowitz, Paula 52
race 61, 70, 71
Raskin, Jonah 133
real estate *see* property ownership
realism 3–5, 7, 13–15, 17–20, 47, 140, 151, 154–156
   American 12, 14, 24, 35, 40–44, 156
   transnational 20, 35–40
   socialist *see* socialism
   avant-garde 7, 18, 21–24
reification 16, 70, 85, 87, 90, 100, 110
"revolting subject" 64, 77–81
Rhys 6, 6
Rooney, Brigid ix, 28
Roosevelt, Franklin D. 47, 51, 56
Roosevelt, Theodore 61
Rourke, Constance 42, 56
Rowley, Hazel 8, 22, 43, 49, 121, 143
Rudd, Steele 30

sea, connection to the 22–28, 50; *see also* oceanic totality and the "sea of story"
Sheridan, Susan 10, 130
Sherrill, Rowland 89
Shih, Shu-mei 5
Shulman, Robert 18
slavery 52, 63, 65, 70–71
socialism 7, 17, 36–38, 51, 144, 151
Stead, Christina
   as a colonial woman writer 3, 6
   death of her mother, the 27
   early life of 23–28
   father *see* Stead, David George (father)
   in London 1, 32, 36, 112
   in Paris 3, 6, 30, 32–40, 151
   publications
      A Little Tea, A Little Chat 3, 8, 11, 21, 35, 45, 86, 87, 100, 104–108, 116, 152
      "A View of the Homestead" 49
      Beauties and the Furies, The 7, 10, 22, 38
      For Love Alone 30
      House of All Nations 22, 35, 38–39, 105, 107
      I'm Dying Laughing 1, 3, 11, 17, 20, 21, 35, 45, 96, 101, 126, 129–150
      "It Is All a Scramble for Boodle" 15–16, 41, 85
      Letty Fox: Her Luck 3, 20, 21, 35, 45, 86–87, 90, 95, 97, 98–100, 107, 152
      "Magic Woman and other Stories, The" 70
      Man Who Loved Children, The 1–5, 8, 11, 17, 20, 21, 35, 41–45, 47–57, 60, 63, 71–77, 93, 118, 125, 152
      "Ocean of Story" 25, 70
      People with the Dogs, The 3, 8, 11, 21, 45, 86, 87, 104, 106, 115–121, 123, 127, 138, 152
      Salzburg Tales The 6, 27, 33, 44, 56
      "Writers' Take Sides, The" 38
   university attendance of 22
Stead, David George (father) 23, 43
Strehle, Susan 59
Sturm, Terry 14
surrealism 22, 23, 30–35, 151

Tocqueville, Alexis De *see* De Tocqueville, Alexis
Tolstoy, Leo 4
traitor, the 143–147
translocation 50
transnational literature 2, 4–8, 19, 50, 151, 153, 154–155
transnationalism 35–36, 153, 156
Twain, Mark 43, 50, 56
Tyler, Imogen 79–81

utopia 86, 87, 106, 115–117, 119, 122, 124–127, 152

vernacular speech 3, 16, 22, 30, 34, 41–44, 48, 54–56, 59, 62, 91, 97, 135, 156
Vials, Chris 18, 44

Walcott, Derek 22
Wald, Alan 41
Ward, Artemus 43, 50, 54, 56
West, Mae 44, 94
Wetherell, Rodney 26
White, Patrick 6

Whitehead, Anne 23, 25
Wicks, Ulrich 89
Wilson, Emma 11
Woolf, Virginia 93
Writers' Congress 22, 38
  American 36, 42
  Popular Front 36
  Soviet 35–37, 43

Yelin, Louise 50, 52, 73, 152

Zatz, Asa 121

www.ingramcontent.com/pod-product-compliance
Lightning Source LLC
Chambersburg PA
CBHW060233240426
43671CB00016B/2927